FACE TO FACE

Praying the Scriptures for Spiritual Growth

Scripture translation and adaptation by

KENNETH BOA

ZondervanPublishingHouse
Grand Rapids, Michigan

A Division of HarperCollins*Publishers*

Face to Face: Praying the Scriptures for Spiritual Growth
Copyright © 1997 by Kenneth Boa

Zondervan Publishing House
Grand Rapids, Michigan 49530
http://www.zondervan.com

Library of Congress Catalog Card Number 97-060199

This edition printed on acid-free paper and meets the American
National Standards Institute Z39.48 standard.

Printed in the United States of America

97 98 99 00 01 02 03 04 / ❖ RRD-C/ 10 9 8 7 6 5 4 3 2 1

CONTENTS

Karen and I dedicate this collection
of Biblical affirmations
with love to our children Heather and Matthew.

INTRODUCTION

The Purpose of this Book

For years I have been frustrated by a hit and (usually) miss approach to catching a few thoughts from the Bible before going to sleep. My morning devotional times have been greatly enhanced by a previous volume, *Face to Face: Praying the Scriptures for Intimate Worship.** This little prayer book is based on the eight forms of prayer modeled in the Lord's Prayer: adoration, confession, renewal, petition, intercession, affirmation, thanksgiving and closing prayer. One of these forms—affirmation—is illustrated in the phrase, "Your kingdom come; Your will be done on earth as it is in heaven" Matthew 6:10). The principle of *affirmation* involves agreeing with God's will for us and submitting to it. It occurred to me, then, that hundreds of affirmations could be derived from Scripture and compiled into a format that would act as a tool to enable people to renew their minds with Biblical truth on a daily basis. And if we pray these affirmations back to God, we are actively and verbally agreeing with His will for us, resulting in our spiritual growth as we become more and more conformed to His image in Christ Jesus.

The germ of truth in the growing body of "self-talk" literature is that people often need to be reminded of their identity and goals so that they have a clear sense of purpose and direction. The problem with this literature is that it often promotes an unbiblical value system and world view. Biblical affirmations are founded in truth; they are not like the self-

---

*previously published as *Handbook to Prayer*, by Kenneth Boa (Atlanta: Trinity House Publishers, 1993).

talk that says, "Every day and in every way, I am getting better and better." The affirmations of Scripture encourage us to walk by faith, not by feelings; when we pray affirmations, we are agreeing with God on the way things really are regardless of our emotional, cultural and theological filters. Though our circumstances may threaten our commitment to the truth— that God is in control of our affairs and has our best interests at heart—Scripture affirms these foundational principles and tells us to cling to them even in the midst of life's pain.

These Biblical affirmations are not merely wishful thinking; they are true of every person who places his or her hope in Jesus Christ. They stress our identity in Him as well as our intimacy with God our Father. They challenge us to value relationships more than objectives. They teach us that *what we do* does not determine *who we are*; rather, our being should shape our doing. They reinforce the realistic perspective that we are strangers and pilgrims, not citizens of this world, and tell us to walk in grace and live in the power of the Spirit of God instead of walking in obedience to a set of external rules and living in the power of the flesh. As we pray these spiritual truths, they counsel us to take the risks of applying Biblical precepts and principles, to place our hope in the character and promises of God, and not in the people, possessions or prestige of this world.

Many of the prayer affirmations in *Face to Face: Praying the Scriptures for Spiritual Growth* are expressed as desires; you will be dialoging with God, agreeing with Him that these are the things you want to be true of your life. Using this book on a regular basis will be a faith-building exercise that will make these affirmations increasingly real in your life, resulting in a change in perspective, without which no genuine spiritual growth can take place. When we renew our minds through praying the affirmations of Scripture, we grow in the knowledge of God and "become mature, attaining to the whole measure of the fullness of Christ" (Ephesians 4:13).

And what better time to use such a tool than just before going to sleep? The thoughts we entertain after we turn out the light have a profound effect on the rest of the night, but few of us make good use of these strategic minutes. Instead, most people carry anxieties and other fleshly thought patterns to bed with them. Throughout the course of the day we are being bombarded by the temporal value system of the world through the things we see, hear and read. Because of this, it is important that we *renew our minds* with the eternal value system of Scripture so that we regain a sense of focus on the crucial issues of who we are, where we came from, why we are here and where we are going.

Face to Face: Praying the Scriptures for Spiritual Growth is designed to assist you in this process of renewing your mind. It can be most effective when used just before going to sleep so that you set, or "program," your conscious and subconscious mind for the rest of the night. This is consistent with David's practice: "When I remember You on my bed, I meditate on You in the night watches" (Psalm 63:6). Rather than being *conformed* to this world, you will be "*transformed* by the renewing of your mind" (Romans 12:2). This will assist you in "taking every thought captive to the obedience of Christ" (2 Corinthians 10:5). *Face to Face: Praying the Scriptures for Spiritual Growth* will help you to "set your mind on the things above, not on the things on the earth" (Colossians 3:2), and to let your mind dwell on "whatever is true, whatever is noble, whatever is right, whatever is pure, whatever is lovely, whatever is of good report—if anything is excellent or praiseworthy" (Philippians 4:8).

The Structure of this Book

To create this collection of Biblical affirmations, I consulted several translations as well as the original language of every passage. The result is essentially my own translation, though it shares much in common with existing translations. My intention in doing this was to remain as close to the Biblical text as possible while still retaining clarity and readability. I then adapted the bulk of the passages into an affirmation format.

Within the *Praying the Scriptures* format, these affirmations are directed to God; as we pray we reflect back to Him and agree with Him about 1) the truths He teaches us about Himself and 2) statements of what we want to be true of our lives. A number of these affirmations were derived from negative statements and evaluations in the Bible and turned into positive statements. In other cases, principles have been derived from the lives of Biblical characters.

To assist you in personalizing these affirmations, I decided to put them in the singular and/or first person whenever possible. However, some (e.g., 1 Corinthians 1:4–5, 7) could not be adapted into the singular without excessive distortion. When you use *Face to Face: Praying the Scriptures for Spiritual Growth* with another person or with a group, turn the singulars into plurals.

Clearly, a large measure of subjectivity is unavoidable in the creation of a book like this. This relates to several issues, like the decision of selecting some passages and not using others; translation decisions; editorial choices involved in adapting passages into the form of affirmations; assignment of passages into categories; and arrangement of these categories. Inevitably, people will wonder why I overlooked some passages or categorized others in the way I did. These are all matters of judgment and interpretation, and I freely admit that there are many other ways in which these affirmations could have been expressed and arranged. In many cases they overlapped my tidy categories, and I had to make choices on the basis of emphasis. Because of all this, I encourage you to make insertions and deletions whenever it will help make this a more effective tool for spiritual growth.

As you can see, there are three major sections in *Face to Face: Praying the Scriptures for Spiritual Growth*: the Daily Guide for Renewal and Growth, the Topical Guide for Renewal and Growth and the Personal Renewal Pages. Some of the passages in the Daily Guide for Renewal and Growth are derived from the Topical Guide for Renewal and Growth. The Topical Guide includes a substantial number of affirmations that have not been used in the Daily Guide.

The Daily Guide for Renewal and Growth was created to expose you to a wide range of affirmations and to give you the opportunity to reaffirm them four times a year. It adopts the five-part structure of the Topical Guide for each of the 31 days of the first, second and third months:

1. **The Attributes of God**
2. **The Works of God**
3. **My Relationship to God**
4. **The Character I Want to Cultivate**
5. **My Relationship to Others**

In these five general categories there is a logical progression from God to self to others. The first two relate to loving God completely, the next two relate to loving self correctly, and the last relates to loving others compassionately. The person, powers and perfection of God are the basis for His work in creation, redemption and consummation. The attributes and works of God are the foundation of my relationship to God, and growth in Christlikeness relates to the character I want to cultivate. When I find my security, significance and sufficiency in Jesus Christ, I can serve others in love as I have been called to do.

Each day includes all five parts for a well-balanced spiritual diet.

How to Use this Book

Face to Face: Praying the Scriptures for Spiritual Growth was designed to be used in two ways: as a tool for daily prayer, and as a topically arranged set of Biblical prayers for focusing on specific areas such as the Person of God; God's grace and love; hope and reward; and courage and perseverance.

The Daily Guide for Renewal and Growth realistically assumes that you are fatigued at the end of your day. For this reason it was structured to be effective with only *five minutes* of use. Each of the five categories has a couplet of passages that are thematically related. Spend a full minute with the first couplet and go beyond reading the prayer affirmations: pray them through, think about them and make them your own. Then do the same for the other four. Obviously you will increase your benefit by spending more than five minutes, but think of the five minutes as a workable minimum. You may use the prayer prompts to add your personal thoughts and prayers as they come to you.

Try to make this the last activity of your day so that, after turning out the light as you go to sleep, you can immediately review the affirmations that were particularly meaningful to you. This will initially require some discipline, since extraneous thoughts will clamor for your attention, but keep returning to the affirmations, and you will increase your skill with daily practice.

Use the Topical Guide when you have more time or when you want to develop in a particular area. You will find the list of topics with page numbers in the Table of Contents. This portion of the book is particularly helpful in guiding you during a retreat or when you schedule a large enough block of time to meditate and pray through one or more entire topics.

I also recommend using Parts One and Two with another person and with small groups. When you use the Daily

Guide for Renewal and Growth with others, try pausing and praying together after each of the five couplets so that you can respond together.

Finally, be sure to use the Personal Prayer Pages at the end of this book to write in the affirmations that are particularly meaningful to you as well as your personal prayer concerns.

We ought always to thank God for other believers, and pray that their faith would grow more and more, and that the love each of them has toward one another would increase. (2 Thessalonians 1:3)

PART ONE

Daily Guide to Renewal
and Growth

THE FIRST MONTH

DAY 1

The Attributes of God

You are my God, and I will give thanks to You;
You are my God, and I will exalt You.
I will give thanks to You, Lord, for You are good;
Your loyal love endures forever. (Psalm 118:28–29)

You, O God, are the blessed and only Sovereign, the King of kings and Lord of lords. You alone have immortality and dwell in unapproachable light; no one has seen You or can see You. To You be honor and eternal dominion. (1 Timothy 6:15–16)

Pause to reflect on these affirmations about the person, powers and perfection of God.

The Works of God

When I consider Your heavens,
    the work of Your fingers,
The moon and the stars, which You have set in place,
    what is man that You are mindful of him,
    and the son of man that You care for him?
You made him a little lower than the heavenly beings
    and crowned him with glory and honor.
You made human beings the rulers over
    the works of Your hands,
        and You put everything under their feet.
    (Psalm 8:3–6)

O Lord of hosts, God of Israel,
Enthroned between the cherubim,
You alone are God over all the kingdoms of the earth.
You have made heaven and earth. (Isaiah 37:16)

Take a moment to consider the greatness of God's wonderful works.

My Relationship to God

O Lord, bless us and keep us;
O Lord, make Your face shine upon us
    and be gracious to us;
O Lord, turn Your face toward us
    and give us peace. (Numbers 6:24–26)

You have loved me, O God, and called me to be a saint; You,
O God my Father, and the Lord Jesus Christ have given me
grace and peace. (Romans 1:7)

*Pause to thank God for the relationship that you enjoy with
Him in Jesus Christ.*

The Character I Want to Cultivate

Lord, who may dwell in Your tabernacle?
Who may live on Your holy mountain?
Those who walk uprightly and work righteousness
    and speak the truth in their hearts;
They do not slander with their tongues or do evil to
    their neighbor or take up a reproach against
        their friends;
They despise the reprobate but honor those who fear You.
They keep their oath even when it hurts,
    lend their money without interest and
    do not accept bribes against the innocent.
Those who do these things will never be shaken.
    (Psalm 15:1–5)

I will let my eyes look straight ahead
   and fix my gaze straight before me.
I will ponder the path of my feet
   so that all my ways will be established.
I will not turn to the right or to the left
   but keep my foot from evil. (Proverbs 4:25–27)

Take a moment to consider the greatness of God's wonderful works.

My Relationship to Others

Friends love at all times;
They are born for times of adversity. (Proverbs 17:17)

We must be devoted to one another in love, honoring one another above ourselves. (Romans 12:10)

Pause to review your relationships with others and to commit them to the Lord.

DAY 2

The Attributes of God

> You, O God, are not a man, that You should lie,
> or a son of man, that You should change Your mind.
> Have You spoken and not done it?
> Have You promised and not fulfilled it?
> (Numbers 23:19)

You who are the Glory of Israel do not lie or change Your mind, for You are not a man, that You should change Your mind. (1 Samuel 15:29)

Pause to reflect on these affirmations about the person, powers and perfection of God.

The Works of God

> One generation shall praise Your works to another,
> O Lord,
> and shall declare Your mighty acts.
> I will meditate on the glorious splendor of Your majesty
> and on Your wonderful works.
> Many shall speak of the might of Your awesome works,
> and I will proclaim Your great deeds.
> (Psalm 145:4–6)

> Who is a God like You, who pardons iniquity
> and forgives the transgression of the remnant of Your
> inheritance?
> You do not stay angry forever but delight to show
> mercy.
> You will have compassion on Your people;

You will tread their iniquities underfoot
  and hurl all their sins into the depths of the sea.
(Micah 7:18–19)

Take a moment to consider the greatness of God's wonderful works.

My Relationship to God

You lifted me out of the slimy pit, O God,
  out of the mud and mire;
You set my feet on a rock
  and gave me a firm place to stand.
You put a new song in my mouth,
  a hymn of praise to You, my God.
Many will see and fear and put their trust in You,
  O Lord. (Psalm 40:2–3)

I shall know the truth, and the truth shall set me free. Everyone who commits sin is a slave of sin. And a slave has no permanent place in the family, but a child belongs to it forever. So if You, the Son of God, set me free, I shall be free indeed. (John 8:32, 34–36)

Pause to thank God for the relationship that you enjoy with Him in Jesus Christ.

The Character I Want to Cultivate

I will not let love and truth leave me;
I will bind them around my neck
  and write them on the tablet of my heart.
(Proverbs 3:3)

The love we have from You, O Lord, is patient, it is kind, it does not envy; love does not boast, it is not arrogant, it does not behave rudely; it does not seek its own, it is not provoked, it keeps no record of wrongs; it does not rejoice in unrighteousness but rejoices with the truth; it bears all things, believes all things, hopes all things, endures all things. Love never fails. (1 Corinthians 13:4–8)

Take a moment to ask the Lord for the grace to grow in godly character.

My Relationship to Others

I will give generously to others without a grudging heart. (Deuteronomy 15:10)

> I will not withhold good from those to whom it is due, when it is within my power to act. (Proverbs 3:27)

Pause to review your relationships with others and to commit them to the Lord.

DAY 3

The Attributes of God

You, O Lord my God, You are God of gods and Lord of lords, the great God, mighty and awesome; You show no partiality and accept no bribes. You execute justice for the fatherless and the widow and love aliens, giving them food and clothing. (Deuteronomy 10:17–18)

As for You, O God, Your way is perfect;
Your word, O Lord, is proven.
You are a shield to all who take refuge in You.
For who is God besides You?
And who is the Rock except You, our God?
(Psalm 18:30–31)

Pause to reflect on these affirmations about the person, powers and perfection of God.

The Works of God

To us a child is born, to us a son is given,
and the government is on Your shoulders.
And You are called Wonderful Counselor, Mighty God,
Everlasting Father, Prince of Peace.
Of the increase of Your government and peace
there will be no end.
You reign on the throne of David and over his kingdom,
establishing and upholding it with justice and
righteousness from this time on and forever.
Your zeal, O Lord of hosts, will accomplish this.
(Isaiah 9:6–7)

You, Jesus, will be great and will be called the Son of the Most High. The Lord God will give You the throne of Your father David, and You will reign over the house of Jacob forever, and Your kingdom will never end. (Luke 1:32–33)

Take a moment to consider the greatness of God's wonderful works.

My Relationship to God

O Lord, You are my rock and my fortress and my deliverer; O God, You are my rock; I will take refuge in You. You are my shield and the horn of my salvation, my stronghold and my refuge—my Savior; You save me from violence; I call on You, Lord; You are worthy of praise, and I am saved from my enemies. (2 Samuel 22:2–4)

Who will bring a charge against those whom You have chosen, O God? You are the One who justifies. Who is he who condemns? It is Christ Jesus who died, who was furthermore raised to life, who is at Your right hand, O God, and is also interceding for me. (Romans 8:33–34)

Pause to thank God for the relationship that you enjoy with Him in Jesus Christ.

The Character I Want to Cultivate

To fear You, Lord, is wisdom;
And to depart from evil is understanding. (Job 28:28)

To fear You, Lord, is the beginning of wisdom;
All who practice Your commandments have good
    understanding.
Your praise endures forever. (Psalm 111:10)

Take a moment to ask the Lord for the grace to grow in godly character.

My Relationship to Others

I will stay away from foolish people,
  for I will not find knowledge on their lips.
  (Proverbs 14:7)

I will not make friends with hot-tempered people
  or associate with those easily angered,
  lest I learn their ways and set a snare for my soul.
  (Proverbs 22:24–25)

*Pause to review your relationships with others and to commit
them to the Lord.*

DAY 4

The Attributes of God

O God, You revealed Yourself to Moses as "I AM WHO I AM." (Exodus 3:14)

Jesus Christ, You are the same yesterday, today and forever. (Hebrews 13:8)

Pause to reflect on these affirmations about the person, powers and perfection of God.

The Works of God

As the Israelites rejoiced in Your works, may I rejoice,
    O God:
    Rejoice greatly, O daughter of Zion!
    Shout, O daughter of Jerusalem!
    Behold, your King is coming to you;
    He is just and having salvation, humble and riding on a
        donkey, on a colt, the foal of a donkey.
    He will proclaim peace to the nations;
    His dominion will extend from sea to sea
        and from the River to the ends of the earth.
    (Zechariah 9:9–10)

God, You sent Your word to the children of Israel, telling the good news of peace through Jesus Christ, who is Lord of all. Jesus commanded the apostles to preach to the people and to testify that He is the One whom You appointed as judge of the living and the dead. To Him all the prophets witness that, through His name, everyone who believes in Him receives forgiveness of sins. (Acts 10:36, 42–43)

Take a moment to consider the greatness of God's wonderful works.

My Relationship to God

O Lord my God, You are one. I want to love You, Lord my God, with all my heart and with all my soul and with all my strength. (Deuteronomy 6:4–5)

Those who love their father or mother more than You are not worthy of You; those who love their son or daughter more than You are not worthy of You. (Matthew 10:37)

Pause to thank God for the relationship that you enjoy with Him in Jesus Christ.

The Character I Want to Cultivate

I will not follow the crowd in doing wrong. (Exodus 23:2)

There are six things You hate, O Lord, seven that are detestable to You:
> Haughty eyes, a lying tongue,
>> hands that shed innocent blood,
>> a heart that devises wicked plans,
>> feet that run swiftly to evil,
>> a false witness who breathes lies
>> and one who causes strife among brothers and sisters.
> (Proverbs 6:16–19)

Take a moment to ask the Lord for the grace to grow in godly character.

My Relationship to Others

Lord God, You said, "It is not good for the man to be alone; I will make a helper suitable for him." And You, the Lord God, made a woman from the rib You had taken out of the man, and You brought her to the man. And the man said, "This is now bone of my bones and flesh of my flesh; she shall be called 'Woman,' because she was taken out of man."

For this reason a man shall leave his father and mother and shall cleave to his wife, and they shall become one flesh. (Genesis 2:18, 22–24)

From the beginning of creation You made us male and female. For this reason a man shall leave his father and mother and shall cleave to his wife, and the two shall become one flesh. So they are no longer two, but one flesh. Therefore what You have joined together, let no one separate. (Matthew 19:4–6; Mark 10:6–9)

Pause to review your relationships with others and to commit them to the Lord.

DAY 5

The Attributes of God

Lord, You are great and greatly to be praised;
You are to be feared above all gods,
    for all the gods of the nations are idols,
        but You made the heavens.
Splendor and majesty are before You;
Strength and joy are in Your place.
I will ascribe to You, O Lord, glory and strength.
I will ascribe to You the glory due Your name
    and worship You in the beauty of holiness.
    (1 Chronicles 16:25–29)

You are the high and lofty One, who inhabits eternity,
    whose name is holy.
You live in a high and holy place but also with those
    who are contrite and lowly in spirit,
        to revive the spirit of the lowly and to revive the
            hearts of the contrite. (Isaiah 57:15)

Pause to reflect on these affirmations about the person, powers and perfection of God.

The Works of God

O God, You completed the heavens and the earth in all their vast array. By the seventh day You finished the work that You had done, and You rested on the seventh day from all Your creative work. And You blessed the seventh day and sanctified it, because on it You rested from all the work of creating that You had done. (Genesis 2:1–3)

O Lord, God of Israel, enthroned between the cherubim, You alone are God over all the kingdoms of the earth. You have made heaven and earth. (2 Kings 19:15)

Take a moment to consider the greatness of God's wonderful works.

My Relationship to God

I glory in Your holy name, O Lord.
Let the hearts of those who seek You rejoice.
I will seek You, O Lord, and Your strength.
I will seek Your face always.
I will remember the wonderful works You have done—
the miracles and the judgments You have pronounced.
(1 Chronicles 16:10–12)

Since I am receiving a kingdom that cannot be shaken, I will be thankful and so worship You , my God, acceptably with reverence and awe, for You are a consuming fire. (Hebrews 12:28–29)

Pause to thank God for the relationship that you enjoy with Him in Jesus Christ.

The Character I Want to Cultivate

I will put away perversity from my mouth and keep corrupt talk far from my lips. (Proverbs 4:24)

I will not let any corrupt word come out of my mouth, but only what is helpful for building others up according to their needs, that it may impart grace to those who hear. (Ephesians 4:29)

Take a moment to ask the Lord for the grace to grow in godly character.

My Relationship to Others

Like Abraham, I should direct my children and my household after me to keep Your way, O Lord, by doing what is right and just. (Genesis 18:19)

I will learn to fear You all the days I live on the earth and teach Your words to my children. (Deuteronomy 4:10)

Pause to review your relationships with others and to commit them to the Lord.

DAY 6

The Attributes of God

Who is like You, O Lord? Who is like You—majestic in holiness, awesome in praises, working wonders? (Exodus 15:11)

You, O Lord, have declared:
"My thoughts are not your thoughts,
    neither are your ways My ways.
As the heavens are higher than the earth,
    so are My ways higher than your ways, and
    My thoughts than your thoughts." (Isaiah 55:8–9)

Pause to reflect on these affirmations about the person, powers and perfection of God.

The Works of God

How great are Your works, O Lord!
Your thoughts are very deep.
Senseless people do not know;
Fools do not understand that though the wicked spring
    up like grass and all the evildoers flourish,
        they will be destroyed forever.
But You, O Lord, are exalted forever. (Psalm 92:5–7)

You, O Lord, are near to all who call upon You,
    to all who call upon You in truth.
You fulfill the desires of those who fear You;
You hear their cry and save them.
You preserve all who love You, but
    all the wicked You will destroy. (Psalm 145:18–20)

Take a moment to consider the greatness of God's wonderful works.

My Relationship to God

I am the salt of the earth, but if the salt loses its flavor, how can it be made salty again? It is no longer good for anything, except to be thrown out and trampled underfoot. I am the light of the world. A city set on a hill cannot be hidden. Neither do people light a lamp and put it under a basket, but on a lampstand, and it gives light to all who are in the house. In the same way, I must let my light shine before all people, that they may see my good deeds and praise You, my Father in heaven. (Matthew 5:13–16)

We are Your temple, O God, and Your Spirit lives in us. (1 Corinthians 3:16)

Pause to thank God for the relationship that you enjoy with Him in Jesus Christ.

The Character I Want to Cultivate

When I am blessed with abundance, I will beware lest my heart become proud, and I forget You, O Lord my God, who provide all good things—lest I think that it was my power and the strength of my hand that brought this wealth. (Deuteronomy 8:12–14, 17)

If I am proud, I will be destroyed;
If I have a haughty spirit, I will fall. (Proverbs 16:18)

Take a moment to ask the Lord for the grace to grow in godly character.

My Relationship to Others

How good and pleasant it is when brothers and sisters live together in unity! (Psalm 133:1)

Lord Jesus, You prayed these words for the unity of all who would believe in You: "I ask that all of them may be one, Father, just as You are in Me and I am in You, that they also may be in Us, that the world may believe that You sent Me. And the glory which You gave Me I have given to them, that they may be one, just as We are one: I in them, and You in Me, that they may be perfected in one, that the world may know that You have sent Me and have loved them, even as You have loved Me." (John 17:21–23)

Pause to review your relationships with others and to commit them to the Lord.

DAY 7

The Attributes of God

I acknowledge this day and take it to my heart that You, Lord, are God in heaven above and on the earth below; there is no other. (Deuteronomy 4:39)

> You are the Lord, and there is no other;
> Apart from You there is no God.
> From the rising of the sun to its setting,
>   we know there is none besides You.
> You are the Lord, and there is no other. (Isaiah 45:5–6)

Pause to reflect on these affirmations about the person, powers and perfection of God.

The Works of God

> Lord, we look forward to the day when Your kingdom
>   will come in all its fullness:
> The wolf will dwell with the lamb,
>   and the leopard will lie down with the goat,
>   and the calf and the lion and the yearling together,
>   and a little child will lead them.
> The cow will feed with the bear;
> Their young will lie down together,
>   and the lion will eat straw like the ox.
> The infant will play near the hole of the cobra,
>   and the young child will put his hand into the viper's
>   hole.
> They will neither harm nor destroy
>   on all Your holy mountain,
>   for the earth will be full of the knowledge of You,
>   O Lord,
>   as the waters cover the sea. (Isaiah 11:6–9)

The heavens will vanish like smoke;
The earth will wear out like a garment,
    and its inhabitants will die in the same way.
But Your salvation, O Lord, will last forever,
    and Your righteousness will never fail. (Isaiah 51:6)

Take a moment to consider the greatness of God's wonderful works.

My Relationship to God

O Lord, You are my strength and my shield;
My heart trusts in You,
    and I am helped.
My heart greatly rejoices,
    and I will give thanks to You in song. (Psalm 28:7)

I will not let my heart be troubled. I will trust in You, Father, and also in Christ. (John 14:1)

Pause to thank God for the relationship that you enjoy with Him in Jesus Christ.

The Character I Want to Cultivate

Instruct those who are wise, and they will be wiser still;
Teach those who are righteous, and they will increase in
    learning. (Proverbs 9:9)

If I heed instruction, I am on the path of life,
    but those who refuse correction go astray.
    (Proverbs 10:17)

Take a moment to ask the Lord for the grace to grow in godly character.

My Relationship to Others

How beautiful on the mountains are the feet of those
who bring good news,
who proclaim Your peace, who bring good tidings,
who proclaim Your salvation.
(Isaiah 52:7; Nahum 1:15)

As I follow You, You will make me a fisher of people.
(Matthew 4:19; Mark 1:17)

*Pause to review your relationships with others and to commit
them to the Lord.*

DAY 8

The Attributes of God

> You are the living God, and there is no god besides You.
> You put to death and You bring to life,
> You have wounded and You will heal, and no one can
>   deliver from Your hand. (Deuteronomy 32:39)

Lord, the God of our fathers, are You not the God who is in heaven? Are You not the ruler over all the kingdoms of the nations? Power and might are in Your hand, and no one is able to withstand You. (2 Chronicles 20:6)

Pause to reflect on these affirmations about the person, powers and perfection of God.

The Works of God

O God, You promised the gospel beforehand through Your prophets in the Holy Scriptures concerning Your Son—who was a descendant of David according to the flesh, and who was declared with power to be Your Son, according to the Spirit of holiness, by Your resurrection from the dead—Jesus Christ our Lord. (Romans 1:2–4)

O God, our Father, You presented Christ as a sacrifice of atonement through faith in His blood. You did this to demonstrate Your righteousness at the present time, because in Your mercy, You passed over the sins committed before Jesus died. You did it to demonstrate Your righteousness in the present time, that You might be just and the justifier of those who have faith in Jesus. (Romans 3:25–26)

Take a moment to consider the greatness of God's wonderful works.

My Relationship to God

By Your grace, O God, I will not despise my birthright for the things of this world. (Genesis 25:33–34)

I will fear You, Lord, and serve You in truth with all my heart, for I consider what great things You have done for me. (1 Samuel 12:24)

Pause to thank God for the relationship that you enjoy with Him in Jesus Christ.

The Character I Want to Cultivate

I will not wear myself out to get rich;
I will have the understanding to cease.
I will not set my desire on what flies away,
    for wealth surely sprouts wings and flies into the
      heavens like an eagle. (Proverbs 23:4–5)

I want to learn to be content in whatever circumstances I am. Whether I am abased or in abundance, whether I am filled or hungry, I want to learn the secret of being content in any and every situation. I can do all things through You who strengthen me. (Philippians 4:11–13)

Take a moment to ask the Lord for the grace to grow in godly character.

My Relationship to Others

I will not hate my brother or sister in my heart. (Leviticus 19:17)

Hatred stirs up strife,
    but love covers all transgressions. (Proverbs 10:12)

Pause to review your relationships with others and to commit them to the Lord.

DAY 9

The Attributes of God

O Lord, O Lord God, You are compassionate and gracious, slow to anger and abounding in lovingkindness and truth, maintaining love to thousands, and forgiving iniquity, transgression and sin. (Exodus 34:6–7)

> Lord, You execute righteousness and justice
> for all who are oppressed.
> You are compassionate and gracious, slow to anger and
> abounding in lovingkindness. (Psalm 103:6, 8)

Pause to reflect on these affirmations about the person, powers and perfection of God.

The Works of God

You, Lord God, formed man from the dust of the ground and breathed into his nostrils the breath of life, and man became a living being. And out of the ground You made every tree grow that is pleasing to the eye and good for food. In the middle of the garden were the tree of life and the tree of the knowledge of good and evil. Then You took the man and put him in the Garden of Eden to cultivate it and take care of it. (Genesis 2:7, 9, 15)

In the day that You, O God, created man and woman, You made them in Your likeness. (Genesis 5:1)

Take a moment to consider the greatness of God's wonderful works.

My Relationship to God

Have You, O Lord, as much delight in burnt offerings and sacrifices as in obedience to Your voice? To obey is better than sacrifice, and to heed is better than the fat of rams. For rebellion is like the sin of divination, and stubbornness is as iniquity and idolatry. (1 Samuel 15:22–23)

I desire not only to call You "Lord" but to do what You say. By Your grace I will come to You, hear Your words and put them into practice. Then I will be like one who built a house, who dug down deep and laid the foundation on rock, and when a flood came, the torrent struck that house but could not shake it, because it was well built. (Luke 6:46–48)

Pause to thank God for the relationship that you enjoy with Him in Jesus Christ.

The Character I Want to Cultivate

Fools show their annoyance at once,
    but if I am prudent, I will overlook an insult.
    (Proverbs 12:16)

I will not be quickly provoked in my spirit,
    for anger rests in the hearts of fools. (Ecclesiastes 7:9)

Take a moment to ask the Lord for the grace to grow in godly character.

My Relationship to Others

I will learn to do good, seek justice, remove the oppressor, defend the orphan and plead for the widow. (Isaiah 1:17)

When You come, O Christ, to reign as king on Your glorious throne, You will say to the sheep on Your right hand, "Come, you who are blessed of My Father, inherit the kingdom prepared for you from the foundation of the world. For I was hungry, and you gave Me something to eat; I was thirsty, and you gave Me something to drink; I was a stranger, and you invited Me in; I was naked, and you clothed Me; I was sick,

and you visited Me; I was in prison, and you came to Me."
Then the righteous will answer You, "Lord, when did we see
You hungry and feed You, or thirsty and give You something
to drink? And when did we see You a stranger and invite You
in, or naked and clothe You? And when did we see You sick
or in prison and come to You?" And You, O King, will answer
and say to them, "I tell you the truth, inasmuch as you did it
to one of the least of these brothers and sisters of Mine, you
did it to Me." (Matthew 25:31, 34–40)

*Pause to review your relationships with others and to commit
them to the Lord.*

DAY 10

The Attributes of God

Great are You, Lord, and most worthy of praise;
You are to be feared above all gods.
For all the gods of the nations are idols,
    but You made the heavens.
Splendor and majesty are before You;
Strength and beauty are in Your sanctuary.
I will ascribe to You, O Lord, glory and strength.
I will ascribe to You the glory due Your name
    and worship You in the beauty of holiness. (Psalm
    96:4–9)

Holy, Holy, Holy are You, Lord of hosts;
The whole earth is full of Your glory. (Isaiah 6:3)

Pause to reflect on these affirmations about the person, powers and perfection of God.

The Works of God

O Lord, You uphold all who fall and lift up all
    who are bowed down.
The eyes of all look to You, and You give them their
    food at the proper time.
You open Your hand and satisfy the desire
    of every living thing. (Psalm 145:14–16)

Lord, You are my God;
I will exalt You and praise Your name,
For You have done wonderful things—things planned
    long ago in perfect faithfulness. (Isaiah 25:1)

Take a moment to consider the greatness of God's wonderful works.

My Relationship to God

> I know, O my Redeemer, that You live,
>   and that in the end You will stand upon the earth.
> And after my skin has been destroyed,
>   yet in my flesh I will see You, O God;
> I myself will see You and behold You with my own eyes
>   and not another.
> How my heart yearns within me! (Job 19:25–27)

I have hope in You, O God, that there will be a resurrection of both the righteous and the wicked. In view of this I strive always to keep my conscience blameless before You and before people. (Acts 24:15–16)

Pause to thank God for the relationship that you enjoy with Him in Jesus Christ.

The Character I Want to Cultivate

I will be strong and courageous; I will not be afraid or discouraged because of my adversaries, for there is a greater power with me than with them, for You, O Lord my God, are with me to help me. (2 Chronicles 32:7–8)

I will not be afraid of my adversaries, but I will remember You, Lord, who are great and awesome. (Nehemiah 4:14)

Take a moment to ask the Lord for the grace to grow in godly character.

My Relationship to Others

Far be it from me that I should sin against You, Lord, by ceasing to pray for others. (1 Samuel 12:23)

I will do nothing out of selfish ambition or vain conceit, but in humility I will esteem others as more important than myself. I will look not only to my own interests, but also to the interests of others. (Philippians 2:3–4)

Pause to review your relationships with others and to commit them to the Lord.

DAY 11

The Attributes of God

> You, O Lord, will guard the feet of Your saints,
>   but the wicked will be silenced in darkness.
> It is not by strength that one prevails;
> Those who contend with You, Lord, will be shattered.
> You will thunder against them from heaven;
> You will judge the ends of the earth.
> You will give strength to Your king
>   and exalt the horn of Your anointed.
>   (1 Samuel 2:9–10)
>
> You have sworn by Yourself;
> The word has gone out of Your mouth in righteousness
>   and will not return.
> Every knee will bow before You, and every tongue will
>   acknowledge You. (Isaiah 45:23)

Pause to reflect on these affirmations about the person, powers and perfection of God.

The Works of God

> You, Lord God, will swallow up death forever,
>   and You will wipe away the tears from every face;
> You will remove the reproach of Your people from all
>   the earth,
>   for You, the Lord, have spoken.
> And it will be said in that day,
> "Behold, this is our God;
> We have waited for Him, and He will save us.

This is the Lord; we have trusted in Him.
Let us rejoice and be glad in His salvation."
(Isaiah 25:8–9)

You will create new heavens and a new earth,
O Sovereign Lord.
The former things will not be remembered,
nor will they come to mind. (Isaiah 65:17)

Take a moment to consider the greatness of God's wonderful works.

My Relationship to God

How great is Your goodness, O Lord, which You have
stored up for those who fear You,
which You have prepared for those who take refuge
in You in the sight of others! (Psalm 31:19)

You know how I am formed;
You remember that I am dust.
As for people, their days are like grass;
They flourish like flowers of the field.
The wind passes over them and they are gone,
and their place remembers them no more.
But Your lovingkindness, O Lord,
is from everlasting to everlasting to those who fear You,
and Your righteousness with their children's children,
to those who keep Your covenant and remember
to obey Your precepts. (Psalm 103:14–18)

*Pause to thank God for the relationship that you enjoy with
Him in Jesus Christ.*

The Character I Want to Cultivate

If I am afraid of people, fear will trap me.
But if I trust in You, O Lord, You will keep me safe.
(Proverbs 29:25)

Cursed is the one who trusts in people,
who depends on human strength
and whose heart turns away from You, O Lord.
But blessed is the one who trusts in You, whose
confidence is in You. (Jeremiah 17:5, 7)

Take a moment to ask the Lord for the grace to grow in godly character.

My Relationship to Others

A virtuous wife is the crown of her husband,
but she who causes shame is like decay in his bones.
(Proverbs 12:4)

Who can find a virtuous wife?
She is worth far more than jewels.
The heart of her husband trusts in her so that he has no
lack of gain.
She brings him good, not harm, all the days of her life.
(Proverbs 31:10–12)

Pause to review your relationships with others and to commit them to the Lord.

DAY 12

The Attributes of God

Your lovingkindness, O Lord, reaches to the heavens,
Your faithfulness to the skies.
Your righteousness is like the mighty mountains;
Your judgments are like the great deep.
O Lord, You preserve people and beasts.
How priceless is Your lovingkindness, O God!
Both the high and low among people find refuge in the
shadow of Your wings.
For with You is the fountain of life;
In Your light we see light. (Psalm 36:5–7, 9)

Your lovingkindness, O Lord, is great toward us,
and Your truth endures forever.
Praise the Lord! (Psalm 117:2)

Pause to reflect on these affirmations about the person, powers and perfection of God.

The Works of God

Your foolishness, O God, is wiser than human wisdom, and Your weakness is stronger than human strength. But You chose the foolish things of the world to shame the wise, and You chose the weak things of the world to shame the strong; the lowly things of this world and the despised things You have chosen, and the things that are not, to nullify the things that are, so that no one may boast before You. (1 Corinthians 1:25, 27–29)

Lord, thank you for the invitation you extended to me when You said, "Behold, I stand at the door and knock. If you hear

My voice and open the door, I will come in to you and dine
with you, and you with Me. To you who overcome, I will
give the right to sit with Me on My throne, just as I overcame and sat down with My Father on His throne." (Revelation 3:20–21)

*Take a moment to consider the greatness of God's wonderful
works.*

My Relationship to God

Have mercy on me, O God, have mercy on me,
  for in You my soul takes refuge.
I will take refuge in the shadow of Your wings
  until destruction passes by.
I cry out to You, O God Most High, to You who fulfill
  Your purpose for me. (Psalm 57:1–2)

This is what You, the Lord God, the Holy One
  of Israel, have said:
"In repentance and rest is your salvation; in quietness
  and trust is your strength." (Isaiah 30:15)

*Pause to thank God for the relationship that you enjoy with
Him in Jesus Christ.*

The Character I Want to Cultivate

You, O Lord, desire mercy, not sacrifice, and the
  knowledge of You more than burnt offerings.
  (Hosea 6:6)

Blessed are the merciful, for they shall obtain mercy.
(Matthew 5:7)

*Take a moment to ask the Lord for the grace to grow in godly
character.*

My Relationship to Others

I will honor my father and my mother. (Exodus 20:12; Deuteronomy 5:16)

> The parents of the righteous will greatly rejoice,
> and those who beget a wise child will be glad.
> May my father and mother be glad;
> May she who gave me birth rejoice.
> (Proverbs 23:24–25)

Pause to review your relationships with others and to commit them to the Lord.

DAY 13

The Attributes of God

> O Lord, our Lord, how majestic is Your name
>   in all the earth!
> You have set Your glory above the heavens! (Psalm 8:1)

> My soul blesses You,
> O Lord my God, You are very great;
> You are clothed with splendor and majesty.
>   (Psalm 104:1)

Pause to reflect on these affirmations about the person, powers and perfection of God.

The Works of God

O Lord, in six days You made the heavens and the earth, the sea, and all that is in them, and rested on the seventh day. Therefore You blessed the Sabbath day and made it holy. (Exodus 20:11)

You alone are the Lord. You made the heavens, even the heaven of heavens, and all their starry host, the earth and all that is on it, the seas and all that is in them. You give life to all that is in them, and the host of heaven worships You. (Nehemiah 9:6)

Take a moment to consider the greatness of God's wonderful works.

My Relationship to God

> You, O Lord, are my shepherd; I shall not be in want.
> You make me lie down in green pastures;
> You lead me beside quiet waters;

You restore my soul.
You guide me in the paths of righteousness
    for Your name's sake.
Even though I walk through the valley of the shadow
    of death,
I will fear no evil, for You are with me.
Your rod and Your staff, they comfort me.
You prepare a table before me in the presence
    of my enemies.
You anoint my head with oil;
My cup overflows.
Surely goodness and mercy will follow me all the days
    of my life,
    and I will dwell in Your house, O Lord, forever.
    (Psalm 23:1–6)

I know that in all things You work for the good of those who love You, O God, of those who have been called according to Your purpose. (Romans 8:28)

Pause to thank God for the relationship that you enjoy with Him in Jesus Christ.

The Character I Want to Cultivate

Lord, make me to know my end and what is the
    measure of my days;
Let me know how fleeting is my life. (Psalm 39:4)

Teach me to number my days, that I may gain
    a heart of wisdom. (Psalm 90:12)

Take a moment to ask the Lord for the grace to grow in godly character.

My Relationship to Others

Since we were called into fellowship with You, Lord Jesus Christ, all of us should agree with one another, so that there may be no divisions among us, and that we may be perfectly joined together in the same mind and in the same judgment. (1 Corinthians 1:9–10)

There is neither Jew nor Greek, there is neither slave nor free, there is neither male nor female, for we are all one in You, Christ Jesus. (Galatians 3:28)

Pause to review your relationships with others and to commit them to the Lord.

DAY 14

The Attributes of God

You, Lord, do not see as people see. People look at my outward appearance, but You look at my heart. (1 Samuel 16:7)

Lord, You have searched me and You know me.
You know when I sit down and when I rise up;
You understand my thoughts from afar.
You scrutinize my path and my lying down and are
    acquainted with all my ways.
Before a word is on my tongue, O Lord,
    You know it completely. (Psalm 139:1–4)

Pause to reflect on these affirmations about the person, powers and perfection of God.

The Works of God

We praise You, Jesus, that God's word is fulfilled in You:

You will come forth a Shoot from the stump of Jesse;
From his roots a Branch will bear fruit.
    the Spirit of the Lord will rest on You—
    the Spirit of wisdom and of understanding,
    the Spirit of counsel and of power,
    the Spirit of knowledge and of the fear of the Lord—
    and You will delight in the fear of the Lord.
You will not judge by what You see with Your eyes,
    or decide by what You hear with Your ears,
    but with righteousness You will judge the poor
    and decide with fairness for the meek of the earth,
    and You will strike the earth with the rod of Your
        mouth;

> with the breath of Your lips You will slay the wicked.
> Righteousness will be Your belt and faithfulness the sash
> around Your waist. (Isaiah 11:1–5)

Behold, a virgin was with child and gave birth to a son, and they called Your name Immanuel, which means, "God with us." (Matthew 1:23)

Take a moment to consider the greatness of God's wonderful works.

My Relationship to God

You, O Lord my God, want me to fear You, to walk in all Your ways, to love You and to serve You, O Lord my God, with all my heart and with all my soul. (Deuteronomy 10:12)

I want to know You, O God, and serve You with a whole heart and with a willing mind; for You search my heart and understand every motive behind my thoughts. (1 Chronicles 28:9)

Pause to thank God for the relationship that you enjoy with Him in Jesus Christ.

The Character I Want to Cultivate

I know, my God, that You test my heart and are pleased with integrity. (1 Chronicles 29:17)

> May those who hope in You not be ashamed
> because of me, O Lord God of hosts.
> May those who seek You not be dishonored
> because of me, O God of Israel. (Psalm 69:6)

Take a moment to ask the Lord for the grace to grow in godly character.

My Relationship to Others

If I acknowledge You before others, Lord Jesus, You will also acknowledge me before Your Father in heaven. But if I deny You before others, You will also deny me before Your Father in heaven. (Matthew 10:32–33)

I will not be ashamed to testify about You, O Lord, but I will join with others in suffering for the gospel according to Your power, O God. (2 Timothy 1:8)

Pause to review your relationships with others and to commit them to the Lord.

DAY 15

The Attributes of God

You, O God, are the Rock; Your work is perfect, for all Your ways are just. A God of faithfulness and without injustice, upright and just are You. (Deuteronomy 32:4)

> Your word, O Lord, is upright, and all Your work
>   is done in faithfulness.
> You love righteousness and justice;
> The earth is full of Your lovingkindness.
>   (Psalm 33:4–5)

Pause to reflect on these affirmations about the person, powers and perfection of God.

The Works of God

Multitudes who sleep in the dust of the earth will awake, some to everlasting life, others to shame and everlasting contempt. Those who are wise will shine like the brightness of the heavens, and those who lead many to righteousness will be like the stars for ever and ever. (Daniel 12:2–3)

An hour is coming when all who are in the graves will hear Your voice, O Son of Man, and will come out—those who have done good will rise to a resurrection of life, and those who have done evil will rise to a resurrection of judgment. (John 5:28–29)

Take a moment to consider the greatness of God's wonderful works.

My Relationship to God

> I will praise You, O Lord my God, with all my heart,
>   and I will glorify Your name forever.
> For great is Your love toward me;
> You have delivered my soul from the depths of the
>   grave. (Psalm 86:12–13)

> I will exult in You, Lord;
> I will rejoice in You, O God of my salvation.
> You, Lord God, are my strength;
> You make my feet like the feet of a deer and enable me
>   to go on the heights. (Habakkuk 3:18–19)

Pause to thank God for the relationship that you enjoy with Him in Jesus Christ.

The Character I Want to Cultivate

I will not spread false reports, nor will I help a wicked person by being a malicious witness. (Exodus 23:1)

> Lying lips are hateful to You, Lord,
>   but You delight in those who deal faithfully.
>   (Proverbs 12:22)

Take a moment to ask the Lord for the grace to grow in godly character.

My Relationship to Others

I will not take vengeance or bear a grudge against others, but I will love my neighbor as myself. (Leviticus 19:18)

Whatever I want others to do to me, I will also do to them, for this is the Law and the Prophets. (Matthew 7:12)

Pause to review your relationships with others and to commit them to the Lord.

DAY 16

The Attributes of God

Lord, there is no one holy like You; there is no one besides You, nor is there any Rock like You, our God. (1 Samuel 2:2)

You are but one God, Father, from whom all things came and for whom I live; and there is but one Lord Jesus Christ, through whom all things came and through whom I live. (1 Corinthians 8:6)

Pause to reflect on these affirmations about the person, powers and perfection of God.

The Works of God

God so loved the world that He gave You, Jesus, His only begotten Son, that whoever believes in You should not perish but have eternal life. For God did not send You into the world to condemn the world, but to save the world through You. (John 3:16–17)

Jesus, You have come as a light into the world, that whoever believes in You should not stay in darkness. You do not judge those who hear Your words but do not keep them, for You did not come to judge the world, but to save the world. (John 12:46–47)

Take a moment to consider the greatness of God's wonderful works.

My Relationship to God

Lord Jesus, You are in Your Father, and I am in You, and You are in me. (John 14:20)

If I have been united with You, O Christ, in the likeness of Your death, I will certainly also be united with You in the likeness of Your resurrection. (Romans 6:5)

Pause to thank God for the relationship that you enjoy with Him in Jesus Christ.

The Character I Want to Cultivate

> When pride comes, then comes dishonor, but with
>   humility comes wisdom. (Proverbs 11:2)

> The proud will be humbled and the lofty will be
>   brought low;
> You alone, O Lord, will be exalted. (Isaiah 2:11)

Take a moment to ask the Lord for the grace to grow in godly character.

My Relationship to Others

> Is this not the fast You have chosen:
>   to loose the bonds of wickedness,
>   to undo the cords of the yoke, and to let the
>   oppressed go free and break every yoke?
> Is it not to share our food with the hungry
>   and to provide the poor wanderer with shelter;
> When we see the naked, to clothe them, and not to
>   turn away from our own flesh?
> Then our light will break forth like the dawn,
>   and our healing will quickly appear,
>   and our righteousness will go before us;
> Your glory, O Lord, will be our rear guard.
> Then we will call, and You will answer;
> We will cry, and You will say, "Here I am."

If we put away the yoke from our midst,
    the pointing of the finger and malicious talk,
and if we extend our souls to the hungry
    and satisfy the afflicted soul,
    then our light will rise in the darkness,
    and our gloom will become like the noonday.
    (Isaiah 58:6–10)

I must help the weak and remember Your words, Lord Jesus,
"It is more blessed to give than to receive." (Acts 20:35)

Pause to review your relationships with others and to commit them to the Lord.

DAY 17

The Attributes of God

O Lord, You will be gracious to whom You will be gracious, and You will have compassion on whom You will have compassion. (Exodus 33:19)

Lord Jesus, You are holy and true; You hold the key of David. What You open no one can shut, and what You shut no one can open. (Revelation 3:7)

Pause to reflect on these affirmations about the person, powers and perfection of God.

The Works of God

O God, You are the maker of the Bear and Orion,
 the Pleiades and the constellations of the south.
You do great things that cannot be fathomed and
 wonderful works that cannot be counted.
 (Job 9:9–10)

The day is Yours, O God; the night also is Yours;
You established the sun and moon.
It was You who set all the boundaries of the earth;
You made both summer and winter. (Psalm 74:16–17)

Take a moment to consider the greatness of God's wonderful works.

My Relationship to God

I will not depend on human strength but on You, O Lord my God, for help and deliverance. (2 Chronicles 16:7–8, 12)

I will trust in You, Lord, and do good;
I will dwell in the land and feed on Your faithfulness.

I will delight myself in You, Lord, and You will give me
the desires of my heart.
I will commit my way to You, Lord, and trust in You,
and You will bring it to pass.
I will rest in You, Lord, and wait patiently for You;
I will not fret because of those who prosper in their
way, because of those who practice evil schemes.
(Psalm 37:3–5, 7)

*Pause to thank God for the relationship that you enjoy with
Him in Jesus Christ.*

The Character I Want to Cultivate

Before I was afflicted, I went astray, O Lord,
but now I keep Your word.
It was good for me to be afflicted, so that I might learn
Your statutes. (Psalm 119:67, 71)

I will not despise Your discipline, O Lord, nor lose heart when
You rebuke me, for whom You love You discipline, and You
chastise every child whom You receive. (Hebrews 12:5–6)

*Take a moment to ask the Lord for the grace to grow in godly
character.*

My Relationship to Others

We who are strong ought to bear the weaknesses of those
who are not strong and not to please ourselves. Each of us
should please our neighbors for their good, to build them
up. (Romans 15:1–2)

I am not to seek my own good, but rather the good of others. (1 Corinthians 10:24)

*Pause to review your relationships with others and to commit
them to the Lord.*

DAY 18

The Attributes of God

You must be treated as holy by those who come near You, O Lord, and before all people You will be honored. (Leviticus 10:3)

> You, O Lord of hosts, will be exalted in judgment;
> and You, the holy God,
> will show Yourself holy in righteousness.
> (Isaiah 5:16)

Pause to reflect on these affirmations about the person, powers and perfection of God.

The Works of God

Your eyes, O Lord, move to and fro throughout the whole earth to strengthen those whose hearts are fully committed to You. (2 Chronicles 16:9)

For those who revere Your name, O Lord Almighty, the sun of righteousness will rise with healing in his wings. And they will go out and leap like calves released from the stall. (Malachi 4:2)

Take a moment to consider the greatness of God's wonderful works.

My Relationship to God

I will not let Your word depart from my mouth, O Lord, but I will meditate on it day and night, so that I may be careful to do all that is written in it; for then I will be prosperous, and I will act wisely. (Joshua 1:8)

I am committed to You, O God, and to the word of Your grace, which is able to build me up and give me an inheritance among all those who are sanctified. (Acts 20:32)

Pause to thank God for the relationship that you enjoy with Him in Jesus Christ.

The Character I Want to Cultivate

I shall not covet my neighbor's house, my neighbor's wife, his manservant or maidservant, his ox or donkey, or anything that belongs to my neighbor. (Exodus 20:17; Deuteronomy 5:21)

I will be on my guard against all covetousness, for my life does not consist in the abundance of my possessions. (Luke 12:15)

Take a moment to ask the Lord for the grace to grow in godly character.

My Relationship to Others

Wives should submit to their own husbands as to You, O Lord. For the husband is the head of the wife, as You, O Christ, also are the head of the church; and You are the Savior of the body. But as the church is subject to You, so wives should be to their husbands in everything. (Ephesians 5:22–24)

Husbands should love their wives, just as You, O Christ, also loved the church and gave Yourself up for her that You might sanctify and cleanse her by the washing with water through the word, that You might present her to Yourself as a glorious church, without spot or wrinkle or any other blemish, but holy and blameless. So husbands ought to love their own wives as their own bodies. He who loves his own wife loves himself; for no one ever hated his own flesh, but nourishes and cherishes it, just as You also do the church, for we are members of Your body. (Ephesians 5:25–30)

Pause to review your relationships with others and to commit them to the Lord.

DAY 19

The Attributes of God

> You, O Lord Most High, are awesome,
>   the great King over all the earth!
> You are the King of all the earth,
>   and I will sing Your praise.
> You reign over the nations;
>   You are seated on Your holy throne. (Psalm 47:2, 7–8)

You, O Son of God, are the radiance of God's glory and the exact representation of His being, upholding all things by Your powerful word. After You cleansed our sins, You sat down at the right hand of the Majesty on high, having become as much superior to angels as the name You have inherited is more excellent than theirs. (Hebrews 1:3–4)

Pause to reflect on these affirmations about the person, powers and perfection of God.

The Works of God

> Behold, You will come with power, Lord God,
>   and Your arm will rule for You.
> Behold, Your reward is with You,
>   and Your recompense accompanies You.
> You will feed Your flock like a shepherd;
> You will gather the lambs in Your arms
>   and carry them close to Your heart;
> You will gently lead those that have young. (Isaiah
>   40:10–11)

When You, O Son of Man, come in Your glory, and all the angels with You, You will sit on Your glorious throne. All the nations will be gathered before You, and You will separate the people one from another as a shepherd separates the sheep from the goats. You will put the sheep on Your right and the goats on Your left. Then You, O King, will say to those on Your right, "Come, you who are blessed by My Father; inherit the kingdom prepared for you since the foundation of the world." (Matthew 25:31–34)

Take a moment to consider the greatness of God's wonderful works.

My Relationship to God

Like Josiah, I want to do what is right in Your sight, O Lord, and walk in all the ways of David, not turning aside to the right or to the left. (2 Kings 22:1–2)

I do not want to be like the rocky places on which the seed was thrown—like those who hear the word and at once receive it with joy, but since they have no root, last only a short time; when affliction or persecution comes because of the word, they quickly fall away. Nor do I want to be like the soil among the thorns on which seed was sown—like those who hear the word, but the worries of this world, the deceitfulness of riches and pleasures, and the desires for other things come in and choke the word, making it immature and unfruitful. Instead, I want to be like the good soil on which seed was sown—like those who with noble and good hearts hear the word, understand and accept it, and with perseverance bear fruit, yielding thirty, sixty or a hundred times what was sown. (Matthew 13:20–23; Mark 4:16–20; Luke 8:13–15)

Pause to thank God for the relationship that you enjoy with Him in Jesus Christ.

The Character I Want to Cultivate

> Blessed are those who do not walk in the counsel of the
>   wicked
>   or stand in the way of sinners
>   or sit in the seat of scorners.
> But their delight is in Your law, O Lord,
>   and on Your law they meditate day and night.
> And they shall be like trees planted by streams of water;
> They yield fruit in season and their leaves do not
>   wither;
> Whatever they do will prosper. (Psalm 1:1–3)

O God, I will be diligent to present myself to You as one approved, a worker who does not need to be ashamed and who correctly handles the word of truth. (2 Timothy 2:15)

Take a moment to ask the Lord for the grace to grow in godly character.

My Relationship to Others

> Those who spare the rod hate their children,
>   but those who love their children are careful
>   to discipline them. (Proverbs 13:24)

> Foolishness is bound up in the hearts of children,
>   but the rod of discipline will drive it far from them.
>   (Proverbs 22:15)

Pause to review your relationships with others and to commit them to the Lord.

DAY 20

The Attributes of God

Yours, O Lord, is the greatness and the power
    and the glory and the victory and the majesty,
    for everything in heaven and earth is Yours.
Yours, O Lord, is the kingdom,
    and You are exalted as head over all.
Both riches and honor come from You,
    and You are the ruler of all things.
In Your hand is power and might to exalt
    and to give strength to all.
Therefore, my God, I give You thanks
    and praise Your glorious name.
All things come from You, and I can only give You what
    comes from Your hand. (1 Chronicles 29:11–14)

Your throne, O God, is for ever and ever;
A scepter of righteousness is the scepter of
    Your kingdom. (Psalm 45:6)

Pause to reflect on these affirmations about the person, powers and perfection of God.

The Works of God

Apart from the law, Your righteousness, O God, has been made known, being witnessed by the Law and the Prophets, even Your righteousness through faith in Jesus Christ to all who believe. For there is no difference, for all have sinned and fall short of Your glory, O God, being justified freely by Your grace through the redemption that is in Christ Jesus. (Romans 3:21–24)

At the right time, when we were helpless, Christ died for the ungodly. For rarely will anyone die for one who is righteous, though perhaps for a good person someone would even dare to die. But You, O God, demonstrate Your own love for us in that while we were still sinners, Christ died for us. (Romans 5:6–8)

Take a moment to consider the greatness of God's wonderful works.

My Relationship to God

No one who waits for You will be ashamed,
>   but the one who is treacherous without cause
>   will be ashamed.
Show me Your ways, O Lord, teach me Your paths;
Lead me in Your truth and teach me,
>   for You are the God of my salvation,
>   and my hope is in You all day long. (Psalm 25:3–5)

You have plans for me, O Lord; You have declared that you have plans to prosper me and not to harm me, plans to give me a future and a hope. (Jeremiah 29:11)

Pause to thank God for the relationship that you enjoy with Him in Jesus Christ.

The Character I Want to Cultivate

I will be strong and courageous, being careful to obey Your word, O Lord; I will not turn from it to the right or to the left, that I may act wisely wherever I go. (Joshua 1:7)

I will take courage and not be afraid, for You, Lord Jesus, are with me. (Mark 6:50)

Take a moment to ask the Lord for the grace to grow in godly character.

My Relationship to Others

We have many members in one body, but all the members do not have the same function; in the same way we who are many are one body in You, O Jesus Christ, and individually members of one another. And we have different gifts, according to the grace You have given to us. (Romans 12:4–6)

There are different kinds of gifts, but the same Spirit. And there are different kinds of service, but the same Lord. And there are different kinds of working, but You are the same God who works all of them in all people. But to each one the manifestation of Your Spirit is given for the common good. (1 Corinthians 12:4–7)

Pause to review your relationships with others and to commit them to the Lord.

DAY 21

The Attributes of God

As for You, O God, Your way is perfect; Your word, O Lord, is proven. You are a shield for all who take refuge in You. For who are You, O God, besides the Lord? And who is the Rock except You, who are our God? (2 Samuel 22:31–32)

> Lord, You long to be gracious
>   and rise to show compassion.
> For You, O Lord, are a God of justice;
>   Blessed are all those who wait for You! (Isaiah 30:18)

Pause to reflect on these affirmations about the person, powers and perfection of God.

The Works of God

> The heavens declare Your glory, O God,
>   and the skies proclaim the work of Your hands.
> Day after day they pour forth speech;
> Night after night they reveal knowledge. (Psalm 19:1–2)

> You, O Lord, are the great God,
>   the great King above all gods.
> In Your hand are the depths of the earth;
> The summits of the mountains are Yours also.
> The sea is Yours, for You made it, and Your hands
>   formed the dry land.
> You are our God and we are the people of Your pasture
>   and the sheep under Your care. (Psalm 95:3–5, 7)

Take a moment to consider the greatness of God's wonderful works.

My Relationship to God

You have loved me with an everlasting love; You have drawn me with lovingkindness. (Jeremiah 31:3)

Who shall separate me from Your love, O Christ? Shall tribulation, or distress, or persecution, or famine, or nakedness, or danger or sword? As it is written: "For Your sake we face death all day long; we are considered as sheep to be slaughtered." Yet in all these things I am more than a conqueror through You who love me. (Romans 8:35–37)

Pause to thank God for the relationship that you enjoy with Him in Jesus Christ.

The Character I Want to Cultivate

I am not trying to win the approval of other people; I want to win Your approval, O God. If I were still trying to please people, I would not be a servant of Christ. (Galatians 1:10)

Since I have been approved by You, O God, to be entrusted with the gospel, I speak not as one who wants to please people but instead so as to please You, the One who tests my heart. I will not seek glory from people. (1 Thessalonians 2:4, 6)

Take a moment to ask the Lord for the grace to grow in godly character.

My Relationship to Others

You have called me to go and proclaim Your kingdom, O God. (Luke 9:60)

As the Father has sent You, You also send us, Lord Jesus. (John 20:21)

Pause to review your relationships with others and to commit them to the Lord.

DAY 22

The Attributes of God

I will arise and bless You, Lord my God; You are from ever-lasting to everlasting. Blessed be Your glorious name, which is exalted above all blessing and praise! (Nehemiah 9:5)

Glory to You, O God, in the highest, and on earth peace to those on whom Your favor rests. (Luke 2:14)

Pause to reflect on these affirmations about the person, powers and perfection of God.

The Works of God

I will remember Your works, O Lord;
Surely I will remember Your wonders of long ago.
I will meditate on all Your works
    and consider all Your mighty deeds.
Your way, O God, is holy.
What god is so great as You?
You are the God who works wonders;
You have revealed Your strength among the peoples.
You redeemed Your people with Your power, the
    descendants of Jacob and Joseph. (Psalm 77:11–15)

As the earth brings forth its sprouts and as a garden
    causes that which is sown to spring up,
So You, Lord God, will make righteousness and praise
    spring up before all nations. (Isaiah 61:11)

Take a moment to consider the greatness of God's wonderful works.

My Relationship to God

We praise You, O Lord;
Day by day You bear our burdens,
  O God of our salvation.
You, our God, are the God of salvation,
  and to You, God the Lord, belongs escape from death.
  (Psalm 68:19–20)

Lord Jesus, all those the Father gives You will come to You, and whoever comes to You, You will never cast out. For You have come down from heaven, not to do Your own will, but the will of Him who sent You. And this is the will of Him who sent You, that You will lose none of all those He has given You, but raise them up at the last day. For Your Father's will is that those who look to You and believe in You may have eternal life, and You will raise them up at the last day. (John 6:37–40)

Pause to thank God for the relationship that you enjoy with Him in Jesus Christ.

The Character I Want to Cultivate

What is desirable in a person is kindness,
  and it is better to be poor than to be a liar.
  (Proverbs 19:22)

As one of Your chosen people, O God, holy and beloved, I will put on a heart of compassion, kindness, humility, gentleness and patience, bearing with others and forgiving others even as You, Lord, forgave me; and above all these things I will put on love, which is the bond of perfection. (Colossians 3:12–14)

Take a moment to ask the Lord for the grace to grow in godly character.

My Relationship to Others

I will love my enemies and pray for those who persecute me. (Matthew 5:44)

I will love my enemies, do good to those who hate me, bless those who curse me, and pray for those who mistreat me. I will do to others as I would have them do to me. (Luke 6:27–28, 31)

Pause to review your relationships with others and to commit them to the Lord.

DAY 23

The Attributes of God

O God, will You indeed dwell on earth? Heaven and the highest heaven cannot contain You. (1 Kings 8:27)

> O God, You sit enthroned above the circle of the earth,
> and its inhabitants are like grasshoppers.
> You stretch out the heavens like a curtain and spread
> them out like a tent to dwell in.
> You reduce rulers to nothing and make the judges
> of this world meaningless. (Isaiah 40:22–23)

Pause to reflect on these affirmations about the person, powers and perfection of God.

The Works of God

You will magnify Yourself and sanctify Yourself, and You will make Yourself known in the sight of many nations, and they will know that You are the Lord. (Ezekiel 38:23)

> The earth will be filled with the knowledge
> of Your glory, O Lord,
> as the waters cover the sea. (Habakkuk 2:14)

Take a moment to consider the greatness of God's wonderful works.

My Relationship to God

> O God, You are my refuge and strength,
> an ever-present help in trouble.
> Therefore I will not fear, though the earth give way
> and the mountains slip into the heart of the sea.
> (Psalm 46:1–2)

I will not fear, for You are with me;
I will not be dismayed, for You are my God.
You will strengthen me and help me;
You will uphold me with Your righteous right hand.
For You are the Lord my God;
You take hold of my right hand and say to me,
"Do not fear; I will help you." (Isaiah 41:10, 13)

Pause to thank God for the relationship that you enjoy with Him in Jesus Christ.

The Character I Want to Cultivate

To fear You, O Lord, is the beginning of knowledge,
but fools despise wisdom and discipline.
(Proverbs 1:7)

Lord, You give wisdom;
From Your mouth come knowledge and understanding.
You store up sound wisdom for the upright;
You are a shield to those who walk in integrity,
guarding the paths of the just and protecting the way
of Your saints.
Then I will understand righteousness and justice and
honesty—every good path,
for wisdom will enter my heart,
and knowledge will be pleasant to my soul.
Discretion will protect me,
and understanding will guard me. (Proverbs 2:6–11)

Take a moment to ask the Lord for the grace to grow in godly character.

My Relationship to Others

As I give, it will be given to me; a good measure, pressed down, shaken together and running over will be poured into my lap. For with the measure I use, it will be measured back to me. (Luke 6:38)

Those who sow sparingly will also reap sparingly, and those who sow bountifully will also reap bountifully. We should give as we have decided in our hearts, not reluctantly or under compulsion; for You, O God, love a cheerful giver. And You are able to make all grace abound to us, so that always having all sufficiency in everything, we may abound in every good work. As it is written: "He has scattered abroad His gifts to the poor; His righteousness endures forever." Now You, the One who supplies seed to the sower and bread for food, will also supply and increase our seed and will increase the fruits of our righteousness. (2 Corinthians 9:6–10)

Pause to review your relationships with others and to commit them to the Lord.

DAY 24

The Attributes of God

Where does wisdom come from?
Where does understanding dwell?
It is hidden from the eyes of every living thing and
  concealed from the birds of the air.
Destruction and Death say, "Only a rumor of it has
  reached our ears."
You understand its way, O God, and You know its place,
  for You look to the ends of the earth and see
  everything under the heavens. (Job 28:20–24)

Oh, the depth of the riches of Your wisdom and knowledge,
O God! How unsearchable are Your judgments and Your
ways past finding out! For who has known Your mind, O
Lord? Or who has been Your counselor? Or who has first
given to You, that You should repay? For from You and
through You and to You are all things. To You be the glory
forever! Amen. (Romans 11:33–36)

*Pause to reflect on these affirmations about the person, powers
and perfection of God.*

The Works of God

O Christ, You were in the world, and the world was made
through You, and the world did not know You. You came to
Your own, but Your own did not receive You. (John 1:10–11)

The light has come into the world, but people loved darkness rather than light because their deeds were evil. For those
who do evil hate the light and will not come into the light,

for fear that their deeds will be exposed. But those who practice the truth come into the light, so that their deeds may be
clearly seen as having been done through You, O God. (John
3:19–21)

*Take a moment to consider the greatness of God's wonderful
works.*

My Relationship to God

I want to love You, Lord my God, obey Your voice, and hold
fast to You. For You are my life and the length of my days.
(Deuteronomy 30:20)

> I love You, O Lord, my strength.
> You are my rock and my fortress and my deliverer;
> My God, You are my rock, in whom I take refuge.
> You are my shield and the horn of my salvation,
>   my stronghold.
> I call upon You, Lord, for You are worthy of praise,
>   and I am saved from my enemies. (Psalm 18:1–3)

*Pause to thank God for the relationship that you enjoy with
Him in Jesus Christ.*

The Character I Want to Cultivate

I will not steal, nor deal falsely, nor deceive others. (Leviticus 19:11)

I will not pervert justice or show partiality. I will not accept
a bribe, for a bribe blinds the eyes of the wise and perverts
the words of the righteous. (Deuteronomy 16:19)

*Take a moment to ask the Lord for the grace to grow in godly
character.*

My Relationship to Others

> Starting a quarrel is like breaching a dam,
>   so I will stop a quarrel before it breaks out.
>   (Proverbs 17:14)

If it is possible, I will live at peace with all people, as far as it depends on me. (Romans 12:18)

Pause to review your relationships with others and to commit them to the Lord.

DAY 25

The Attributes of God

O God, You are exalted beyond our understanding; the
number of Your years is unsearchable. (Job 36:26)

You are He; You are the first, and You are also the last.
(Isaiah 48:12)

*Pause to reflect on these affirmations about the person, powers
and perfection of God.*

The Works of God

The earth is Yours, O Lord, and everything in it,
    the world and all who dwell in it.
For You founded it upon the seas and established it
    upon the waters. (Psalm 24:1–2)

O Lord, You cover Yourself in light as with a garment;
You stretch out the heavens like a tent curtain
    and lay the beams of Your upper chambers in the
        waters.
You make the clouds Your chariot and walk on the
    wings of the wind.
You make the winds Your messengers,
    flames of fire Your servants.
You set the earth on its foundations so that it can never
    be moved.
You covered it with the deep as with a garment;
The waters stood above the mountains.

At Your rebuke the waters fled;
At the sound of Your thunder they hurried away.
They flowed over the mountains and went down into
    the valleys, to the place You assigned for them.
You set a boundary they cannot cross,
    that they will not return to cover the earth.
O Lord, how manifold are Your works!
In wisdom You made them all;
The earth is full of Your possessions.
    (Psalm 104:2–9, 24)

Take a moment to consider the greatness of God's wonderful works.

My Relationship to God

I will give thanks to You, O Lord,
    and call upon Your name
    and make known to others what You have done.
I will sing to You, sing praises to You,
    and tell of all Your wonderful acts. (1 Chronicles
    16:8–9)

I trust in Your loyal love;
My heart rejoices in Your salvation.
I will sing to You, O Lord, for You have dealt
    bountifully with me. (Psalm 13:5–6)

Pause to thank God for the relationship that you enjoy with Him in Jesus Christ.

The Character I Want to Cultivate

In a multitude of words, transgression does not cease,
    but those who restrain their lips are wise.
    (Proverbs 10:19)

Fools have no delight in understanding
But only in airing their own opinions. (Proverbs 18:2)

Take a moment to ask the Lord for the grace to grow in godly character.

My Relationship to Others

Love is as strong as death; its jealousy is as cruel as the grave; its flames are a blazing fire from You, O Lord. Many waters cannot quench love, nor can rivers overflow it. If a man were to give all the wealth of his house for love, it would be utterly scorned. (Song of Songs 8:6–7)

A husband should not break his promises to the wife of his youth, because she is a companion and a wife by covenant. Lord God of hosts, You seek a godly offspring and hate divorce; therefore we must take heed to our spirit and not break faith. (Malachi 2:14–16)

Pause to review your relationships with others and to commit them to the Lord.

DAY 26

The Attributes of God

Nothing is too difficult for You, O Lord. (Genesis 18:14)

All things are possible with You, O God. (Matthew 19:26; Mark 10:27)

Pause to reflect on these affirmations about the person, powers and perfection of God.

The Works of God

O Servant of God, people despised and rejected You;
You were a man of sorrows and acquainted with grief.
And like one from whom people hide their faces,
    you were despised, and we did not esteem You.
Surely You have borne our infirmities and carried our
    sorrows,
    yet we considered You stricken, smitten by God and
      afflicted.
But You were pierced for our transgressions,
    You were crushed for our iniquities;
The punishment that brought us peace was upon You,
    and by Your wounds we are healed.
All of us like sheep have gone astray, all of us have
    turned to our own way,
    and the Lord has laid on You the iniquity of us all.
    (Isaiah 53:3–6)

Jesus, You who are the Son of Man, did not come to be served, but to serve and to give Your life as a ransom for many. (Matthew 20:28)

Take a moment to consider the greatness of God's wonderful works.

My Relationship to God

I know that my old self was crucified with You, O Christ, so that the body of sin might be done away with, that I should no longer be a slave to sin; for anyone who has died has been freed from sin. (Romans 6:6–7)

Through the law I died to the law so that I might live for God. I have been crucified with You, O Christ, and it is no longer I who live, but You live in me. The life that I now live in the flesh, I live by faith in You, the Son of God, who loved me and gave Yourself for me. (Galatians 2:19–20)

Pause to thank God for the relationship that you enjoy with Him in Jesus Christ.

The Character I Want to Cultivate

> To fear You, Lord, is instruction for wisdom, and
>   humility comes before honor. (Proverbs 15:33)

O Lord, thank You for the truth You have spoken when You said, "Let not those who are wise boast of wisdom, and let not those who are strong boast of strength, and let not those who are rich boast of riches; but let those who boast boast about this: that they understand and know Me, that I am the Lord, who exercises lovingkindness, justice and righteousness on earth; for in these I delight." (Jeremiah 9:23–24)

Take a moment to ask the Lord for the grace to grow in godly character.

My Relationship to Others

Your commandments will be upon my heart, and I will teach them diligently to my children and talk about them when I sit in my house and when I walk along the way and when I lie down and when I rise up. (Deuteronomy 6:6–7)

> Wise children heed their parent's instruction,
>   but a scoffer does not listen to rebuke.
>   (Proverbs 13:1)

Pause to review your relationships with others and to commit them to the Lord.

DAY 27

The Attributes of God

You, Lord God, are the faithful God. You keep Your covenant and Your lovingkindness to a thousand generations of those who love You and keep Your commands. (Deuteronomy 7:9)

> I call this to mind, and therefore I have hope:
> Your mercies, O Lord, never cease,
>   for Your compassions never fail.
> They are new every morning;
> Great is Your faithfulness. (Lamentations 3:21–23)

Pause to reflect on these affirmations about the person, powers and perfection of God.

The Works of God

O Son of Man, You are going to come in the glory of Your Father with Your angels, and then You will reward people according to their works. (Matthew 16:27)

As the lightning comes from the east and flashes to the west, so will be Your coming, O Son of Man. Your sign will appear in the sky, and all the nations of the earth will mourn, and they will see You coming on the clouds of the sky with power and great glory. (Matthew 24:27, 30)

Take a moment to consider the greatness of God's wonderful works.

My Relationship to God

O Lord, You are my light and my salvation;
Whom shall I fear?
You are the strength of my life;
Of whom shall I be afraid? (Psalm 27:1)

When I am afraid, I will trust in You.
When I am afraid, I will trust in You whose word I
    praise.
In You I have put my trust.
I will not fear; what can mortals do to me?
    (Psalm 56:3–4)

Pause to thank God for the relationship that you enjoy with Him in Jesus Christ.

The Character I Want to Cultivate

Those who listen to a life-giving rebuke will be at home
    among the wise.
Those who refuse instruction despise themselves,
    but those who heed correction gain understanding.
    (Proverbs 15:31–32)

A rebuke goes deeper into one who is wise
    than a hundred lashes into a fool. (Proverbs 17:10)

Take a moment to ask the Lord for the grace to grow in godly character.

My Relationship to Others

O God, You are the One who gives endurance and encouragement; grant that we be of the same mind toward one
another, according to Christ Jesus, so that with one accord
and one mouth we may glorify You, the God and Father of
our Lord Jesus Christ. (Romans 15:5–6)

Lord, we know that there should be no division in the body, but its members should have concern for each other. If one member suffers, all the members suffer with it; if one member is honored, all the members rejoice with it. Now we are Your body, O Christ, and each one of us is a member of it. (1 Corinthians 12:25–27)

Pause to review your relationships with others and to commit them to the Lord.

The Attributes of God

> I will exalt You, my God and King;
> I will bless Your name for ever and ever.
> Every day I will bless You,
>   and I will praise Your name for ever and ever.
> Great are You, Lord, and most worthy of praise;
> Your greatness is unsearchable. (Psalm 145:1–3)

I rejoice in the knowledge that one day, every creature in heaven and on earth and under the earth and on the sea and all that is in them will sing of You, Almighty King: "To Him who sits on the throne and to the Lamb be blessing and honor and glory and power for ever and ever!" (Revelation 5:13)

Pause to reflect on these affirmations about the person, powers and perfection of God.

The Works of God

We know Your grace, O Lord Jesus Christ, that though You were rich, yet for our sakes You became poor, that we, through Your poverty, might become rich. (2 Corinthians 8:9)

You, O Lord, are one God, and there is only one Mediator between You and people, the Man Christ Jesus, who gave Himself as a ransom for all—the testimony given in its proper time. (1 Timothy 2:5–6)

Take a moment to consider the greatness of God's wonderful works.

My Relationship to God

> Naked I came from my mother's womb, and naked I
>   will depart.

O Lord, You give, and You take away;
Blessed be Your name, O Lord. (Job 1:21)

If I wish to come after You, Jesus Christ, I must deny myself
and take up my cross and follow You. For if I want to save
my life, I will lose it, but if I lose my life for You and for the
gospel, I will find it. For what profit will I have if I gain the
whole world, yet forfeit my soul? Or what will I give in
exchange for my soul? (Matthew 16:24–26; Mark 8:34–37;
Luke 9:23–25)

*Pause to thank God for the relationship that you enjoy with
Him in Jesus Christ.*

The Character I Want to Cultivate

If I love money, I will not be satisfied with money; if I love
abundance, I will not be satisfied with its increase. (Ecclesiastes 5:10)

Those who want to get rich fall into temptation and a snare
and into many foolish and harmful desires that plunge people
into ruin and destruction. For the love of money is a root of
all kinds of evil, and some by longing for it have wandered
from the faith and pierced themselves with many sorrows.
But I will flee from these things, and pursue righteousness,
godliness, faith, love, patience and gentleness. (1 Timothy
6:9–11)

*Take a moment to ask the Lord for the grace to grow in godly
character.*

My Relationship to Others

The harvest is plentiful, but the workers are few. Therefore,
I pray that You, Lord of the harvest, will send out workers
into Your harvest. (Matthew 9:37–38; Luke 10:2)

You say to me, O Lord, "Behold, lift up your eyes and look at the fields, for they are white for harvest. Even now the reaper draws his wages and gathers fruit for eternal life, that those who sow and those who reap may rejoice together." (John 4:35–36)

Pause to review your relationships with others and to commit them to the Lord.

DAY 29

The Attributes of God

O Lord, You bring death and make alive;
You bring down to the grave and raise up.
You, Lord, send poverty and wealth;
You humble and You exalt.
You raise the poor from the dust
    and lift the needy from the ash heap,
To seat them with princes and make them inherit a
    throne of honor.
For the foundations of the earth are Yours, O Lord,
    and You have set the world upon them.
    (1 Samuel 2:6–8)

Lord, whatever pleases You, You do in the heavens and
    on the earth, in the seas and all their depths. (Psalm
    135:6)

*Pause to reflect on these affirmations about the person, powers
and perfection of God.*

The Works of God

By Your word, O Lord, the heavens were made,
And by the breath of Your mouth their starry host.
    (Psalm 33:6)

You, O Holy One, have asked,
"To whom will you compare Me?
Or who is My equal?"
We lift our eyes to the heavens and see
    who has created them.
You bring out the starry host by number
    and call them each by name.

Because of Your great might and the strength of Your
power, not one of them is missing.
Do we not know?
Have we not heard?
You are the everlasting God, the Lord, the Creator
of the ends of the earth.
You do not grow tired or weary.
No one can fathom Your understanding. (Isaiah 40:25–
26, 28)

Take a moment to consider the greatness of God's wonderful works.

My Relationship to God

Lord Jesus, those who have Your commandments and obey
them are the ones who love You; and those who love You
will be loved by Your Father, and You will love them and
manifest Yourself to them. (John 14:21)

I want to be a doer of the word and not merely a hearer who
deceives myself. For those who hear the word and do not do
it are like people who look at their natural faces in a mirror
and, after looking at themselves, go away and immediately
forget what kind of people they are. But those who look
intently into the perfect law of freedom and continue in it,
who hear and do not forget the word but do it, these will be
blessed in what they do. (James 1:22–25)

*Pause to thank God for the relationship that you enjoy with
Him in Jesus Christ.*

The Character I Want to Cultivate

Those who are slow to anger are better than the mighty,
and those who rule their spirits than those who take
a city. (Proverbs 16:32)

In my anger I will not sin; I will not let the sun go down
while I am still angry, and I will not give the devil a foothold.
(Ephesians 4:26–27)

*Take a moment to ask the Lord for the grace to grow in godly
character.*

My Relationship to Others

The foremost commandment is this: "Hear, O Israel; the Lord
our God, the Lord is one; and you shall love the Lord your
God with all your heart and with all your soul and with all your
mind and with all your strength." The second is this: "You shall
love your neighbor as yourself." There is no commandment
greater than these, O God. To love You with all my heart and
with all my understanding and with all my strength, and to
love my neighbor as myself are more important than all burnt
offerings and sacrifices. (Mark 12:29–31, 33)

I will owe nothing to anyone except to love them, for those
who love their neighbor have fulfilled the law. For the commandments, "You shall not commit adultery," "You shall not
murder," "You shall not steal," "You shall not covet," and
any other commandments there may be are summed up in
this saying: "You shall love your neighbor as yourself." Love
does no harm to a neighbor; therefore love is the fulfillment
of the law. (Romans 13:8–10)

*Pause to review your relationships with others and to commit
them to the Lord.*

DAY 30

The Attributes of God

To You, O God, belong wisdom and power;
Counsel and understanding are Yours. (Job 12:13)

Hallelujah! Salvation and glory and power belong
  to You, our God,
    because Your judgments are true and righteous.
  (Revelation 19:1–2)

*Pause to reflect on these affirmations about the person, powers
and perfection of God.*

The Works of God

O Lord, what are human beings that You take care of
  them, or people that You think of them?
Their lives are like breaths; their days are like passing
  shadows. (Psalm 144:3–4)

O God, You give strength to the weary
  and increase the power of the weak.
Even youths grow tired and weary,
  and young men stumble and fall;
But we who wait for You, O Lord,
  will renew our strength.
We will mount up with wings like eagles;
We will run and not grow weary;
We will walk and not be faint. (Isaiah 40:29–31)

*Take a moment to consider the greatness of God's wonderful
works.*

My Relationship to God

Why is my soul so downcast?
Why am I so disturbed deep within my being?
I will hope in You, O God, for I will yet praise You
    for the help of Your presence.
O my God, my soul is downcast within me;
Therefore I will remember You.
Why is my soul so downcast?
Why am I so disturbed within my being?
I will hope in You, my God, for I will yet praise You—
The help of my countenance and my God. (Psalm
    42:5–6, 11)

I rejoice in my tribulations, knowing that tribulation produces perseverance; and perseverance, character; and character, hope. And hope does not disappoint, because Your
love, O God, has been poured out into my heart through
the Holy Spirit whom You have given to me. (Romans
5:3–5)

*Pause to thank God for the relationship that you enjoy with
Him in Jesus Christ.*

The Character I Want to Cultivate

I will be strong and courageous; I will not be afraid or discouraged, for You, O Lord my God, will be with me wherever I go. (Joshua 1:9)

I will be strong and courageous and act. I will not be afraid
or discouraged, for You, Lord God, are with me. You will
not fail me or forsake me. (1 Chronicles 28:20)

*Take a moment to ask the Lord for the grace to grow in godly
character.*

My Relationship to Others

If I am generous, I will prosper;
  if I water others, I will myself be refreshed.
  (Proverbs 11:25)

Those who are generous will be blessed,
  for they share their food with the poor.
  (Proverbs 22:9)

Pause to review your relationships with others and to commit them to the Lord.

DAY 31

The Attributes of God

I will sing to You, Lord, for You are highly exalted.
You, O Lord, are my strength and my song;
You have become my salvation.
You are my God, and I will praise You,
    my father's God, and I will exalt You. (Exodus 15:1–2)

My Redeemer, the Lord of hosts is Your name;
You are the Holy One of Israel. (Isaiah 47:4)

Pause to reflect on these affirmations about the person, powers and perfection of God.

The Works of God

I must be ready, for You, Jesus, the Son of Man, will come at an hour when I do not expect You. (Matthew 24:44; Luke 12:40)

Many will see You, O Son of Man, coming in clouds with great power and glory. And You will send Your angels and gather Your elect from the four winds, from the ends of the earth to the ends of the heavens. We must take heed and be watchful, for we do not know when that time will come. (Mark 13:26–27, 33)

Take a moment to consider the greatness of God's wonderful works.

My Relationship to God

Having been justified by faith, I have peace with You, O God, through the Lord Jesus Christ, through whom I have gained access by faith into this grace in which I stand; and I rejoice in the hope of Your glory. (Romans 5:1–2)

I am convinced that neither death nor life, nor angels nor principalities, nor things present nor things to come, nor powers, nor height nor depth, nor anything else in all creation, will be able to separate me from Your love, O God, that is in Christ Jesus my Lord. (Romans 8:38–39)

Pause to thank God for the relationship that you enjoy with Him in Jesus Christ.

The Character I Want to Cultivate

I will teach my children to fear You, O Lord:
Who are they who love life and desire many days
that they may see good?
They are to keep their tongues from evil
and their lips from speaking guile.
They are to depart from evil and do good,
to seek peace and pursue it.
Your eyes, O Lord, are on the righteous, and Your ears
are attentive to their cry. (Psalm 34:11–15)

I was once darkness, but now I am light in You, Lord. I will walk as a child of light (for the fruit of the light consists in all goodness and righteousness and truth), learning what is pleasing to You. (Ephesians 5:8–10)

Take a moment to ask the Lord for the grace to grow in godly character.

My Relationship to Others

I will not defraud my neighbors or rob them. (Leviticus 19:13)

I will not mistreat my neighbors, but I will fear You, God; for You are the Lord my God. (Leviticus 25:17)

Pause to review your relationships with others and to commit them to the Lord.

THE SECOND MONTH

❧
DAY 1

The Attributes of God

God, You reveal deep things out of darkness
    and bring the shadow of death into the light.
You make nations great and destroy them;
You enlarge nations and disperse them. (Job 12:22–23)

Blessed be Your name, O God, for ever and ever,
    for wisdom and power belong to You.
You change the times and the seasons;
You raise up kings and depose them.
You give wisdom to the wise and knowledge to those
    who have understanding.
You reveal deep and hidden things;
You know what is in the darkness,
    and light dwells with You. (Daniel 2:20–22)

Pause to reflect on these affirmations about the person, powers and perfection of God.

The Works of God

You, O Son of Man, did not come to be served, but to serve, and to give Your life as a ransom for many. (Mark 10:45)

Lord Jesus, how can I thank You for the suffering You endured for my sake?:

During Your trials some began to spit at You and blindfold You and strike You with their fists and say to You, "Prophesy!" And the guards received You with slaps in the face. The soldiers put a purple robe on You, then twisted together a crown of thorns and set it on You. And they began to call out to You, "Hail, king of the Jews!" Again and again they struck You on the head with a staff and spit on You, and bending their knees, they paid mock homage to You. When they crucified You, those who passed by hurled insults at You, wagging their heads and saying, "Ha! You who are going to destroy the temple and build it in three days, save Yourself and come down from the cross!" And at the ninth hour You cried out in a loud voice, "Eloi, Eloi, lama sabachthani?" which means, "My God, My God, why have You forsaken Me?" (Mark 14:65; 15:17–19, 29–30, 34)

Take a moment to consider the greatness of God's wonderful works.

My Relationship to God

Who are those that fear You, O Lord?
You will instruct them in the way they should choose.
(Psalm 25:12)

You will instruct me and teach me
in the way I should go;
You will counsel me and watch over me. (Psalm 32:8)

Pause to thank God for the relationship that you enjoy with Him in Jesus Christ.

The Character I Want to Cultivate

If we pursue righteousness and love, we will find life,
righteousness and honor. (Proverbs 21:21)

The goal of the instruction of Your Word, O Lord, is love that comes from a pure heart and a good conscience and a sincere faith. (1 Timothy 1:5)

Take a moment to ask the Lord for the grace to grow in godly character.

My Relationship to Others

> Houses and wealth are inherited from fathers,
>   but a prudent wife is from You, Lord. (Proverbs 19:14)

> Charm is deceptive, and beauty is fleeting;
>   but a woman who fears You, Lord, shall be praised.
>   (Proverbs 31:30)

Pause to review your relationships with others and to commit them to the Lord.

DAY 2

The Attributes of God

O Lord, God of Israel, there is no God like You in heaven above or on earth below; You keep Your covenant and mercy with Your servants who walk before You with all their heart. (1 Kings 8:23; 2 Chronicles 6:14)

I know that You are a gracious and compassionate God, slow to anger and abounding in lovingkindness, a God who relents from sending calamity. (Jonah 4:2)

Pause to reflect on these affirmations about the person, powers and perfection of God.

The Works of God

Every animal of the forest is Yours,
   and the cattle on a thousand hills, O God.
You know every bird in the mountains, and everything
   that moves in the field is Yours. (Psalm 50:10–11)

The heavens are Yours; the earth also is Yours;
You founded the world and all its fullness. (Psalm 89:11)

Take a moment to consider the greatness of God's wonderful works.

My Relationship to God

Joy in You, my Lord, is my strength. (Nehemiah 8:10)

Better is one day in Your courts than a thousand
   elsewhere, O Lord Almighty.
I would rather be a doorkeeper in Your house, my God,
   than dwell in the tents of the wicked.
For You, Lord God, are a sun and shield.
You will give grace and glory;

No good thing do You withhold from those who walk
  in integrity.
O Lord of hosts, blessed are those who trust in You!
  (Psalm 84:10–12)

Pause to thank God for the relationship that you enjoy with Him in Jesus Christ.

The Character I Want to Cultivate

I will receive the words of wisdom and treasure her
  commands within me,
Turning my ear to wisdom and applying my heart
  to understanding.
If I cry for discernment and lift up my voice
  for understanding,
If I seek her as silver and search for her as for hidden
  treasures,
Then I will understand what it is to fear You, O Lord,
And what it is to know You, O God. (Proverbs 2:1–5)

To fear You, O Lord, is the beginning of wisdom,
  and to know You, O Holy One, is understanding.
  (Proverbs 9:10)

Take a moment to ask the Lord for the grace to grow in godly character.

My Relationship to Others

I will discipline my children while there is hope and
  not be a willing party to their death. (Proverbs 19:18)

The rod and reproof impart wisdom,
  but children left to themselves bring shame to their
  mother. (Proverbs 29:15)

Pause to review your relationships with others and to commit them to the Lord.

DAY 3

The Attributes of God

> Great are You, Lord, and most worthy of praise
>   in Your city, O God, Your holy mountain.
> As is Your name, O God, so is Your praise
>   to the ends of the earth;
> Your right hand is filled with righteousness.
>   (Psalm 48:1, 10)

Lord Jesus Christ, You received honor and glory from God the Father when the voice came to You from the Majestic Glory, saying, "This is My beloved Son, with whom I am well pleased." (2 Peter 1:17)

Pause to reflect on these affirmations about the person, powers and perfection of God.

The Works of God

God's grace was given to us in You, Christ Jesus, before the beginning of time and has now been revealed through Your appearing, O Savior, You who abolished death and brought life and immortality to light through the gospel. (2 Timothy 1:9–10)

We see You, Jesus—the One who was made a little lower than the angels—now crowned with glory and honor because You suffered death, so that by the grace of God You might taste death for everyone. In bringing many of us to glory, it was fitting that God, for whom and through whom everything exists, should make You—the author of our salvation—perfect through suffering. (Hebrews 2:9–10)

Take a moment to consider the greatness of God's wonderful works.

My Relationship to God

I will praise You, O Lord, with all my heart;
I will tell of all Your wonders.
I will be glad and rejoice in You;
I will sing praise to Your name, O Most High.
(Psalm 9:1–2)

The righteous will rejoice in You, O Lord,
for praise is becoming to the upright. (Psalm 33:1)

Pause to thank God for the relationship that you enjoy with Him in Jesus Christ.

The Character I Want to Cultivate

I will not be dishonest in judgment, in measurement of weight or quantity. I will be honest and just in my business affairs. (Leviticus 19:35–36)

The integrity of the upright guides them,
but the unfaithful are destroyed by their duplicity.
(Proverbs 11:3)

Take a moment to ask the Lord for the grace to grow in godly character.

My Relationship to Others

I will pursue the things that lead to peace and to mutual edification. (Romans 14:19)

We should bear with one another in love and make every effort to keep the unity of Your Spirit in the bond of peace. (Ephesians 4:2–3)

Pause to review your relationships with others and to commit them to the Lord.

DAY 4

The Attributes of God

You are the great, the mighty and the awesome God; You keep Your covenant of lovingkindness. (Nehemiah 9:32)

> To whom can I liken You or count Your equal, O Lord?
> To whom can I compare You that You may be alike?
> (Isaiah 46:5)

Pause to reflect on these affirmations about the person, powers and perfection of God.

The Works of God

An hour is coming, and now is, when the dead will hear Your voice, O Son of God, and those who hear will live. For as the Father has life in Himself, so He has granted You to have life in Yourself, and He has given You authority to execute judgment, because You are the Son of Man. (John 5:25–27)

We will all stand before Your judgment seat, O Lord. For You have said, "As I live, every knee will bow before Me, and every tongue will confess to God." So then, each of us will give an account of himself to You. (Romans 14:10–12)

Take a moment to consider the greatness of God's wonderful works.

My Relationship to God

There is now no condemnation for those who are in You, Christ Jesus, because the law of the Spirit of life in You has set us free from the law of sin and death. (Romans 8:1–2)

I did not receive a spirit of slavery again to fear, but I received Your Spirit of adoption by whom I cry, "Abba, Father." The Spirit Himself testifies with my spirit that I am Your child, O God. (Romans 8:15–16)

Pause to thank God for the relationship that you enjoy with Him in Jesus Christ.

The Character I Want to Cultivate

A talebearer reveals secrets,
> but the person who is trustworthy conceals a matter.
(Proverbs 11:13)

These are the things I shall do: speak the truth to others, judge with truth and justice for peace. I shall not plot evil against my neighbor and not love a false oath; for these things You hate, O Lord. (Zechariah 8:16–17)

Take a moment to ask the Lord for the grace to grow in godly character.

My Relationship to Others

You have called us to go and make disciples of all nations, baptizing them in the name of the Father and of You, the Son, and of the Holy Spirit, teaching them to observe everything You have commanded us. And surely You are with us always, even to the end of the age. (Matthew 28:19–20)

As You, Father, sent Your Son into the world, Your Son also has sent us into the world. And He has prayed for those who will believe in You through our message. (John 17:18, 20)

Pause to review your relationships with others and to commit them to the Lord.

DAY 5

The Attributes of God

I will give thanks to You, Lord, for You are good; Your love endures forever. (1 Chronicles 16:34)

> Lovingkindness and truth meet together;
> Righteousness and peace kiss each other.
> Truth springs forth from the earth,
>   and righteousness looks down from heaven.
>   (Psalm 85:10–11)

Pause to reflect on these affirmations about the person, powers and perfection of God.

The Works of God

Jesus, I praise You, for You have fulfilled the words of the prophet Isaiah:

"The Spirit of the Lord is upon Me, because He has anointed Me to preach good news to the poor. He has sent Me to proclaim freedom for the captives and recovery of sight to the blind, to set free those who are downtrodden, to proclaim the acceptable year of the Lord." (Luke 4:18–19)

You, Jesus, the Son of Man, came to seek and to save that which was lost. (Luke 19:10)

Take a moment to consider the greatness of God's wonderful works.

My Relationship to God

> I will trust in You, Lord, with all my heart
>   and lean not on my own understanding;
> In all my ways I will acknowledge You,
>   and You will make my paths straight.

I will not be wise in my own eyes,
>   but I will fear You, Lord, and depart from evil.
>   (Proverbs 3:5–7)

Not by might nor by power, but by Your Spirit, O Lord God of hosts. (Zechariah 4:6)

Pause to thank God for the relationship that you enjoy with Him in Jesus Christ.

The Character I Want to Cultivate

Before my downfall my heart is haughty,
>   but I must have humility before I have honor.
>   (Proverbs 18:12)

Blessed are the poor in spirit, for theirs is the kingdom of heaven. Blessed are those who mourn, for they will be comforted. Blessed are the meek, for they will inherit the earth. (Matthew 5:3–5)

Take a moment to ask the Lord for the grace to grow in godly character.

My Relationship to Others

May I learn the importance of forgiveness from You, Lord Jesus, who were asked by Peter: "Lord, how often shall my brother sin against me, and I forgive him? Up to seven times?" You said to him, "I tell you, not seven times, but up to seventy times seven." (Matthew 18:21–22)

I will love my enemies, do good to them, and lend to them, expecting nothing in return. Then my reward will be great, and I will be Your child, O Most High; for You are kind to the ungrateful and evil. I will be merciful just as You, Father, are merciful. (Luke 6:35–36)

Pause to review your relationships with others and to commit them to the Lord.

DAY 6

The Attributes of God

> I will be still and know that You are God.
> You will be exalted among the nations.
> You will be exalted in the earth. (Psalm 46:10)

O God and Father of the Lord Jesus—You are blessed forever. (2 Corinthians 11:31)

Pause to reflect on these affirmations about the person, powers and perfection of God.

The Works of God

> O Lord, You formed my inward parts.
> You wove me together in my mother's womb.
> I thank You because I am fearfully
>   and wonderfully made.
> Your works are wonderful,
>   and my soul knows it full well.
> My frame was not hidden from You when I was made
>   in secret and skillfully wrought in the depths
>   of the earth.
> Your eyes saw my embryo,
>   and all the days ordained for me were written
>   in Your book before one of them came to be.
>   (Psalm 139:13–16)

Through You, O Christ, all things were made, and without You nothing was made that has been made. In You was life, and that life was our light. (John 1:3–4)

Take a moment to consider the greatness of God's wonderful works.

My Relationship to God

As for me and my household, we will serve You, O Lord. (Joshua 24:15)

By Your grace, O Lord, I want to hear You say to me, "Well done, good and faithful servant; you have been faithful with a few things; I will put you in charge of many things. Enter into the joy of your Lord." (Matthew 25:21)

Pause to thank God for the relationship that you enjoy with Him in Jesus Christ.

The Character I Want to Cultivate

Those who love instruction love knowledge,
    but those who hate correction are stupid.
    (Proverbs 12:1)

Pride breeds nothing but strife,
    but wisdom is found in those who take advice.
    (Proverbs 13:10)

Take a moment to ask the Lord for the grace to grow in godly character.

My Relationship to Others

I will contribute to the needs of the saints and practice hospitality. (Romans 12:13)

I will not forget to do good and to share with others, for with such sacrifices You, my God, are well pleased. (Hebrews 13:16)

Pause to review your relationships with others and to commit them to the Lord.

DAY 7

The Attributes of God

You, O God, are wise in heart and mighty in strength.
Who has resisted You without harm? (Job 9:4)

Your eyes, O Lord, are everywhere, keeping watch
on the evil and the good. (Proverbs 15:3)

*Pause to reflect on these affirmations about the person, powers
and perfection of God.*

The Works of God

O Christ, You have appeared once for all at the end of the ages
to do away with sin by sacrificing Yourself. And as it is
appointed for people to die once and after that to face judgment, so You were offered once to bear the sins of many; and
You will appear a second time, not to bear sin but to bring salvation to those who eagerly wait for You. (Hebrews 9:26–28)

I have come to Mount Zion, to the heavenly Jerusalem, Your
city, O living God. I have come to myriad angels, and to the
assembly and church of the firstborn who are enrolled in
heaven. I have come to You, the Judge of all people, to the
spirits of the righteous made perfect, to Jesus the mediator of
a new covenant, and to the sprinkled blood that speaks of better things than the blood of Abel. (Hebrews 12:22–24)

Take a moment to consider the greatness of God's wonderful works.

My Relationship to God

I want to follow Abraham's example of willingness and offer
all that I have to You, holding nothing back and trusting in
Your character and in Your promises. (Genesis 22:2–11)

Like Josiah, I want a tender and responsive heart, so that I will humble myself before You when I hear Your word. (2 Chronicles 34:27)

Pause to thank God for the relationship that you enjoy with Him in Jesus Christ.

The Character I Want to Cultivate

I will not lay up for myself treasures on earth, where moth and rust destroy and where thieves break in and steal. But I will lay up for myself treasures in heaven, where moth and rust do not destroy and where thieves do not break in and steal. For where my treasure is, there my heart will be also. (Matthew 6:19–21; Luke 12:34)

I do not want to lay up treasure for myself without being rich toward You, O God. (Luke 12:21)

Take a moment to ask the Lord for the grace to grow in godly character.

My Relationship to Others

The people of this world are more shrewd in dealing with their own kind than are the people of light. I would be wise to use worldly wealth to help others, making friends for myself, so that when it is gone, they may welcome me into Your eternal dwellings. (Luke 16:8–9)

What is my hope or joy or crown of rejoicing in Your presence, Lord Jesus, at Your coming? My glory and joy is the people in whose lives I have been privileged to have a ministry. (1 Thessalonians 2:19–20)

Pause to review your relationships with others and to commit them to the Lord.

DAY 8

The Attributes of God

Let me fall into Your hands, O Lord, for Your mercies are very great; but do not let me fall into the hands of people. (1 Chronicles 21:13)

> You, Lord, are good and ready to forgive and abundant in mercy to all who call upon You. (Psalm 86:5)

Pause to reflect on these affirmations about the person, powers and perfection of God.

The Works of God

We are not to be ignorant about those who fall asleep or grieve like other people, who have no hope. For if we believe that You, Jesus, died and rose again, even so the Father will bring with You those who have fallen asleep in You. According to Your own word, we who are alive and remain until Your coming will not precede those who have fallen asleep. For You Yourself will come down from heaven, with a loud command, with the voice of the archangel, and with the trumpet of God, and the dead in You will rise first. Then we who are alive and remain will be caught up together with them in the clouds to meet You in the air. And so we will be with You forever. (1 Thessalonians 4:13–17)

We are looking for Your blessed hope and Your glorious appearing, Christ Jesus, our great God and Savior. You gave Yourself for us to redeem us from all iniquity and to purify for Yourself a people for Your own possession, a people zealous for good works. (Titus 2:13–14)

Take a moment to consider the greatness of God's wonderful works.

My Relationship to God

> I am confident that I will see Your goodness, O Lord,
>   in the land of the living.
> I will hope in You and be of good courage,
>   and You will strengthen my heart.
> Yes, I will hope in You, Lord. (Psalm 27:13–14)

> I wait for You, O Lord;
> My soul waits, and in Your word I put my hope.
> I hope in You, O Lord, for with You is unfailing love
>   and abundant redemption. (Psalm 130:5, 7)

Pause to thank God for the relationship that you enjoy with Him in Jesus Christ.

The Character I Want to Cultivate

I want to be above reproach, temperate, sensible, respectable, hospitable, able to teach, not given to drunkenness, not violent but gentle, not quarrelsome, not a lover of money. I want to manage my family well and keep my children under control with proper respect. And I want a good reputation with outsiders, so that I will not fall into disgrace and the snare of the devil. (1 Timothy 3:2–4, 7)

I want to be above reproach, blameless as Your steward, O God, not self-willed, not quick-tempered, not given to wine, not violent, not fond of dishonest gain, but hospitable, a lover of what is good, sensible, just, holy and self-controlled. (Titus 1:6–8)

Take a moment to ask the Lord for the grace to grow in godly character.

My Relationship to Others

The husband should fulfill his marital duty to his wife, and likewise the wife to her husband. The wife's body does not belong to her alone, but also to her husband. In the same way, the husband's body does not belong to him alone, but also to his wife. (1 Corinthians 7:3–4)

Each husband must love his own wife as he loves himself, and each wife must respect her husband. (Ephesians 5:33)

Pause to review your relationships with others and to commit them to the Lord.

DAY 9

The Attributes of God

> You have chosen me as Your witness and servant
> so that I may know and believe You
> and understand that You are the Lord.
> Before You no god was formed,
> nor will there be one after You. (Isaiah 43:10)

Lord God, You are the Alpha and the Omega, who is, and who was, and who is to come, the Almighty. (Revelation 1:8)

Pause to reflect on these affirmations about the person, powers and perfection of God.

The Works of God

Blessed are You, O Lord, God of Israel, because You have visited us and have redeemed Your people. You have raised up a horn of salvation for us in the house of Your servant David (as You spoke by the mouth of Your holy prophets of long ago), salvation from our enemies and from the hand of all who hate us—to show mercy to our fathers and to remember Your holy covenant, the oath You swore to our father Abraham: to rescue us from the hand of our enemies, and to enable us to serve You without fear in holiness and righteousness before You all our days. (Luke 1:68–75)

The Scriptures predicted that You, Christ Jesus, would suffer and rise from the dead on the third day, and that repentance and forgiveness of sins would be preached in Your name to all nations, beginning at Jerusalem. (Luke 24:46–47)

Take a moment to consider the greatness of God's wonderful works.

My Relationship to God

O God, I know that You will keep me strong to the end, so that I will be blameless on the day of our Lord Jesus Christ. You are faithful; through You I was called into fellowship with Your Son, Jesus Christ our Lord. (1 Corinthians 1:8–9)

Thanks be to You, O God, who always lead us in triumph in Christ and through us spread everywhere the fragrance of the knowledge of You. (2 Corinthians 2:14)

Pause to thank God for the relationship that you enjoy with Him in Jesus Christ.

The Character I Want to Cultivate

I will rejoice in hope, persevere in affliction and continue steadfastly in prayer. (Romans 12:12)

I will fight the good fight of faith and lay hold of the eternal life to which I was called, Father, when I made the good confession in the presence of many witnesses. You are the One who gives life to all things; in Your sight, and in the sight of Your Son, Christ Jesus, who testified the good confession before Pontius Pilate, I want to keep this command without blemish or reproach until the appearing of our Lord Jesus Christ, which You will bring about in Your own time. (1 Timothy 6:12–15)

Take a moment to ask the Lord for the grace to grow in godly character.

My Relationship to Others

Children should obey their parents as believers in You, O Lord, for this is right. "Honor your father and mother"— which is the first commandment with a promise—"that it may go well with you, and that you may live long on the earth." (Ephesians 6:1–3)

Children should obey their parents in everything, for this is well pleasing to You, Lord. (Colossians 3:20)

Pause to review your relationships with others and to commit them to the Lord.

DAY 10

The Attributes of God

Lord, You have been our dwelling place
    throughout all generations.
Before the mountains were born
    or You brought forth the earth and the world,
    from everlasting to everlasting,
    You are God.
You turn people back into dust and say, "Return to dust."
For a thousand years in Your sight are like yesterday
    when it passes by or like a watch in the night.
    (Psalm 90:1–4)

My days are like a lengthened shadow,
And I wither away like grass.
But You, O Lord, will endure forever,
    and the remembrance of Your name
        to all generations.
In the beginning You laid the foundations of the earth,
    and the heavens are the work of Your hands.
They will perish, but You will endure.
They will all wear out like a garment;
Like clothing You will change them,
    and they will be discarded.
But You are the same,
    and Your years will have no end.
    (Psalm 102:11–12, 25–27)

*Pause to reflect on these affirmations about the person, powers
and perfection of God.*

The Works of God

Lord Jesus Christ, You have been raised from the dead, the firstfruits of those who have fallen asleep. For since death came through a man, the resurrection of the dead comes also through a Man. For as in Adam all die, so in You all will be made alive. But each in his own order: You, the firstfruits; afterward, those who are Yours at Your coming. Then the end will come, when You deliver the kingdom to God the Father—after You have abolished all rule and all authority and power. For You must reign until You have put all Your enemies under Your feet. The last enemy that will be destroyed is death. (1 Corinthians 15:20–26)

We will not all sleep, but we will all be changed in a moment—in the twinkling of an eye—at the last trumpet. For the trumpet will sound, and the dead will be raised imperishable, and we shall be changed. For this perishable must clothe itself with the imperishable, and this mortal with immortality. (1 Corinthians 15:51–53)

Take a moment to consider the greatness of God's wonderful works.

My Relationship to God

I give You thanks that to all who receive You, Lord Jesus Christ, and believe in Your name, You give the right to become children of God—children born not of natural descent, nor of human decision or a husband's will, but born of God. (John 1:12–13)

We cannot see Your kingdom, O God, without being born again; we cannot enter into Your kingdom unless we are born of water and the Spirit. That which is born of the flesh is flesh, and that which is born of the Spirit is spirit. The wind blows wherever it pleases, and we hear its sound, but we cannot tell where it comes from or where it is going. So it is with everyone born of the Spirit. (John 3:3, 5–6, 8)

Pause to thank God for the relationship that you enjoy with Him in Jesus Christ.

The Character I Want to Cultivate

Who may ascend Your hill, O Lord?
Who may stand in Your holy place?
Those who have clean hands and pure hearts,
    who have not lifted up their souls to idols
        or sworn by what is false. (Psalm 24:3–4)

The path of the righteous is like the first gleam of dawn,
    shining ever brighter until the full light of day.
But the way of the wicked is like darkness;
They do not know what makes them stumble.
    (Proverbs 4:18–19)

Take a moment to ask the Lord for the grace to grow in godly character.

My Relationship to Others

I want to speak words of encouragement to other believers. (Acts 20:2)

We should encourage one another and build each other up in You, Christ Jesus. (1 Thessalonians 5:11)

Pause to review your relationships with others and to commit them to the Lord.

DAY 11

The Attributes of God

O Lord, You reign forever.
You have established Your throne for judgment.
You will judge the world in righteousness,
  and You will govern the peoples with justice.
You, O Lord, will also be a refuge for the oppressed,
  a stronghold in times of trouble.
Those who know Your name will trust in You,
  for You, Lord, have never forsaken those who seek You.
  (Psalm 9:7–10)

You, O Lord, are righteous in all Your ways
  and gracious in all Your works. (Psalm 145:17)

Pause to reflect on these affirmations about the person, powers and perfection of God.

The Works of God

You died for our sins, O Christ, according to the Scriptures; You were buried, and You were raised on the third day according to the Scriptures. (1 Corinthians 15:3–4)

Lord Jesus Christ, You gave Yourself for our sins to rescue us from the present evil age, according to the will of our God and Father, to whom be glory for ever and ever. (Galatians 1:3–5)

Take a moment to consider the greatness of God's wonderful works.

My Relationship to God

O My Father, You know what I need before I ask You. (Matthew 6:8)

Holy Spirit, help me in my weakness, for I do not know what I ought to pray for, but You Yourself intercede for me with groans that words cannot express. And He who searches my heart knows Your mind, O Spirit, because You intercede for the saints according to the will of God. (Romans 8:26–27)

Pause to thank God for the relationship that you enjoy with Him in Jesus Christ.

The Character I Want to Cultivate

Show me how to love, O Lord, for if I speak in human language and the language of angels, but have not love, I am only a resounding gong or a clanging cymbal. And if I have the gift of prophecy and understand all mysteries and all knowledge, and if I have all faith so as to remove mountains, but have not love, I am nothing. And if I give all my possessions to the poor, and if I deliver my body to be burned, but have not love, it profits me nothing. (1 Corinthians 13:1–3)

I want everything I do to be done in love. (1 Corinthians 16:14)

Take a moment to ask the Lord for the grace to grow in godly character.

My Relationship to Others

You teach us concerning the lost, Lord Jesus, when You said, "What man among you, if he has a hundred sheep and loses one of them, does not leave the ninety-nine in the open country and go after the one that is lost until he finds it? And when he finds it, he lays it on his shoulders, rejoicing. And when he comes into his house, he calls his friends and neighbors together and says to them, 'Rejoice with me, for I have found my sheep which was lost!' I tell you that, in the same way, there will be more joy in heaven over one sinner who repents than over ninety-nine righteous people who need no repentance. There is joy in the presence of the angels of God over one sinner who repents." (Luke 15:4–7, 10)

From now on I will regard no one only according to the flesh. (2 Corinthians 5:16)

Pause to review your relationships with others and to commit them to the Lord.

DAY 12

The Attributes of God

> Your righteousness, O God, reaches to the heavens.
> You who have done great things,
> O God, who is like You? (Psalm 71:19)

> You, the Lord, alone have declared what is to come
>   from the distant past.
> There is no god apart from You,
>   a righteous God and a Savior.
> There is none besides You.
> You are God, and there is no other. (Isaiah 45:21–22)

Pause to reflect on these affirmations about the person, powers and perfection of God.

The Works of God

Everything exposed by the light becomes visible, for it is light that makes everything visible. For this reason it is said, "Awake, you who sleep; arise from the dead, and Christ will shine on you." (Ephesians 5:13-14)

Your day, O Lord, will come like a thief. The heavens will pass away with a roar, and the elements will be destroyed by intense heat, and the earth and its works will be laid bare. Your day, O God, will bring about the destruction of the heavens by fire, and the elements will melt with intense heat. (2 Peter 3:10, 12)

Take a moment to consider the greatness of God's wonderful works.

My Relationship to God

Father in heaven, hallowed be Your name. Your kingdom come; Your will be done on earth as it is in heaven. (Matthew 6:9–10)

Though I have not seen You, Jesus, I love You; and though I do not see You now, I believe in You; I rejoice with joy inexpressible and full of glory, for I am receiving the end of my faith, the salvation of my soul. (1 Peter 1:8–9)

Pause to thank God for the relationship that you enjoy with Him in Jesus Christ.

The Character I Want to Cultivate

Wisdom is foremost;
Therefore I will get wisdom, and though it cost all I
    have, I will get understanding.
I will esteem her, and she will exalt me;
I will embrace her, and she will honor me.
    (Proverbs 4:7–8)

Blessed are those who listen to wisdom, watching daily
    at her gates, waiting at her doorposts.
For whoever finds wisdom finds life
    and obtains favor from You, Lord.
But those who fail to find her injure their own souls;
All who hate her love death. (Proverbs 8:34–36)

Take a moment to ask the Lord for the grace to grow in godly character.

My Relationship to Others

O Lord, You have given us a new commandment: to love one another even as You have loved us, so we must love one another. By this all people will know that we are Your disciples, if we have love for one another. (John 13:34)

This is Your commandment, that we love one another as You have loved us. (John 15:12)

Pause to review your relationships with others and to commit them to the Lord.

DAY 13

The Attributes of God

Where can I go from Your Spirit?
Or where can I flee from Your presence?
If I ascend to heaven, You are there.
If I make my bed in Sheol, You are there.
If I take the wings of the dawn,
 if I dwell in the depths of the sea,
 even there Your hand will lead me.
Your right hand will lay hold of me.
If I say, "Surely the darkness will cover me,"
 even the night will be light around me.
The darkness is not dark to You,
 and the night shines as the day;
Darkness and light are alike to You. (Psalm 139:7–12)

You know me, O Lord; You see me and test my thoughts
about You. (Jeremiah 12:3)

*Pause to reflect on these affirmations about the person, powers
and perfection of God.*

The Works of God

Surely Your hand, O Lord, is not too short to save,
 nor Your ear too dull to hear.
But our iniquities have separated us from You, our God.
Our sins have hidden Your face from us,
 so that You will not hear.
Yet You, Lord, saw that there was no one to intervene;
So Your own arm worked salvation for You,

and Your righteousness sustained You.
You put on righteousness as Your breastplate,
   and the helmet of salvation on Your head.
You put on the garments of vengeance
   and wrapped Yourself in zeal as a cloak.
From the west, many will fear Your name, O Lord,
   and from the rising of the sun,
      they will revere Your glory.
For You will come like a flood that Your breath drives
   along. (Isaiah 59:1–2, 16–19)

You led Your people with cords of human kindness,
   O Lord, with bands of love;
You lifted the yoke from their neck and bent down
   to feed them. (Hosea 11:4)

Take a moment to consider the greatness of God's wonderful works.

My Relationship to God

I will sing of Your strength, yes,
   I will sing of Your mercy in the morning,
   for You have been my stronghold,
   my refuge in times of trouble.
To You, O my Strength,
   I will sing praises
   for You are my fortress, my loving God.
   (Psalm 59:16–17)

My soul will bless You, Lord,
   and not forget all Your benefits.
You forgive all my iniquities and heal all my diseases.
You redeem my life from the pit
   and crown me with love and compassion.

You satisfy my desires with good things,
  so that my youth is renewed like the eagle's.
  (Psalm 103:2–5)

Pause to thank God for the relationship that you enjoy with Him in Jesus Christ.

The Character I Want to Cultivate

I will have accurate and honest standards in my business practices. (Deuteronomy 25:15)

Those who walk in integrity walk securely,
  but those who pervert their ways will be found out.
  (Proverbs 10:9)

Take a moment to ask the Lord for the grace to grow in godly character.

My Relationship to Others

Those who oppress the poor reproach You, our Maker,
  but whoever is kind to the needy honors You.
  (Proverbs 14:31)

Those who are kind to the poor lend to You, Lord,
  and You will reward them for what they have done.
  (Proverbs 19:17)

Pause to review your relationships with others and to commit them to the Lord.

DAY 14

The Attributes of God

Your law, O Lord, is perfect, restoring the soul.
Your testimony, O Lord, is sure, making wise the simple.
Your precepts, O Lord, are right, rejoicing the heart.
Your commandment, O Lord, is pure,
    enlightening the eyes.
The fear of You, O Lord, is clean, enduring forever.
Your judgments, O Lord, are true and altogether
    righteous.
They are more desirable than gold, than much pure gold.
They are sweeter than honey, than honey from the comb.
Moreover, by them is Your servant warned—in keeping
    them there is great reward. (Psalm 19:7–11)

The sum of Your words is truth, and all of Your
    righteous judgments are eternal. (Psalm 119:160)

*Pause to reflect on these affirmations about the person, powers
and perfection of God.*

The Works of God

We know, O Lord, that You are God.
It is You who made us.
We are Your people and the sheep of Your pasture.
    (Psalm 100:3)

O God, You have made everything beautiful in its time. You
have also set eternity in our hearts; yet we cannot fathom what
You have done from beginning to end. (Ecclesiastes 3:11)

*Take a moment to consider the greatness of God's wonderful
works.*

My Relationship to God

It is because of You, O God, that I am in Christ Jesus, who has become for me wisdom from You—that is, my righteousness, sanctification and redemption. (1 Corinthians 1:30)

You, O God, raised me up with Christ Jesus and seated me with You in the heavenly realms in Him, in order that, in the coming ages, You might show the surpassing riches of Your grace in kindness toward me in Christ Jesus. (Ephesians 2:6–7)

Pause to thank God for the relationship that you enjoy with Him in Jesus Christ.

The Character I Want to Cultivate

Reckless words pierce like a sword,
> but the tongue of the wise brings healing.
> (Proverbs 12:18)

Do you see those who are hasty in their words?
There is more hope for fools than for them. (Proverbs 29:20)

Take a moment to ask the Lord for the grace to grow in godly character.

My Relationship to Others

I will do no injustice in judgment, nor show partiality to the poor or favoritism to the great, but I will judge my neighbor fairly. (Leviticus 19:15)

In my faith in You, my glorious Lord Jesus Christ, I will not show partiality to some people above others. (James 2:1)

Pause to review your relationships with others and to commit them to the Lord.

DAY 15

The Attributes of God

> You, O Lord, are the true God;
> You are the living God and the everlasting King.
> At Your wrath the earth trembles, and the nations
>   cannot endure Your indignation. (Jeremiah 10:10)

You, Lord Jesus, are the first and the last and the Living One; You were dead, and behold, You are alive forevermore and hold the keys of death and of Hades. (Revelation 1:17–18)

Pause to reflect on these affirmations about the person, powers and perfection of God.

The Works of God

Your power, O God, toward us who believe is power according to the working of Your mighty strength, which You exerted in Christ when You raised Him from the dead and seated Him at Your right hand in the heavenly realms, far above all rule and authority, power and dominion, and every title that can be given, not only in the present age but also in the one to come. (Ephesians 1:19–21)

By common confession, great is the mystery of godliness: You, Jesus, were revealed in the flesh, vindicated in the Spirit, seen by angels, preached among the nations, believed on in the world, taken up in glory. (1 Timothy 3:16)

Take a moment to consider the greatness of God's wonderful works.

My Relationship to God

O Jesus, peace You leave with me; Your peace You give to me. You do not give to me as the world gives. I will not let my heart be troubled nor let it be fearful. (John 14:27)

It is in You, Lord Jesus, that I have peace. In this world I will have tribulation, but I will be of good cheer, because You have overcome the world. (John 16:33)

Pause to thank God for the relationship that you enjoy with Him in Jesus Christ.

The Character I Want to Cultivate

I will not boast about tomorrow,
>   for I do not know what that day may bring.
>   (Proverbs 27:1)

I should not say, "Today or tomorrow I will go to this or that city, spend a year there, carry on business, and make a profit." For I do not even know what my life will be tomorrow. I am a vapor that appears for a little while and then vanishes away. Instead I ought to say, "If the Lord wills, I will live and do this or that." Otherwise, I boast in my arrogance, and all such boasting is evil. (James 4:13–16)

Take a moment to ask the Lord for the grace to grow in godly character.

My Relationship to Others

Wives should be submissive to their own husbands, so that if any of them do not believe the word, they may be won without a word by the behavior of their wives, when they see their purity and reverence. (1 Peter 3:1–2)

Husbands should be considerate as they live with their wives and treat them with respect as the weaker vessel and as co-heirs of the grace of life. (1 Peter 3:7)

Pause to review your relationships with others and to commit them to the Lord.

DAY 16

The Attributes of God

> I know that You can do all things and that no purpose
>   of Yours can be thwarted. (Job 42:2)

> From the rising of the sun to its setting,
>   Your name, O Lord, is to be praised.
> You are high above all nations,
>   Your glory is above the heavens.
> Who is like You, O Lord our God,
>   the One who is enthroned on high,
> You who humble Yourself to behold the things that are
>   in the heavens and in the earth? (Psalm 113:3–6)

*Pause to reflect on these affirmations about the person, powers
and perfection of God.*

The Works of God

In the resurrection of the dead, the body that is sown is perishable, but it is raised imperishable; it is sown in dishonor, but it is raised in glory; it is sown in weakness, but it is raised in power; it is sown a natural body, but it is raised a spiritual body. If there is a natural body, there is also a spiritual body. (1 Corinthians 15:42–44)

The first man was of the dust of the earth; You, Jesus Christ, the second Man, are from heaven. As was the earthly man, so are those who are of the earth; and as You, the Man from heaven are, so also are those who are of heaven. And just as we have borne the image of the earthly man, so shall we bear Your likeness—You who are the heavenly Man. (1 Corinthians 15:47–49)

Take a moment to consider the greatness of God's wonderful works.

My Relationship to God

Those who do not take their cross and follow after You, O Jesus, are not worthy of You. Those who find their lives will lose them, and those who lose their lives for Your sake will find them. (Matthew 10:38–39)

Those who wish to become great among others must become their servant, and those who wish to be first among others must be their slave. (Matthew 20:26–27; Mark 10:43–44)

Pause to thank God for the relationship that you enjoy with Him in Jesus Christ.

The Character I Want to Cultivate

Your commandment is a lamp, O Lord;
Your teaching is a light, and Your reproofs of discipline
are the way to life. (Proverbs 6:23)

All Scripture is God-breathed and is useful for teaching, for reproof, for correction and for training in righteousness, that we Your people may be thoroughly equipped for every good work. (2 Timothy 3:16–17)

Take a moment to ask the Lord for the grace to grow in godly character.

My Relationship to Others

I will train up my children in the way they should go;
Even when they are old they will not depart from it.
(Proverbs 22:6)

I will correct my children, and they will give me rest;
They will bring delight to my soul. (Proverbs 29:17)

Pause to review your relationships with others and to commit them to the Lord.

DAY 17

The Attributes of God

O Lord, God of heaven, You are the great and awesome God, keeping Your covenant of loyal love with those who love You and obey Your commands. (Nehemiah 1:5)

> Great and marvelous are Your works,
>   Lord God Almighty!
> Righteous and true are Your ways, King of the nations!
> Who will not fear You, O Lord, and glorify Your name?
> For You alone are holy.
> All nations will come and worship before You,
>   for Your righteous acts have been revealed.
>   (Revelation 15:3–4)

Pause to reflect on these affirmations about the person, powers and perfection of God.

The Works of God

John was called Your prophet, O Most High; for he went on before You to prepare the way for You, and to give Your people the knowledge of salvation through the forgiveness of their sins because of Your tender mercy, O God, with which the sunrise from on high came from heaven to shine on those living in darkness and in the shadow of death, to guide their feet into the path of peace. (Luke 1:76–79)

Jesus, You are the Lamb of God, who takes away the sin of the world. (John 1:29)

Take a moment to consider the greatness of God's wonderful works.

My Relationship to God

Your grace, Lord Jesus Christ, and the love of God, and the fellowship of the Holy Spirit are with me. (2 Corinthians 13:14)

In You, O Christ, I have obtained an inheritance, having been predestined according to the plan of Him who works all things according to the counsel of His will, that I who have trusted in You should be to the praise of His glory. (Ephesians 1:11–12)

Pause to thank God for the relationship that you enjoy with Him in Jesus Christ.

The Character I Want to Cultivate

I cannot serve two masters; for either I will hate the one and love the other, or I will be devoted to the one and despise the other. I cannot serve both You, O God, and wealth. (Matthew 6:24; Luke 16:13)

I will not love the world or the things in the world. If I love the world, Your love, O Father, is not in me. For all that is in the world—the lust of the flesh, the lust of the eyes and the pride of life—is not of You but of the world. And the world and its lusts are passing away, but the one who does Your will, O God, abides forever. (1 John 2:15–17)

Take a moment to ask the Lord for the grace to grow in godly character.

My Relationship to Others

In Christ Jesus, Your whole building, O God, is joined together and growing into a holy temple in You, in whom we also are being built together into Your dwelling in the Spirit. (Ephesians 2:21–22)

Grace has been given to each one of us according to the measure of Your gift, Christ Jesus. And You gave some to be apostles, some to be prophets, some to be evangelists, and some to be pastors and teachers, to equip the saints for the work of ministry so that Your body will be built up. (Ephesians 4:7, 11–12)

Pause to review your relationships with others and to commit them to the Lord.

DAY 18

The Attributes of God

I will regard You as holy, Lord of hosts.
You shall be my fear, and You shall be my dread.
(Isaiah 8:13)

You, O Lord, are in Your holy temple;
Let all the earth be silent before You. (Habakkuk 2:20)

Pause to reflect on these affirmations about the person, powers and perfection of God.

The Works of God

It is You, O Lord, who measured the waters
in the hollow of Your hand.
You marked off the heavens
with the breadth of Your hand.
You have calculated the dust of the earth in a measure,
and weighed the mountains in the balance and the
hills in scales. (Isaiah 40:12)

It is You, Lord God, who created the heavens and
stretched them out,
who spread out the earth and all that grows on it.
You give breath to its people,
and spirit to those who walk on it. (Isaiah 42:5)

Take a moment to consider the greatness of God's wonderful works.

My Relationship to God

My soul waits in hope for You, Lord;
You are my help and my shield.

My heart rejoices in You, because I trust
   in Your holy name. (Psalm 33:20–21)

Since I am Your child, O God, I am Your heir, and a joint
heir with Christ, if indeed I share in His sufferings in order
that I may also share in His glory. For I consider that the sufferings of this present time are not worth comparing with
the glory that will be revealed to me. (Romans 8:17–18)

*Pause to thank God for the relationship that you enjoy with
Him in Jesus Christ.*

The Character I Want to Cultivate

Since I belong to the day, I will be self-controlled, putting on
faith and love as a breastplate and the hope of salvation as a
helmet. (1 Thessalonians 5:8)

I will prepare my mind for action and be self-controlled, setting my hope fully on the grace to be given to me at Your
revelation, Christ Jesus. (1 Peter 1:13)

*Take a moment to ask the Lord for the grace to grow in godly
character.*

My Relationship to Others

I will seek to walk in wisdom toward outsiders, making the
most of every opportunity. My speech is always to be grace-
ful, seasoned with salt, so that I may know how to answer
each person. (Colossians 4:5–6)

I will sanctify You, O Christ, as Lord in my heart, always
being ready to give an answer, but with gentleness and
respect, to everyone who asks me to give the reason for the
hope that is in me. (1 Peter 3:15)

*Pause to review your relationships with others and to commit
them to the Lord.*

DAY 19

The Attributes of God

> I will ascribe to You glory and strength, O Lord.
> I will ascribe to You the glory due Your name
>   and worship You, Lord, in the beauty of holiness.
>   (Psalm 29:1–2)

> You reign, O Lord; You are clothed with majesty;
> You are robed in majesty and armed with strength.
> Indeed, the world is firmly established;
> It cannot be moved.
> Your throne is established from of old;
> You are from everlasting.
> Your testimonies stand firm;
> Holiness adorns Your house, O Lord, forever.
>   (Psalm 93:1–2, 5)

Pause to reflect on these affirmations about the person, powers and perfection of God.

The Works of God

Jesus, You are the stone that was rejected by the builders, but that has become the chief cornerstone. Salvation is found in no one else, for there is no other name under heaven given to us by which we can be saved. (Acts 4:11–12)

In the past, O God, You overlooked the times of ignorance, but now You command all people everywhere to repent. For You have set a day when You will judge the world with justice by the Man You have appointed. You have given assurance of this to all people by raising Him from the dead. (Acts 17:30–31)

Take a moment to consider the greatness of God's wonderful works.

My Relationship to God

All of us have become like those who are unclean,
    and all our righteous acts are like filthy rags.
We all shrivel up like leaves, and our iniquities,
    like the wind, sweep us away.
But now, O Lord, You are our Father.
We are the clay;
You are the potter;
We are all the work of Your hand. (Isaiah 64:6, 8)

You have declared to us, O Lord,
"Even now, return to Me with all your heart,
    with fasting and weeping and mourning."
So we will rend our hearts and not our garments.
We will return to You, O Lord our God,
    for You are gracious and compassionate,
    slow to anger and abounding in lovingkindness;
And You relent from sending calamity. (Joel 2:12–13)

Pause to thank God for the relationship that you enjoy with Him in Jesus Christ.

The Character I Want to Cultivate

Thanks be to You, O God, the One who gives me the victory through our Lord Jesus Christ. Therefore I will be steadfast, immovable, abounding in Your work, Lord, knowing that my labor in You is not in vain. (1 Corinthians 15:57–58)

May our Lord Jesus Christ Himself and You, God our Father, who have loved us and have given us eternal consolation and good hope by grace, comfort our hearts and strengthen us in every good work and word. (2 Thessalonians 2:16–17)

Take a moment to ask the Lord for the grace to grow in godly character.

My Relationship to Others

In obedience to the truth I will purify my soul for a sincere love of my brothers and sisters and love others fervently from the heart. (1 Peter 1:22)

This is the message we heard from the beginning: that we should love one another. We know that we have passed out of death into life, because we love our brothers and sisters. The one who does not love abides in death. By this we know love, that You, O Jesus Christ, laid down Your life for us, and we ought to lay down our lives for our brothers and sisters. (1 John 3:11, 14, 16)

Pause to review your relationships with others and to commit them to the Lord.

DAY 20

The Attributes of God

One thing You have spoken; two things I have heard:
That You, O God, are strong
    and that You, O Lord, are loving.
For You reward us according to what we have done.
    (Psalm 62:11–12)

You, O Lord, are our judge,
You are our lawgiver,
You are our king;
It is You who will save us. (Isaiah 33:22)

Pause to reflect on these affirmations about the person, powers and perfection of God.

The Works of God

Father, we look for the time when the Holy City, the new Jerusalem, will come down out of heaven prepared as a bride adorned for her husband. A loud voice from the throne will say, "Behold, God makes His home with people, and He will dwell with them, and they will be His people, and God Himself will be with them and be their God, and He will wipe every tear from their eyes. There will be no more death or mourning or crying or pain, for the first things have passed away." You, O God, who are seated on the throne will say, "Behold, I make all things new." (Revelation 21:2–5)

You, Lord Jesus, are coming quickly. Your reward is with You, and You will give to everyone according to what they have done. You are the Alpha and the Omega, the First and the

Last, the Beginning and the End. Yes, You are coming quickly. Amen. Come, Lord Jesus. (Revelation 22:12–13, 20)

Take a moment to consider the greatness of God's wonderful works.

My Relationship to God

No temptation has overtaken me except what is common to all people. And You, O God, are faithful; You will not let me be tempted beyond what I am able, but with the temptation You will also provide a way out, so that I may be able to endure it. (1 Corinthians 10:13)

You, O Lord, are faithful; You will strengthen me and protect me from the evil one. (2 Thessalonians 3:3)

Pause to thank God for the relationship that you enjoy with Him in Jesus Christ.

The Character I Want to Cultivate

Direct my footsteps according to Your word, O Lord,
and let no iniquity have dominion over me.
(Psalm 119:133)

The hour has come for me to wake up from sleep, for my salvation is nearer now than when I first believed. The night is nearly over; the day is almost here. Therefore I will cast off the works of darkness and put on the armor of light. (Romans 13:11–12)

Take a moment to ask the Lord for the grace to grow in godly character.

My Relationship to Others

I will remember those in prison as though bound with them, and those who are mistreated, as though suffering with them. (Hebrews 13:3)

This is pure and undefiled religion before You, my God and Father: to visit orphans and widows in their affliction and to keep oneself unspotted from the world. (James 1:27)

Pause to review your relationships with others and to commit them to the Lord.

DAY 21

The Attributes of God

In the beginning was the Word, and the Word was with You,
O God, and the Word was You. The Word was in the beginning with You. (John 1:1–2)

The Word became flesh and dwelt among us. We have seen
His glory, the glory of Your only begotten, O Father, full of
grace and truth. (John 1:14)

*Pause to reflect on these affirmations about the person, powers
and perfection of God.*

The Works of God

You, O God, will impute righteousness to us who believe in
You who raised Jesus our Lord from the dead. Jesus was
delivered over to death because of our sins and was raised in
order to make us right with You. (Romans 4:24–25)

If many died because of the sin of the one man, Adam, how
much more did Your grace, O God, and the gift that came
by the grace of the one Man, Jesus Christ, abound to the
many? And the result of Your gift, O God, is not like the
result of the one man's sin, for judgment followed one sin
and brought condemnation, but Your gift followed many
sins and brought justification. (Romans 5:15–16)

*Take a moment to consider the greatness of God's wonderful
works.*

My Relationship to God

As the deer pants for the water brooks,
so my soul pants for You, O God.

My soul thirsts for You, for the living God.
When shall I come and appear before You?
   (Psalm 42:1–2)

God, You are my God.
Earnestly I seek You;
My soul thirsts for You.
My body longs for You in a dry and weary land
   where there is no water. (Psalm 63:1)

Pause to thank God for the relationship that you enjoy with Him in Jesus Christ.

The Character I Want to Cultivate

I want to abound in faith, in speech, in knowledge, in all diligence, in love and in the grace of giving. (2 Corinthians 8:7)

I want to abound in love and faith toward You, Lord Jesus, and toward all the saints. (Philemon 5)

Take a moment to ask the Lord for the grace to grow in godly character.

My Relationship to Others

I will trust in You enough to honor You, O Lord, as holy in the sight of others. (Numbers 20:12)

As iron sharpens iron,
   so one person sharpens another. (Proverbs 27:17)

Pause to review your relationships with others and to commit them to the Lord.

DAY 22

The Attributes of God

> All Your works will praise you, O Lord,
> and Your saints will bless You.
> They will speak of the glory of Your kingdom
> and talk of Your power,
> so that all people may know of Your mighty acts
> and the glorious majesty of Your kingdom.
> Your kingdom is an everlasting kingdom,
> and Your dominion endures through all generations.
> (Psalm 145:10–13)

In Your majesty, O Lord, You dwell in the likeness of a throne of sapphire above the expanse that is over the cherubim. (Ezekiel 10:1)

Pause to reflect on these affirmations about the person, powers and perfection of God.

The Works of God

> By wisdom, O Lord, You founded the earth;
> By understanding You established the heavens;
> By Your knowledge the deeps were divided,
> and the clouds drop down the dew.
> (Proverbs 3:19–20)

> You made the earth and created people upon it.
> Your own hands stretched out the heavens,
> And You ordered their starry hosts. (Isaiah 45:12)

Take a moment to consider the greatness of God's wonderful works.

My Relationship to God

We should not get drunk on wine, for that is dissipation. Instead, we should be filled with the Spirit, speaking to one another with psalms, hymns and spiritual songs; singing and making music in our hearts to You, always giving thanks to You, Father, for everything, in the name of our Lord Jesus Christ. (Ephesians 5:18–20)

O God, I will rejoice always, pray without ceasing, and give thanks in all circumstances, for this is Your will for us in Christ Jesus. (1 Thessalonians 5:16–18)

Pause to thank God for the relationship that you enjoy with Him in Jesus Christ.

The Character I Want to Cultivate

Blessed are those who find wisdom
    and those who gain understanding,
      for wisdom's profit is greater than that of silver,
    and her gain is more than fine gold.
She is more precious than jewels,
    and nothing I desire can compare with her.
Long life is in her right hand;
In her left hand are riches and honor.
Her ways are pleasant ways, and all her paths are peace.
She is a tree of life to those who embrace her,
    and happy are those who hold her fast.
    (Proverbs 3:13–18)

Those who get wisdom love their own soul;
Those who keep understanding will find good.
    (Proverbs 19:8)

Take a moment to ask the Lord for the grace to grow in godly character.

My Relationship to Others

Lord Jesus Christ, grant that as Your body, we might reach unity of the faith and in the knowledge of You, the Son of God, so that we will become mature and attain to the whole measure of Your fullness. Then we will no longer be infants, being blown and carried by every wind of doctrine and by the cunning and craftiness of people who scheme deceitfully. Instead we will speak the truth in love; we will grow up in every way in You, our Head. (Ephesians 4:13–15)

We must not forsake meeting together, as some are in the habit of doing, but encourage one another all the more as we see the day approaching. (Hebrews 10:25)

Pause to review your relationships with others and to commit them to the Lord.

DAY 23

The Attributes of God

You, O Lord, are a compassionate and gracious God,
 slow to anger and abounding in lovingkindness
 and truth. (Psalm 86:15)

Great are Your works, O Lord;
They are pondered by all who delight in them.
Splendid and majestic is Your work,
 and Your righteousness endures forever.
You have caused Your wonderful acts
 to be remembered;
You, Lord, are gracious and compassionate.
 (Psalm 111:2–4)

*Pause to reflect on these affirmations about the person, powers
and perfection of God.*

The Works of God

My attitude should be the same as Yours, Christ Jesus;
though You are in Your very nature God, You did not consider equality with God something to be grasped, but emptied Yourself, becoming like a servant and being made in
human form. And appearing as a human being, You humbled Yourself and became obedient to death, even death on
a cross. (Philippians 2:5–8)

We thank You, O Christ, that You were made like Your
brothers and sisters in every way, in order that You might
become a merciful and faithful high priest in things pertaining to God, to make propitiation for our sins. Because

You Yourself suffered when You were tempted, You are able to help us who are being tempted. (Hebrews 2:17–18)

Take a moment to consider the greatness of God's wonderful works.

My Relationship to God

All of us who were baptized into You, Christ Jesus, were baptized into Your death. We are therefore buried with You through baptism into death, in order that, just as You were raised from the dead through the glory of the Father, so we too may walk in newness of life. (Romans 6:3–4)

Those who are in You, O Christ, are new creations; the old things have passed away; behold, they have become new. (2 Corinthians 5:17)

Pause to thank God for the relationship that you enjoy with Him in Jesus Christ.

The Character I Want to Cultivate

I will have respect for You, Lord, and serve You faithfully. May I do it with all my heart, for with You, Lord my God, there is no injustice or partiality or bribery. (2 Chronicles 19:7)

Whoever is faithful with very little is also faithful with much, and whoever is dishonest with very little will also be dishonest with much. If I am not faithful in handling worldly wealth, who will trust me with true riches? And if I am not faithful with someone else's property, who will give me property of my own? (Luke 16:10–12)

Take a moment to ask the Lord for the grace to grow in godly character.

My Relationship to Others

We are the fragrance of Christ to You, O God, among those who are being saved and among those who are perishing; to the one, we are an aroma from death to death; to the other, an aroma from life to life. And who is sufficient for these things? (2 Corinthians 2:15–16)

I pray that I may share my faith effectively through the knowledge of every good thing I have in You, Christ Jesus. (Philemon 6)

Pause to review your relationships with others and to commit them to the Lord.

DAY 24

The Attributes of God

Jesus is Your beloved Son, O God, in whom You are well pleased. (Matthew 3:17; Mark 1:11; Luke 3:22)

No one has ever seen You, O God, but the only begotten God who is at your side, Father; He has made You known. (John 1:18)

Pause to reflect on these affirmations about the person, powers and perfection of God.

The Works of God

God highly exalted You, Christ Jesus, and gave You the name that is above every name, that at Your name, Jesus, every knee should bow, in heaven and on earth and under the earth, and every tongue should confess that You are Lord, to the glory of God the Father. (Philippians 2:9–11)

Jesus Christ, You are coming with the clouds, and every eye will see You, even those who pierced You; and all the peoples of the earth will mourn because of You. Even so, Amen. (Revelation 1:7)

Take a moment to consider the greatness of God's wonderful works.

My Relationship to God

You are the light of the world, O Lord. Those who follow You will not walk in the darkness but will have the light of life. (John 8:12)

You are the true vine, Jesus, and Your Father is the gardener. He cuts off every branch in You that bears no fruit, while every branch that does bear fruit He prunes, that it may bear more fruit. I will abide in You, and You will abide in me. As the branch cannot bear fruit of itself, unless it abides in the vine, neither can I bear fruit, unless I abide in You. (John 15:1–2, 4)

Pause to thank God for the relationship that you enjoy with Him in Jesus Christ.

The Character I Want to Cultivate

Those who are simple believe everything,
   but prudent people consider their steps.
   (Proverbs 14:15)

Prudent people see evil and hide themselves,
   but the simple keep going and suffer for it.
   (Proverbs 22:3; 27:12)

Take a moment to ask the Lord for the grace to grow in godly character.

My Relationship to Others

I will bless those who persecute me; I will bless and not curse. (Romans 12:14)

I will bear with others and forgive whatever complaints I have against them; I will forgive just as You, Lord, forgave me. (Colossians 3:13)

Pause to review your relationships with others and to commit them to the Lord.

DAY 25

The Attributes of God

Who has understood what is in Your mind, O Lord,
    or instructed You as Your counselor?
Whom did You consult to enlighten You,
    and who taught You the path of justice?
Who taught You knowledge or showed You the way of
    understanding?
Surely the nations are like a drop in a bucket;
They are regarded as dust on the scales;
You weigh the islands as though they were fine dust.
Before You all the nations are as nothing;
You regard them as less than nothing and worthless.
To whom, then, will I compare You, O God?
Or what likeness will I compare with You? (Isaiah
    40:13–15, 17–18)

You are the Lord, the God of all people. Nothing is too difficult for You. (Jeremiah 32:27)

Pause to reflect on these affirmations about the person, powers and perfection of God.

The Works of God

Through You, Jesus, the forgiveness of sins is proclaimed. Through You everyone who believes is justified from all things from which they could not be justified by the law of Moses. (Acts 13:38–39)

What the law was powerless to do, in that it was weakened through the flesh, You did, O God, by sending Your own Son in the likeness of sinful flesh, on account of sin; You condemned sin in the flesh, in order that the requirement of the law might be fully met in us, who do not walk according to the flesh, but according to Your Spirit. (Romans 8:3–4)

Take a moment to consider the greatness of God's wonderful works.

My Relationship to God

You must increase, O Christ; I must decrease. (John 3:30)

Lord Jesus, I thank you for Your word of truth, that unless a grain of wheat falls to the ground and dies, it remains alone. But if it dies, it bears much fruit. Those who love their lives will lose them, and those who hate their lives in this world will keep them for eternal life. (John 12:24–25)

Pause to thank God for the relationship that you enjoy with Him in Jesus Christ.

The Character I Want to Cultivate

Should I seek great things for myself? I will seek them not. (Jeremiah 45:5)

Those who exalt themselves will be humbled, and those who humble themselves will be exalted. (Matthew 23:12; Luke 14:11; 18:14)

Take a moment to ask the Lord for the grace to grow in godly character.

My Relationship to Others

I will submit myself to the governing authorities. For there is no authority except from You, O God, and the authorities that exist have been established by You. Consequently, those who resist authority have opposed Your ordinance, O God, and those who do so will bring judgment on themselves. (Romans 13:1–2)

I will submit myself for Your sake, O Lord, to every human authority, whether to a king as being supreme, or to the governors he sends to punish evildoers and to praise those who do right; for it is Your will, O God, that by doing good I may silence the ignorance of foolish people. (1 Peter 2:13–15)

Pause to review your relationships with others and to commit them to the Lord.

DAY 26

The Attributes of God

Be exalted, O God, above the heavens;
Let Your glory be over all the earth.
For Your mercy reaches to the heavens,
    and Your faithfulness reaches to the clouds.
    (Psalm 57:5, 10)

Your word is settled in heaven forever, O Lord.
Your faithfulness continues through all generations.
You established the earth, and it stands.
Your laws continue to this day
    according to Your purposes,
    for all things serve You. (Psalm 119:89–91)

Pause to reflect on these affirmations about the person, powers and perfection of God.

The Works of God

You are the Lord who created the heavens;
You are God.
You fashioned and made the earth and established it;
You did not create it to be empty
    but formed it to be inhabited.
You are the Lord, and there is no other. (Isaiah 45:18)

You made the earth by Your power, O God; You established the world by Your wisdom and stretched out the heavens by Your understanding. (Jeremiah 10:12)

Take a moment to consider the greatness of God's wonderful works.

My Relationship to God

By this is Your Father glorified, Lord Jesus: that I bear much fruit, showing myself to be Your disciple. (John 15:8)

Just as I presented the members of my body as slaves to impurity and to ever-increasing lawlessness, so I now present my members as slaves to righteousness, leading to holiness. (Romans 6:19)

Pause to thank God for the relationship that you enjoy with Him in Jesus Christ.

The Character I Want to Cultivate

If I am foolish, my ways will seem right in my own eyes,
    but if I am wise, I will listen to counsel.
    (Proverbs 12:15)

I will listen to counsel and accept instruction,
    that I may be wise in my latter days.
    (Proverbs 19:20)

Take a moment to ask the Lord for the grace to grow in godly character.

My Relationship to Others

We are always to thank You, God, for other believers, mentioning them in our prayers. (1 Thessalonians 1:2)

We should ask for one another's prayers. (1 Thessalonians 5:25)

Pause to review your relationships with others and to commit them to the Lord.

DAY 27

The Attributes of God

O Sovereign Lord, You are God! Your words are true, and You have promised good things to Your servant. (2 Samuel 7:28)

You, O Lord, are the Spirit, and where the Spirit of the Lord is, there is freedom. (2 Corinthians 3:17)

Pause to reflect on these affirmations about the person, powers and perfection of God.

The Works of God

Lord, thank You for Your promise to us:
"I will put My law within you and write it on your
 hearts.
I will be your God, and you will be My people.
No longer will you teach your neighbor,
Nor will you teach a friend, saying, 'Know the Lord,'
 because You shall all know Me,
 from the least of you to the greatest.
For I will forgive your iniquity
 and will remember your sins no more."
 (Jeremiah 31:33–34)

Jesus, we praise You that You taught us to remember You—You took bread, gave thanks, broke it, and gave it to Your disciples, saying, "Take and eat; this is My body." You took the cup, gave thanks and offered it to them, saying, "Drink from it, all of you. This is My blood of the new covenant, which is poured out for many for the forgiveness of sins." (Matthew 26:26–28)

Take a moment to consider the greatness of God's wonderful works.

My Relationship to God

Having the firstfruits of Your Spirit, O Lord, I groan inwardly as I wait eagerly for my adoption, the redemption of my body. For in hope I have been saved, but hope that I can see is not hope; for who hopes for what is already there? But if I hope for what I do not yet have, I eagerly wait for it with patience. (Romans 8:23–25)

God of hope, You will fill me with all joy and peace as I trust in You, so that I may overflow with hope by the power of Your Holy Spirit. (Romans 15:13)

Pause to thank God for the relationship that you enjoy with Him in Jesus Christ.

The Character I Want to Cultivate

I will not worry about my life, what I will eat or what I will drink; or about my body, what I will wear. Life is more than food, and the body more than clothes. The birds of the air do not sow or reap or gather into barns, and yet You, my heavenly Father, feed them. Am I not much more valuable than they? Can I add a single hour to my life by worrying? And why do I worry about clothes? I will consider how the lilies of the field grow; they neither labor nor spin, yet not even Solomon in all his splendor was dressed like one of these. But if You, O God, so clothe the grass of the field, which is here today and tomorrow is thrown into the fire, will You not much more clothe me? So I will not worry, saying, "What shall I eat?" or "What shall I drink?" or "What shall I wear?" For the pagans run after all these things, and You, my heavenly Father, know that I need them. But I will seek first Your kingdom and Your righteousness, and all these things will be added to me. (Matthew 6:25–33; Luke 12:22–31)

I will keep my life free from the love of money and be content with what I have, for You have said, "I will never leave you, nor will I forsake you." (Hebrews 13:5)

Take a moment to ask the Lord for the grace to grow in godly character.

My Relationship to Others

I pray that words may be given to me, that I may open my mouth boldly to make known the mystery of the gospel. (Ephesians 6:19)

I pray that You, O God, may open to me a door for the word, so that I may speak the mystery of Christ and proclaim it clearly, as I ought. (Colossians 4:3–4)

Pause to review your relationships with others and to commit them to the Lord.

DAY 28

The Attributes of God

You are the righteous God, who searches my heart
and secret thoughts. (Psalm 7:9)

What I do may seem right to me,
but You, Lord, know what I am thinking.
(Proverbs 21:2)

*Pause to reflect on these affirmations about the person, powers
and perfection of God.*

The Works of God

Like the roar of rushing waters and like loud peals of thunder, a great multitude will shout, "Hallelujah! For the Lord God Almighty reigns. Let us rejoice and be glad and give Him glory! For Your marriage, O Lamb, has come, and Your bride has made herself ready." Blessed are those who are invited to Your marriage supper, O Lamb. (Revelation 19:6–7, 9)

We praise You, O Jesus, our Messiah, for the vision we have from John: He saw heaven opened, and there before him was a white horse. You are its rider, called Faithful and True; and in righteousness You judge and make war. Your eyes are like a flame of fire, and on Your head are many crowns. You have a name written on You that no one knows except Yourself. You are clothed in a robe dipped in blood, and Your name is the Word of God. The armies of heaven, riding on white horses and dressed in fine linen, white and clean, are following You. Out of Your mouth goes a sharp sword with which You will strike down the nations; You will rule them with a rod of iron. You tread the winepress of the fury of the wrath of God Almighty. And on Your robe and on Your thigh You have a name written: KING OF KINGS AND LORD OF LORDS. (Revelation 19:11–16)

Take a moment to consider the greatness of God's wonderful works.

My Relationship to God

O Lord my God, many are the wonders You have done,
and Your thoughts toward us no one can recount
to You;
Were I to speak and tell of them,
they would be too many to declare. (Psalm 40:5)

O God, You chose me in Christ, before the foundation of the world, to be holy and blameless in Your sight. In love You predestined me to be adopted as Your child through Jesus Christ, according to the good pleasure of Your will, to the praise of the glory of Your grace, which You bestowed upon me in the One You love. (Ephesians 1:4–6)

Pause to thank God for the relationship that you enjoy with Him in Jesus Christ.

The Character I Want to Cultivate

I want to be worthy of respect, not double-tongued, not addicted to wine, not fond of dishonest gain, but holding the mystery of the faith with a clear conscience. (1 Timothy 3:8–9)

Your grace, O God, has appeared, bringing salvation to all people, teaching us to deny ungodliness and worldly passions and to live sensibly, righteously and godly in the present age. (Titus 2:11–12)

Take a moment to ask the Lord for the grace to grow in godly character.

My Relationship to Others

Above all, I will love others fervently, because love covers a multitude of sins. (1 Peter 4:8)

In this is love, not that we loved You, O God, but that You loved us and sent Your Son to be the propitiation for our sins. Since You so loved us, we also ought to love one another. No one has ever seen You; but if we love one another, You abide in us, and Your love is perfected in us. (1 John 4:10–12)

Pause to review your relationships with others and to commit them to the Lord.

DAY 29

The Attributes of God

You, O Lord, are righteous;
You love righteousness; the upright will see Your face.
(Psalm 11:7)

Your eyes are too pure to look at evil;
You cannot look on wickedness, my holy God.
(Habakkuk 1:13)

Pause to reflect on these affirmations about the person, powers and perfection of God.

The Works of God

In Your Father's house are many dwellings, Lord Jesus; if it were not so, You would have told us. You went there to prepare a place for us. And as You went to prepare a place for us, You will come again and receive us to Yourself, that we also may be where You are. (John 14:2–3)

May I witness Your glory, O Lord, as John did when he looked and heard the voice of many angels encircling the throne and the living creatures and the elders. The number of angles was myriad myriads, and thousands of thousands, saying to You with a loud voice, "Worthy is the Lamb who was slain, to receive power and riches and wisdom and strength and honor and glory and blessing!" (Revelation 5:11–12)

Take a moment to consider the greatness of God's wonderful works.

My Relationship to God

> You, O God, will not always strive with us,
> > nor will You harbor Your anger forever.
> You do not treat us as our sins deserve
> > or repay us according to our iniquities.
> For as high as the heavens are above the earth,
> > so great is Your love for those who fear You;
> As far as the east is from the west,
> > so far have You removed our transgressions from us.
> As a father has compassion on his children,
> > so You, O Lord, have compassion on us who fear You.
> > (Psalm 103:9–13)

> You, O Lord, have said,
> "Come now, let us reason together.
> Though your sins are like scarlet,
> > they shall be as white as snow;
> Though they are red as crimson,
> > they shall be like wool." (Isaiah 1:18)

Pause to thank God for the relationship that you enjoy with Him in Jesus Christ.

The Character I Want to Cultivate

I will be on my guard; I will stand firm in the faith, act with courage and be strong. (1 Corinthians 16:13)

I will be self-controlled in all things, endure hardship, do the work of an evangelist and fulfill my ministry. (2 Timothy 4:5)

Take a moment to ask the Lord for the grace to grow in godly character.

My Relationship to Others

May I obey those who are in authority over me with fear and trembling and with sincerity of heart, as I would obey Christ, not with external service as one who wants to please people, but as a slave of Christ, doing Your will, O God, from my heart. With good will may I serve as if I were serving you, O Lord, and not people, knowing that I will receive back from You whatever good I do. (Ephesians 6:5–8)

I will treat subordinates with respect, not threatening them, knowing that You, O Lord, are both their Master and mine and that You are in heaven, and there is no partiality with You. (Ephesians 6:9)

Pause to review your relationships with others and to commit them to the Lord.

DAY 30

The Attributes of God

I will proclaim Your name, O Lord, and praise Your greatness, O my God. (Deuteronomy 32:3)

> Your name is the Lord:
> I know that You alone are the Most High over all the earth. (Psalm 83:18)

Pause to reflect on these affirmations about the person, powers and perfection of God.

The Works of God

> O Lord God of hosts—You who touch the earth
>   and it melts,
>   and all who live in it mourn;
> You who build Your staircase in the heavens
>   and set its foundation over the earth;
> You who call for the waters of the sea and
>   pour them out over the face of the earth—
>   the Lord is Your name. (Amos 9:5–6)

God, You made the world and everything in it. You are Lord of heaven and earth; You do not dwell in temples built by hands. You are not served by human hands, as though You needed anything, since You Yourself give life and breath and everything else to all people. (Acts 17:24–25)

Take a moment to consider the greatness of God's wonderful works.

My Relationship to God

> I will lie down in peace and sleep, for You alone,
>   O Lord, make me dwell in safety. (Psalm 4:8)

May You, O God of peace—who through the blood of the
eternal covenant brought back from the dead our Lord Jesus,
our great Shepherd of the sheep—equip me with every good
thing to do Your will, and may You work in me what is pleasing in Your sight, through Jesus Christ, to whom be glory
for ever and ever. (Hebrews 13:20–21)

*Pause to thank God for the relationship that you enjoy with
Him in Jesus Christ.*

The Character I Want to Cultivate

You have shown me what is good, O Lord.
And what do You require of me but to act justly
and to love mercy and to walk humbly
with You, my God? (Micah 6:8)

I will seek Your interests, Christ Jesus, rather than my own.
(Philippians 2:21)

*Take a moment to ask the Lord for the grace to grow in godly
character.*

My Relationship to Others

Just as the body is one, but has many parts, and all the parts
of the body, being many, are one body, so also are You, O
Christ Jesus. (1 Corinthians 12:12)

You are the Head, O Christ, and under Your control the
whole body is being joined and held together by every sup-
porting ligament, even as each individual part works effectively, so that the body grows and edifies itself in love.
(Ephesians 4:16)

*Pause to review your relationships with others and to commit
them to the Lord.*

DAY 31

The Attributes of God

> All people are like grass
>   and all their glory is like the flower of the field.
> The grass withers and the flower fades,
>   because Your breath, O Lord, blows on it.
> Surely the people are like grass.
> The grass withers and the flower fades,
>   but Your word, O God, stands forever.
>   (Isaiah 40:6–8)

> How great are Your signs, O God,
>   and how mighty are Your wonders!
> Your kingdom is an eternal kingdom;
> Your dominion endures from generation to generation.
>   (Daniel 4:3)

Pause to reflect on these affirmations about the person, powers and perfection of God.

The Works of God

You are the good Shepherd, Lord Jesus; You lay down Your life for the sheep. You are the good Shepherd; You know Your sheep and Your sheep know You—just as the Father knows You and You know the Father—and You lay down Your life for the sheep. (John 10:11, 14–15)

Greater love has no one than this, that he lay down his life for his friends. (John 15:13)

Take a moment to consider the greatness of God's wonderful works.

My Relationship to God

> Whom have I in heaven but You?
> And there is nothing on earth I desire besides You.
> My flesh and my heart may fail, but You, O God,
>   are the strength of my heart and my portion forever.
> Those who are far from You will perish;
> You have cut off all who are unfaithful to You.
> But as for me, it is good to be near You.
> I have made You my refuge, Lord God,
>   that I may tell of all Your works. (Psalm 73:25–28)

> I will give You my heart and let my eyes delight
>   in Your ways. (Proverbs 23:26)

Pause to thank God for the relationship that you enjoy with Him in Jesus Christ.

The Character I Want to Cultivate

I will imitate You, O God, as Your beloved child, and I will walk in love, just as Christ loved me and gave Himself up for me as a fragrant offering and sacrifice to You. (Ephesians 5:1–2)

This is love: that I walk in obedience to Your commandments, O God. And this is the commandment I have heard from the beginning: I should walk in love. (2 John 6)

Take a moment to ask the Lord for the grace to grow in godly character.

My Relationship to Others

Knowing the fear of You, Lord, I will seek to persuade others. (2 Corinthians 5:11)

All things are from You, O God, who reconciled us to Yourself through Christ and gave us the ministry of reconciliation: namely, that You were reconciling the world to Yourself in Christ, not counting our trespasses against us. And You have committed to us the message of reconciliation. Therefore we are ambassadors for Christ, as though You, O God, were appealing to others through us—we implore them on Christ's behalf to be reconciled to You. (2 Corinthians 5:18–20)

Pause to review your relationships with others and to commit them to the Lord.

THE THIRD MONTH

🌿

DAY 1

The Attributes of God

I will sing of Your mercies forever, O Lord.
With my mouth I will make Your faithfulness known
    through all generations.
I will declare that Your lovingkindness
    will be built up forever,
      that You will establish Your faithfulness in the heavens.
The heavens will praise Your wonders, O Lord,
    and Your faithfulness in the assembly of the holy ones.
For who in the heavens can be compared with You,
    Lord?
Who is like You among the children of the mighty?
You, O God, are greatly feared in the council
    of the holy ones
And You are more awesome than all who surround You.
O Lord God of hosts, who is like You?
O mighty Lord, Your faithfulness surrounds You.
    (Psalm 89:1–2, 5–8)

I will sing of Your lovingkindness and justice.
To You, O Lord, I will sing praises. (Psalm 101:1)

Pause to reflect on these affirmations about the person, powers and perfection of God.

The Works of God

Nothing is hidden that will not be revealed, and nothing is secret that will not be known and come out into the open. (Luke 8:17)

If I am ashamed of You and Your words, Jesus, then You, O Son of Man, will be ashamed of me when You come in Your glory and in the glory of Your Father and with the holy angels. (Luke 9:26)

Take a moment to consider the greatness of God's wonderful works.

My Relationship to God

Blessed are those who have learned to acclaim You,
    who walk in the light of Your presence, O Lord.
We rejoice in Your name all day long;
We exalt in Your righteousness. (Psalm 89:15–16)

Through Jesus, I will continually offer to You, O God, a sacrifice of praise—the fruit of lips that give thanks to Your name. (Hebrews 13:15)

Pause to thank God for the relationship that you enjoy with Him in Jesus Christ.

The Character I Want to Cultivate

Wisdom is better than jewels, and all desirable things
    cannot be compared with her.
Wisdom dwells together with prudence and finds
    knowledge and discretion. (Proverbs 8:11–12)

The wisdom that comes from above is first pure, then peaceable, gentle, submissive, full of mercy and good fruits, without partiality and hypocrisy. And the fruit of righteousness is sown in peace by those who make peace. (James 3:17–18)

Take a moment to ask the Lord for the grace to grow in godly character.

My Relationship to Others

I will not judge my brothers and sisters or regard them with contempt. Instead of judging them, I will resolve not to put a stumbling block or obstacle in their way. (Romans 14:10, 13)

I will accept others just as You, O Jesus Christ, accepted me to the glory of God. (Romans 15:7)

Pause to review your relationships with others and to commit them to the Lord.

The Attributes of God

> You live, O Lord!
> Blessed are You, my Rock!
> You are exalted, O God, Rock of my salvation!
> (2 Samuel 22:47)

> I will trust in You forever, for in You, Yahweh, the Lord,
> I have an everlasting Rock. (Isaiah 26:4)

Pause to reflect on these affirmations about the person, powers and perfection of God.

The Works of God

The wages of sin is death, but Your gift, O God, is eternal life in Christ Jesus our Lord. (Romans 6:23)

Since the children God has given You, Jesus, have bodies made of flesh and blood, You shared in their humanity so that by Your death You might destroy him who holds the power of death—that is, the devil—and free those who all their lives were held in slavery by their fear of death. (Hebrews 2:14–15)

Take a moment to consider the greatness of God's wonderful works.

My Relationship to God

If I died with You, Jesus Christ, I believe that I will also live with You, knowing that You, having been raised from the dead, cannot die again; death no longer has dominion over You. For the death that You died, You died to sin once for all; but the life that You live, You live to God. In the same way,

I must consider myself to be dead to sin but alive to God in You. (Romans 6:8–11)

With regard to my former way of life, I am to put off my old self, which is being corrupted by its deceitful desires, and be renewed in the spirit of my mind; I am to put on the new self, which was created according to You, O God, in righteousness and true holiness. (Ephesians 4:22–24)

Pause to thank God for the relationship that you enjoy with Him in Jesus Christ.

The Character I Want to Cultivate

To fear You, Lord, is to hate evil;
Wisdom hates pride and arrogance and the evil way
    and the perverse mouth. (Proverbs 8:13)

I will walk properly as in the daytime, not in partying and drunkenness, not in sexual immorality and evil conduct, not in dissension and jealousy. Instead, I will put on You, Lord Jesus Christ, like clothing, rather than thinking about how to satisfy my fleshly lusts. (Romans 13:13–14)

Take a moment to ask the Lord for the grace to grow in godly character.

My Relationship to Others

I will not become conceited, provoking and envying others. (Galatians 5:26)

I will do all things without complaining or arguing, so that I may become blameless and pure—Your child, O God, without fault in the midst of a crooked and perverse generation, among whom I shine as a light in the world, holding out the word of life. (Philippians 2:14–16)

Pause to review your relationships with others and to commit them to the Lord.

DAY 3

The Attributes of God

> You, Almighty God, are beyond our reach;
> You are exalted in power,
>   and in Your justice and great righteousness,
> You do not oppress. (Job 37:23)

> Great are You, Lord, and mighty in power;
> Your understanding is infinite. (Psalm 147:5)

Pause to reflect on these affirmations about the person, powers and perfection of God.

The Works of God

> You, O Lord, appoint the number of the stars
>   and call them each by name. (Psalm 147:4)

You, O Lord, give the sun for light by day and decree the moon and stars for light by night; You stir up the sea so that its waves roar—the Lord of hosts is Your name. (Jeremiah 31:35)

Take a moment to consider the greatness of God's wonderful works.

My Relationship to God

I am always confident and know that as long as I am at home in the body, I am away from You, Lord. For I live by faith, not by sight. I am of good courage and would prefer to be absent from the body and to be at home with You. (2 Corinthians 5:6–8)

Faith is the certainty of things hoped for and the conviction of things not seen. (Hebrews 11:1)

Pause to thank God for the relationship that you enjoy with Him in Jesus Christ.

The Character I Want to Cultivate

A gentle answer turns away wrath,
> but a harsh word stirs up anger.
The tongue of the wise uses knowledge rightly,
> but the mouth of the fool pours out folly.
> (Proverbs 15:1–2)

I will put away all of these things: anger, wrath, malice, slander and abusive language from my mouth. (Colossians 3:8)

Take a moment to ask the Lord for the grace to grow in godly character.

My Relationship to Others

We should bear one another's burdens and so fulfill Your law, O Christ. (Galatians 6:2)

We should submit to one another out of reverence for You, O Christ. (Ephesians 5:21)

Pause to review your relationships with others and to commit them to the Lord.

DAY 4

The Attributes of God

> It is good to give thanks to You, Lord, to sing praises to
>   Your name, O Most High,
> To declare Your lovingkindness in the morning and
>   Your faithfulness at night. (Psalm 92:1–2)

> How precious are Your thoughts to me, O God!
> How vast is the sum of them!
> If I should count them, they would outnumber the
>   grains of sand.
> When I awake, I am still with You. (Psalm 139:17–18)

*Pause to reflect on these affirmations about the person, powers
and perfection of God.*

The Works of God

O Son of Man, You went up to Jerusalem where You were
delivered to the chief priests and to the scribes. They condemned You to death and handed You over to the Gentiles,
who mocked You and spat upon You, scourged You and
killed You. But on the third day You rose again. (Mark
10:33–34)

After Your resurrection, Jesus, You said to the two disciples
on the road to Emmaus, "Did not the Christ have to suffer these things and then enter His glory?" And beginning
with Moses and all the Prophets, You explained to them
what was said in all the Scriptures concerning Yourself.
Later You appeared to Your disciples and said to them,
"These are the words I spoke to you while I was still with
you, that everything must be fulfilled that is written about

Me in the Law of Moses, the Prophets and the Psalms."
(Luke 24:26–27, 44)

Take a moment to consider the greatness of God's wonderful works.

My Relationship to God

I will not let sin reign in my mortal body that I should obey
its lusts. Nor will I present the parts of my body to sin as
instruments of wickedness, but I will present myself to You,
my God, as one who is alive from the dead. I will present
my body to You as an instrument of righteousness. (Romans
6:12–13)

In view of Your mercy, O God, I present my body as a living sacrifice, holy and pleasing to You, which is my reason-
able service. (Romans 12:1)

*Pause to thank God for the relationship that you enjoy with
Him in Jesus Christ.*

The Character I Want to Cultivate

The one You esteem is humble and contrite of spirit
and trembles at Your word. (Isaiah 66:2)

Who makes me different from anyone else? And what do I
have that I did not receive? And if I did receive it, why should
I boast as though I had not received it? (1 Corinthians 4:7)

*Take a moment to ask the Lord for the grace to grow in godly
character.*

My Relationship to Others

My love must be sincere. I will hate what is evil and cling to
what is good. (Romans 12:9)

I will rejoice with those who rejoice and weep with those who weep. (Romans 12:15)

Pause to review your relationships with others and to commit them to the Lord.

DAY 5

The Attributes of God

Jesus, You are the Christ, the Son of the living God. (Matthew 16:16)

Jesus, You are the way and the truth and the life. No one comes to the Father except through You. (John 14:6)

Pause to reflect on these affirmations about the person, powers and perfection of God.

The Works of God

The kingdom of the world has become Your kingdom, O Lord, and of Your Christ, and You will reign for ever and ever. (Revelation 11:15)

Lord Jesus, You are the Alpha and the Omega, the Beginning and the End. To anyone who is thirsty, You will give to drink without cost from the spring of the water of life. Those who overcome will inherit all this, and You will be their God and they will be Your children. (Revelation 21:6–7)

Take a moment to consider the greatness of God's wonderful works.

My Relationship to God

I will incline my ear and come to You;
I will hear You, that my soul may live. (Isaiah 55:3)

Everyone who hears Your words, Lord Jesus, and does them is like a wise man who built his house on the rock. (Matthew 7:24)

Pause to thank God for the relationship that you enjoy with Him in Jesus Christ.

The Character I Want to Cultivate

I will endure discipline, for You, O God, are treating me as Your child. For what child is not disciplined by its father? If I am without discipline, (and all of us undergo discipline), then I am an illegitimate child and not a true child. Moreover, we have all had human fathers who disciplined us, and we respected them; how much more should I be disciplined by You, the Father of my spirit, and live? (Hebrews 12:7–9)

Our fathers disciplined us for a little while as they thought best; but You, O God, discipline us for our good, that we may share in Your holiness. No discipline seems pleasant at the time, but painful; later on, however, it produces the peaceable fruit of righteousness in those who have been trained by it. (Hebrews 12:10–11)

Take a moment to ask the Lord for the grace to grow in godly character.

My Relationship to Others

I will not repay anyone evil for evil, but I will seek to do what is right in the sight of all people. (Romans 12:17)

I will not repay evil for evil to anyone, but I will pursue what is good for others. (1 Thessalonians 5:15)

Pause to review your relationships with others and to commit them to the Lord.

DAY 6

The Attributes of God

> You are in Your holy temple, O Lord;
> You are on Your heavenly throne.
> You observe all people;
> Your eyes examine them. (Psalm 11:4)

The heart is deceitful above all things and incurably sick. Who can understand it? You, Lord, search human hearts and test people's minds to reward them according to their ways, according to the fruit of their deeds. (Jeremiah 17:9–10)

Pause to reflect on these affirmations about the person, powers and perfection of God.

The Works of God

Triune God, we rejoice in the unity we have in You, in which there is one body and one Spirit, just as we were called in one hope of our calling—one Lord, one faith, one baptism, one God and Father of all—who is over all and through all and in all. (Ephesians 4:4–6)

I give honor and praise to You, O Christ, for You are the head of the body, the church; You are the beginning and the firstborn from among the dead, so that in everything You might have supremacy. (Colossians 1:18)

Take a moment to consider the greatness of God's wonderful works.

My Relationship to God

No eye has seen, no ear has heard, no mind has conceived, O God, what You have prepared for those who love You. (1 Corinthians 2:9)

Now I see dimly, as in a mirror, but then I shall see face to face. Now I know in part, but then I shall know fully, even as I am fully known. (1 Corinthians 13:12)

Pause to thank God for the relationship that you enjoy with Him in Jesus Christ.

The Character I Want to Cultivate

I will not worry about tomorrow, for tomorrow will worry about itself. Each day has enough trouble of its own. (Matthew 6:34)

I will not be worried and troubled about many things, for only one thing is needed. Like Mary, I want to choose what is better, that which will not be taken away from me. (Luke 10:41–42)

Take a moment to ask the Lord for the grace to grow in godly character.

My Relationship to Others

We must encourage one another daily, as long as it is still called "Today," lest any of us be hardened by sin's deceitfulness. (Hebrews 3:13)

We should consider how to stir up one another to love and to do good works. (Hebrews 10:24)

Pause to review your relationships with others and to commit them to the Lord.

DAY 7

The Attributes of God

I will give thanks to You, O Lord,
  because of Your righteousness.
I will sing praise to Your name, O Lord Most High.
  (Psalm 7:17)

My soul magnifies You, O Lord, and my spirit rejoices in
You, God my Savior, for You, Mighty One, have done great
things for me, and holy is Your name. Your mercy is on those
who fear You, from generation to generation. (Luke 1:46–
47, 49–50)

*Pause to reflect on these affirmations about the person, powers
and perfection of God.*

The Works of God

Your hand, O Lord, laid the foundations of the earth,
  and Your right hand spread out the heavens;
When You summon them, they all stand up together.
  (Isaiah 48:13)

Heaven is Your throne, O Lord,
  and the earth is Your footstool.
Your hand made all these things,
  and so they came into being. (Isaiah 66:1–2)

Take a moment to consider the greatness of God's wonderful works.

My Relationship to God

I believe, Lord Jesus, that it is through Your grace that I am saved. (Acts 15:11)

By grace I have been saved through faith, and this not of myself; it is Your gift to me, O God, and not of works, so that I cannot boast. (Ephesians 2:8–9)

Pause to thank God for the relationship that you enjoy with Him in Jesus Christ.

The Character I Want to Cultivate

Your word is a lamp to my feet and a light to my path.
I have inclined my heart to perform Your statutes
   to the very end. (Psalm 119:105, 112)

We are all children of the light and children of the day. We do not belong to the night or to the darkness. So then, let us not be like others who are asleep, but instead be alert and self-controlled. (1 Thessalonians 5:5–6)

Take a moment to ask the Lord for the grace to grow in godly character.

My Relationship to Others

I will accept those whose faith is weak, without passing judgment on their opinions. Who am I to judge another's servant? Whether or not they stand or fall is their own master's concern. And they will stand, for You, O Lord, are able to make them stand. (Romans 14:1, 4)

Knowledge puffs up, but love builds up. (1 Corinthians 8:1)

Pause to review your relationships with others and to commit them to the Lord.

DAY 8

The Attributes of God

Before Abraham was born, You always exist, Jesus Christ. (John 8:58)

In You, O Christ, all the fullness of the Godhead lives in bodily form. (Colossians 2:9)

Pause to reflect on these affirmations about the person, powers and perfection of God.

The Works of God

Lord Jesus, I thank You for the marvelous promise of Your resurrection when You said, "Destroy this temple, and I will raise it again in three days." But You were speaking of the temple of Your body. After You were raised from the dead, Your disciples remembered that You had said this to them, and they believed the Scripture and the words that You had spoken. (John 2:19, 21–22)

Lord Jesus, we thank You that You expressed Your willingness to die for us when You said, "My Father loves Me because I lay down My life that I may take it up again. No one takes it from Me, but I lay it down of My own accord. I have authority to lay it down and authority to take it up again. This command I received from My Father." (John 10:17–18)

Take a moment to consider the greatness of God's wonderful works.

My Relationship to God

If we drink ordinary water, we will be thirsty again; but if we drink the water You give, O Jesus, we will never thirst.

Indeed, the water You give becomes in us a spring of water welling up to eternal life. (John 4:13–14)

I believe Your promise, O God, that because I hear the word of Jesus and believe You who sent Him, I have eternal life and will not come into judgment—I have passed over from death to life. (John 5:24)

Pause to thank God for the relationship that you enjoy with Him in Jesus Christ.

The Character I Want to Cultivate

Establish our hearts as blameless and holy in Your presence, O God and Father, at the coming of our Lord Jesus with all His saints. (1 Thessalonians 3:13)

I desire to be diligent so that I can have full assurance of hope to the end. I do not want to become sluggish but to imitate those who through faith and patience inherit what has been promised. (Hebrews 6:11–12)

Take a moment to ask the Lord for the grace to grow in godly character.

My Relationship to Others

If I am righteous, I will be cautious
about the friends I choose,
but the ways of the wicked will lead me astray.
(Proverbs 12:26)

I will not give cause for offense in anything, so that my ministry will not be discredited. (2 Corinthians 6:3)

Pause to review your relationships with others and to commit them to the Lord.

DAY 9

The Attributes of God

To You, Lord my God, belong the heavens, even the highest heavens, the earth and everything in it. (Deuteronomy 10:14)

> There is none like You, O Lord;
> You are great, and Your name is mighty in power.
> Who should not revere You, O King of the nations?
> It is Your rightful due.
> For among all the wise of the nations
>   and in all their kingdoms,
>   there is no one like You. (Jeremiah 10:6–7)

Pause to reflect on these affirmations about the person, powers and perfection of God.

The Works of God

We rejoice, O Lord, that there will no longer be any curse. Your throne, O God, and the throne of the Lamb will be in the new Jerusalem, and Your servants will serve You. They will see Your face, and Your name will be on their foreheads. And there will be no night there; they will not need the light of a lamp or the light of the sun, for You, Lord God, will give them light. And they shall reign for ever and ever. (Revelation 22:3–5)

There will be no temple in the new Jerusalem, because You, Lord God Almighty, and the Lamb are its temple. The city will not need the sun or the moon to shine on it, for Your glory, O God, gives it light, and the Lamb is its lamp. The nations will walk by the city's light, and the kings of the earth will bring their splendor into it. And its gates will never be shut by day, for there will be no night there. (Revelation 21:22–25)

Take a moment to consider the greatness of God's wonderful works.

My Relationship to God

I lift up my eyes to the hills—where does my help
    come from?
My help comes from You, O Lord,
    who made heaven and earth.
You will not allow my foot to slip;
You who watch over me will not slumber.
You are my keeper;
You, Lord, are my shade at my right hand.
The sun will not harm me by day,
    nor the moon by night.
You will keep me from all evil;
You will preserve my soul.
You will watch over my coming and going from this
    time forth and forever. (Psalm 121:1–3, 5–8)

Even to my old age, You are the same, O Lord,
And even when my hair is gray, You will carry me.
You have made me, and You will bear me.
You will sustain me, and You will deliver me.
    (Isaiah 46:4)

Pause to thank God for the relationship that you enjoy with Him in Jesus Christ.

The Character I Want to Cultivate

I will commit my works to You, O Lord,
    and my plans will be established. (Proverbs 16:3)

I want my conscience to testify that I have conducted myself in the world in the holiness and sincerity that are from You, not in fleshly wisdom but in Your grace, O God, especially in my relationships with others. (2 Corinthians 1:12)

Take a moment to ask the Lord for the grace to grow in godly character.

My Relationship to Others

If someone is caught in a trespass, we who are spiritual should restore that person in a spirit of gentleness, taking care lest we ourselves should be tempted. (Galatians 6:1)

May we let Your word, O Christ, dwell in us richly as we teach and admonish one another with all wisdom, and as we sing psalms, hymns and spiritual songs with gratitude in our hearts to You, our God. (Colossians 3:16)

Pause to review your relationships with others and to commit them to the Lord.

DAY 10

The Attributes of God

Righteousness and justice are the foundation
of Your throne;
Lovingkindness and truth go before You. (Psalm 89:14)

I will give thanks to You, O Lord, for You are good;
Your lovingkindness endures forever.
I will give thanks to You, Lord, for Your unfailing love
and Your wonderful acts to Your people,
for You satisfy the thirsty soul and fill the hungry
soul with good things. (Psalm 107:1, 8–9)

Pause to reflect on these affirmations about the person, powers and perfection of God.

The Works of God

Lord Jesus, You are the resurrection and the life. Those who believe in You will live, even though they die, and those who live and believe in You will never die. (John 11:25–26)

Everything You have created, O God, eagerly waits in expectation of the time when Your children will appear in their full and final glory. (Romans 8:19)

Take a moment to consider the greatness of God's wonderful works.

My Relationship to God

As the Father has loved You, Jesus, You also have loved me. I must abide in Your love. If I keep Your commandments, I will abide in Your love, just as You kept Your Father's commandments and abide in His love. You have told me this so that Your joy may be in me and that my joy may be full. (John 15:9–11)

This is eternal life: that I may know You, the only true God, and Jesus Christ, whom You have sent. (John 17:3)

Pause to thank God for the relationship that you enjoy with Him in Jesus Christ.

The Character I Want to Cultivate

I will keep the pattern of sound teaching that I have heard, in the faith and love that are in You, Christ Jesus. (2 Timothy 1:13)

I will not love with words or tongue but will strive to love in deed and in truth. By this I will know that I am of the truth and my heart will be assured before You; for if my heart condemns me, You, O God, are greater than my heart, and You know all things. If my heart does not condemn me, I have confidence before You and receive from You whatever I ask, because I keep Your commandments and do the things that are pleasing in Your sight. (1 John 3:18–22)

Take a moment to ask the Lord for the grace to grow in godly character.

My Relationship to Others

I was called to freedom, but I will not use my freedom to indulge the flesh, but through love I will serve others. For the whole law is summed up in this Your word, O God: "You shall love your neighbor as yourself." (Galatians 5:13–14)

Concerning love among believers: You have taught us, O God, to love each other, and we are to love each other more and more. (1 Thessalonians 4:9–10)

Pause to review your relationships with others and to commit them to the Lord.

DAY 11

The Attributes of God

Lord Jesus Christ, Your works have proved that the Father is in You, and that You are in the Father. (John 10:38)

You knew, Jesus, that the Father had given all things into Your hands and that You had come from God and were returning to God. (John 13:3)

Pause to reflect on these affirmations about the person, powers and perfection of God.

The Works of God

O Lord, You stretch out the heavens, lay the foundation of the earth and form the spirits of people within them. (Zechariah 12:1)

Since the creation of the world, Your invisible attributes, O God—Your eternal power and divine nature—have been clearly seen, revealed in what You have made, so that people are without excuse. (Romans 1:20)

Take a moment to consider the greatness of God's wonderful works.

My Relationship to God

With the righteous I shall rejoice in You, Lord,
   and trust in You,
      and with all the upright in heart, I shall be full of joy.
   (Psalm 64:10)

I will sing to You, Lord, as long as I live;
I will sing praise to You my God, while I have my being.

May my meditation be pleasing to You;
   I will be glad in You, Lord. (Psalm 104:33–34)

Pause to thank God for the relationship that you enjoy with Him in Jesus Christ.

The Character I Want to Cultivate

I will guard my heart with all diligence,
   for out of it flow the issues of life. (Proverbs 4:23)

Whatever is true, whatever is noble, whatever is right, whatever is pure, whatever is lovely, whatever is of good report—if anything is excellent or praiseworthy—I will think about such things. The things I have learned and received and heard and seen in those who walk with You, Christ Jesus, I will practice, and You, the God of peace, will be with me. (Philippians 4:8–9)

Take a moment to ask the Lord for the grace to grow in godly character.

My Relationship to Others

I will avoid foolish and ignorant disputes, knowing that they produce quarrels. As Your servant, O Lord, I must not quarrel but be gentle toward all, able to teach and patient. (2 Timothy 2:23–24)

I will not return evil for evil or insult for insult, but I will give blessing instead, because to this You called me, Lord, that I may inherit a blessing. (1 Peter 3:9)

Pause to review your relationships with others and to commit them to the Lord.

DAY 12

The Attributes of God

> You fashion the hearts of all and understand
> all their works, O God. (Psalm 33:15)

> Death and Destruction lie open before You, Lord;
> How much more do human hearts! (Proverbs 15:11)

Pause to reflect on these affirmations about the person, powers and perfection of God.

The Works of God

We can come to You, Lord Jesus Christ, for to all of us who are weary and burdened, You will give rest. We can take up Your yoke and learn from You, for You are gentle and humble in heart, and we will find rest for our souls. For Your yoke is easy, and Your burden is light. (Matthew 11:28–30)

As Moses lifted up the snake in the desert, so You, O Son of Man, had to be lifted up, that everyone who believes in You may have eternal life. (John 3:14–15)

Take a moment to consider the greatness of God's wonderful works.

My Relationship to God

Jesus, You have asked the Father, and He has given me another Comforter to be with me forever, even the Spirit of truth, whom the world cannot receive, because it neither sees Him nor knows Him. But I know Him, for He lives in me. (John 14:16–17)

I am not in the flesh but in the Spirit, since Your Spirit, O God, lives in me. And whoever does not have the Spirit of Christ does not belong to Him. (Romans 8:9)

Pause to thank God for the relationship that you enjoy with Him in Jesus Christ.

The Character I Want to Cultivate

I will not show partiality in judgment; I will hear both small and great alike. I will not be afraid of anyone, for judgment belongs to God. (Deuteronomy 1:17)

I do not want even a hint of immorality, or any impurity or greed in my life, as these are improper for a saint. Nor will I give myself over to obscenity, foolish talk or coarse joking, which are not fitting, but rather I will give myself to thanksgiving. (Ephesians 5:3–4)

Take a moment to ask the Lord for the grace to grow in godly character.

My Relationship to Others

As we have opportunity, we should do good to all people, especially to those who belong to the family of faith. (Galatians 6:10)

You, O God, are not unjust so that You forget our work and the love we have shown for Your name when we have ministered and continue to minister to Your saints. (Hebrews 6:10)

Pause to review your relationships with others and to commit them to the Lord.

DAY 13

The Attributes of God

> You, O Lord, are upright;
> You are my Rock,
>   and there is no unrighteousness in You.
>   (Psalm 92:15)
>
> Lord of hosts, You judge righteously and test my heart
>   and mind.
> To You I have committed my cause. (Jeremiah 11:20)

Pause to reflect on these affirmations about the person, powers and perfection of God.

The Works of God

Blessed are those who die in You, Lord, from now on. They will rest from their labor, for their works will follow them. (Revelation 14:13)

There will be a new heaven and a new earth, for the first heaven and the first earth will pass away, and there will no longer be any sea. (Revelation 21:1)

Take a moment to consider the greatness of God's wonderful works.

My Relationship to God

Your grace is sufficient for me, for Your power is made perfect in weakness. Therefore I will boast all the more gladly in my weaknesses, that Your power, O Christ, may rest upon me. Therefore I can be content in weaknesses, in insults, in hardships, in persecutions and in difficulties, for

Your sake. For when I am weak, then I am strong. (2 Corinthians 12:9–10)

Since I have in You, Jesus, the Son of God, a great high priest who has passed through the heavens, I will hold firmly to the faith I confess. For in You I do not have a high priest who is unable to sympathize with my weaknesses, but One who has been tempted in every way, just as I am, yet one who is without sin. Therefore I will approach the throne of grace with confidence, so that I may receive mercy and find grace to help me in my time of need. (Hebrews 4:14–16)

Pause to thank God for the relationship that you enjoy with Him in Jesus Christ.

The Character I Want to Cultivate

Better is open rebuke than love that is concealed.
  (Proverbs 27:5)

Faithful are the wounds of a friend,
  but the kisses of an enemy are deceitful.
  (Proverbs 27:6)

Take a moment to ask the Lord for the grace to grow in godly character.

My Relationship to Others

I will put away all bitterness and anger and wrath and shouting and slander, along with all malice. And I will be kind and compassionate to others, forgiving them just as You, O God, in Christ also forgave me. (Ephesians 4:31–32)

I will not slander other believers. Those who slander their brother or sister or judge their brother or sister slander the law and judge the law. When I judge the law, I am not a doer of the law, but a judge. You are only one Lawgiver and Judge, O God, the One who is able to save and to destroy. Who am I to judge my neighbor? (James 4:11–12)

Pause to review your relationships with others and to commit them to the Lord.

DAY 14

The Attributes of God

Jesus, You are in the Father, and the Father is in You. You spoke the words of Your Father and did the works of Your Father who dwells in You. You claimed to be in the Father and the Father in You, and You proved it through Your works. (John 14:10–11)

Jesus, You are my Lord and my God. (John 20:28)

Pause to reflect on these affirmations about the person, powers and perfection of God.

The Works of God

You are able to do immeasurably more than all that we ask or think, O God, according to Your power that is at work within us. To You be glory in the church and in Christ Jesus throughout all generations, for ever and ever. (Ephesians 3:20–21)

The mystery that has been kept hidden for ages and generations is now disclosed to the saints. You, Lord God, have chosen to make known among the Gentiles the glorious riches of this mystery, which is Christ in us, the hope of glory. (Colossians 1:26–27)

Take a moment to consider the greatness of God's wonderful works.

My Relationship to God

The greatest among us should be like the youngest, and the one who rules like the one who serves. For who is greater, the one who is at the table or the one who serves? Is it not the one who is at the table? But You, Jesus, came among us as the One who serves. (Luke 22:26–27)

If I serve You, Jesus, I must follow You; and where You are, Your servant also will be. If I serve You, the Father will honor me. (John 12:26)

Pause to thank God for the relationship that you enjoy with Him in Jesus Christ.

The Character I Want to Cultivate

I will not trust in myself or in my own righteousness, nor will I view others with contempt. (Luke 18:9)

I will be of the same mind with others; I will not be haughty in mind or wise in my own estimation, but I will associate with the humble. (Romans 12:16)

Take a moment to ask the Lord for the grace to grow in godly character.

My Relationship to Others

We should love one another, for love is from You, O God, and everyone who loves has been born of You and knows You. Whoever does not love does not know You, for You, O God, are love. (1 John 4:7–8)

We love because You, O God, first loved us. Those who say, "I love God," and hate their neighbors are liars; for those who do not love their neighbors whom they have seen cannot love You whom they have not seen. And we have this commandment from You: that those who love You must also love their neighbors. (1 John 4:19–21)

Pause to review your relationships with others and to commit them to the Lord.

DAY 15

The Attributes of God

> Surely as You, O Lord of hosts,
>   have thought, so it will be,
>   and as You have purposed, so it will stand.
> For You, Lord of hosts, have purposed,
>   and who can annul it?
> Your hand is stretched out,
>   and who can turn it back? (Isaiah 14:24, 27)

> You are the Lord, and there is no savior besides You.
> From ancient days You are He,
>   and no one can deliver out of Your hand;
> You act, and who can reverse it? (Isaiah 43:11, 13)

Pause to reflect on these affirmations about the person, powers and perfection of God.

The Works of God

You, Lord God, give life to the dead and call into being things that do not exist. (Romans 4:17)

The whole family in heaven and on earth derives its name from You, the God and Father of our Lord Jesus Christ. (Ephesians 3:14–15)

Take a moment to consider the greatness of God's wonderful works.

My Relationship to God

I will not lose heart; even though my outward self is perishing, yet my inner self is being renewed day by day. For this light affliction, which is momentary, is working for me a far more exceeding and eternal weight of glory. So I do not look at the things that are seen but at the things that are unseen. For the things that are seen are temporary, but the things that are unseen are eternal. (2 Corinthians 4:16–18)

My citizenship is in heaven; from there I also eagerly await You, my Savior, Lord Jesus Christ. You will transform my lowly body and conform it to Your glorious body by the power that enables You to subject all things to Yourself. (Philippians 3:20–21)

Pause to thank God for the relationship that you enjoy with Him in Jesus Christ.

The Character I Want to Cultivate

I will be anxious for nothing, but in everything, by prayer and petition with thanksgiving, I will let my requests be known to You. And Your peace, O God, which transcends all understanding, will guard my heart and my mind in Christ Jesus. (Philippians 4:6–7)

I will let Your peace, O Christ, to which I was called as a member of one body, rule in my heart, and I will be thankful. (Colossians 3:15)

Take a moment to ask the Lord for the grace to grow in godly character.

My Relationship to Others

I will give to all what they are due: taxes to whom taxes are due, custom to whom custom, respect to whom respect, honor to whom honor. (Romans 13:7)

I will honor all people, love the community of believers, fear You, O God, and honor the king. (1 Peter 2:17)

Pause to review your relationships with others and to commit them to the Lord.

DAY 16

The Attributes of God

I will express the memory of Your abundant goodness
and joyfully sing of Your righteousness.
You, O Lord, are gracious and compassionate,
slow to anger and great in lovingkindness.
You are good to all, and Your tender mercies
are over all Your works. (Psalm 145:7–9)

O Lord, You are not slow concerning Your promise, as some
count slowness, but are patient with us, not wanting anyone
to perish, but for all to come to repentance. (2 Peter 3:9)

*Pause to reflect on these affirmations about the person, powers
and perfection of God.*

The Works of God

You, Lord God, take no pleasure in the death of the wicked
but are pleased when the wicked turn from their ways and
live. (Ezekiel 18:23; 33:11)

Jesus, You said, "It is not the healthy who need a physician,
but those who are sick." You did not come to call the righteous, but sinners. (Matthew 9:12–13)

*Take a moment to consider the greatness of God's wonderful
works.*

My Relationship to God

I am confident of this, that You, the One who began a good
work in me, will carry it on to completion until Your day,
Christ Jesus. (Philippians 1:6)

In Your great grace, O God, You called me to Your eternal glory in Christ. After I have suffered a little while, You Yourself will perfect, confirm, strengthen and establish me. (1 Peter 5:10)

Pause to thank God for the relationship that you enjoy with Him in Jesus Christ.

The Character I Want to Cultivate

> If I am hot-tempered, I will stir up dissension,
>   but if I am slow to anger, I will calm a quarrel.
>   (Proverbs 15:18)

We should be quick to hear, slow to speak and slow to anger, for our anger does not produce Your righteousness, O God. (James 1:19–20)

Take a moment to ask the Lord for the grace to grow in godly character.

My Relationship to Others

I will not provoke my children to wrath but bring them up in Your discipline and instruction, O Lord. (Ephesians 6:4)

I will not provoke my children, or they will become discouraged. (Colossians 3:21)

Pause to review your relationships with others and to commit them to the Lord.

DAY 17

The Attributes of God

Jesus, You are the Christ, the Son of God, who came into the world. (John 11:27)

Anyone who has seen You, Jesus, has seen the Father. (John 14:9)

Pause to reflect on these affirmations about the person, powers and perfection of God.

The Works of God

Jesus Christ, You are the faithful witness, the firstborn from the dead, and the ruler of the kings of the earth. To You—who love us and have freed us from our sins by Your blood and have made us to be a kingdom and priests to serve Your God and Father—be glory and power for ever and ever. (Revelation 1:5–6)

Lamb of God, You are worthy to take the scroll and to open its seals, because You were slain, and with Your blood You purchased us for God from every tribe and language and people and nation. You have made us to be a kingdom and priests to serve our God, and we will reign on the earth. (Revelation 5:9–10)

Take a moment to consider the greatness of God's wonderful works.

My Relationship to God

Jesus, You are the door; whoever enters through You will be saved and will come in and go out and find pasture. The thief comes only to steal and kill and destroy; You have come that we may have life and have it abundantly. (John 10:9–10)

Your sheep hear Your voice, and You know them, and they follow You. You give them eternal life, and they shall never perish; no one can snatch them out of Your hand. The Father, who has given them to You, is greater than all; no one can snatch them out of the Father's hand. (John 10:27–29)

Pause to thank God for the relationship that you enjoy with Him in Jesus Christ.

The Character I Want to Cultivate

I will fight the good fight, finish the race, and keep the faith, so that there will be laid up for me the crown of righteousness, which You, Lord, the righteous Judge, will award to me on that day; and not only to me, but also to all who have longed for Your appearing. (2 Timothy 4:7–8)

Since I have a great cloud of witnesses surrounding me, I want to lay aside every impediment and the sin that so easily entangles, and run with endurance the race that is set before me, fixing my eyes on You, Jesus, the author and perfecter of my faith, who for the joy set before You endured the cross, despising the shame, and sat down at the right hand of the throne of God. I will consider You who endured such hostility from sinners, so that I will not grow weary and lose heart. (Hebrews 12:1–3)

Take a moment to ask the Lord for the grace to grow in godly character.

My Relationship to Others

We always pray for other believers, that You, our God, may count them worthy of Your calling and fulfill with power every desire for goodness and every work of faith. (2 Thessalonians 1:11)

We ask that Your name, O Lord Jesus, may be glorified in others, and they in You, according to the grace of our God. (2 Thessalonians 1:12)

Pause to review your relationships with others and to commit them to the Lord.

DAY 18

The Attributes of God

> Though You are on high, Lord,
>   You look upon the lowly,
>   but the proud You know from afar.
>   (Psalm 138:6)

I know, O Lord, that my life is not my own;
It is not for me to direct my steps. (Jeremiah 10:23)

Pause to reflect on these affirmations about the person, powers and perfection of God.

The Works of God

> You answer us with awesome deeds of righteousness,
>   O God of our salvation,
> You who are the hope of all the ends of the earth
>   and of the farthest seas.
> You formed the mountains by Your strength,
>   having armed Yourself with power.
> You stilled the roaring of the seas,
>   the roaring of their waves,
>   and the tumult of the peoples. (Psalm 65:5–7)

Jesus Christ, You are the image of the invisible God, the first-born over all creation. For by You all things were created that are in heaven and on earth, visible and invisible, whether thrones or dominions or rulers or authorities; all things were created by You and for You. And You are before all things, and in You all things hold together. (Colossians 1:15–17)

Take a moment to consider the greatness of God's wonderful works.

My Relationship to God

If You, O God, are for me, who can be against me? You who did not spare Your own Son, but delivered Him up for us all, how will You not also, with Him, freely give us all things? (Romans 8:31–32)

Your divine power, O God, has given me all things that pertain to life and godliness, through the knowledge of You who called me by Your own glory and virtue. Through these You have given me Your very great and precious promises, so that I may be a partaker of the divine nature, having escaped the corruption that is in the world by lust. (2 Peter 1:3–4)

Pause to thank God for the relationship that you enjoy with Him in Jesus Christ.

The Character I Want to Cultivate

Blessed are those who hunger and thirst for righteousness, for they shall be satisfied. (Matthew 5:6)

Your kingdom, O God, is not a matter of eating and drinking, but of righteousness and peace and joy in Your Holy Spirit. (Romans 14:17)

Take a moment to ask the Lord for the grace to grow in godly character.

My Relationship to Others

May You, O Lord, make me increase and abound in my love for believers and for unbelievers. (1 Thessalonians 3:12)

Those who love their brothers and sisters abide in the light, and there is no cause for stumbling in them. But those who hate their brothers and sisters are in the darkness and walk in the darkness and do not know where they are going, because the darkness has blinded their eyes. (1 John 2:10–11)

Pause to review your relationships with others and to commit them to the Lord.

DAY 19

The Attributes of God

> I will enter Your gates with thanksgiving, O Lord,
>   and Your courts with praise;
> I will give thanks to You and bless Your name.
> For You are good and Your lovingkindness
>   endures forever;
> Your faithfulness continues through all generations.
>   (Psalm 100:4–5)

Blessed are You, the God and Father of our Lord Jesus Christ, the Father of mercies and the God of all comfort. (2 Corinthians 1:3)

Pause to reflect on these affirmations about the person, powers and perfection of God.

The Works of God

> Lord, You save the humble
>   but bring low those whose eyes are haughty.
>   (Psalm 18:27)

> Lord, You guide the humble in what is right
>   and teach the humble Your way. (Psalm 25:9)

Take a moment to consider the greatness of God's wonderful works.

My Relationship to God

> I have set You always before me, O Lord;
> Because You are at my right hand, I will not be shaken.
> Therefore my heart is glad, and my glory rejoices;

My body also will rest in hope.
You will make known to me the path of life;
In Your presence is fullness of joy;
In Your right hand are pleasures forever.
  (Psalm 16:8–9, 11)

"You, O Lord, are my portion," says my soul; therefore I will wait for You. You are good to those who wait for You, Lord, to the soul who seeks You. It is good to hope silently for Your salvation. (Lamentations 3:24–26)

Pause to thank God for the relationship that you enjoy with Him in Jesus Christ.

The Character I Want to Cultivate

The waywardness of the simple will kill them,
    and the complacency of fools will destroy them;
But if I listen to wisdom, I will live securely
    and be at ease from the fear of evil. (Proverbs 1:32–33)

If I trust in my own heart, I am foolish,
    but if I walk in wisdom, I will be delivered.
  (Proverbs 28:26)

Take a moment to ask the Lord for the grace to grow in godly character.

My Relationship to Others

An anxious heart weighs one down,
    but a good word makes a person glad. (Proverbs 12:25)

God, You comfort us in all our afflictions, so that we can comfort those in any affliction with the comfort we ourselves have received from You. (2 Corinthians 1:4)

Pause to review your relationships with others and to commit them to the Lord.

DAY 20

The Attributes of God

In my heart I plan my way,
    but You, O Lord, determine my steps.
    (Proverbs 16:9)

Many are the plans in my heart,
    but it is Your counsel, O Lord, that will stand.
    (Proverbs 19:21)

Pause to reflect on these affirmations about the person, powers and perfection of God.

The Works of God

In the past, O God, You spoke to the fathers through the prophets at many times and in various ways, but in these last days You have spoken to us by Your Son, whom You appointed heir of all things, and through whom You made the universe. (Hebrews 1:1–2)

By faith I understand that the universe was formed by Your word, O God, so that what is seen was not made out of things which are visible. (Hebrews 11:3)

Take a moment to consider the greatness of God's wonderful works.

My Relationship to God

To me, to live is You, O Christ, and to die is gain. (Philippians 1:21)

Whatever was gain to me I now consider loss for Your sake, O Christ. What is more, I consider all things loss compared to the surpassing greatness of knowing You as my Lord; for Your sake I suffer the loss of all things and consider them rubbish, that I may gain You and be found in You, not having a righteousness of my own that comes from the law, but that which is through faith in You—the righteousness that comes from God on the basis of faith. (Philippians 3:7–9)

Pause to thank God for the relationship that you enjoy with Him in Jesus Christ.

The Character I Want to Cultivate

I will flee from sexual immorality. All other sins people commit are outside their bodies, but sexually immoral people sin against their own bodies. (1 Corinthians 6:18)

I will consider the parts of my earthly body as dead to immorality, impurity, passion, evil desires and greed, which is idolatry. Because of these, O God, Your wrath is coming. I used to walk in these ways in the life I once lived. (Colossians 3:5–7)

Take a moment to ask the Lord for the grace to grow in godly character.

My Relationship to Others

If we have any encouragement from being united with You, O Christ, if any comfort from Your love, if any fellowship of the Spirit, if any affection and compassion, we should also be like-minded, having the same love, being one in spirit and one in purpose. (Philippians 2:1–2)

We should all be of one mind and be sympathetic, loving as brothers and sisters, compassionate and humble. (1 Peter 3:8)

Pause to review your relationships with others and to commit them to the Lord.

DAY 21

The Attributes of God

> Your merciful love is higher than the heavens, O Lord,
> and Your truth reaches to the skies. (Psalm 108:4)

> I will give thanks to You, the God of heaven,
> for Your merciful love endures forever.
> (Psalm 136:26)

Pause to reflect on these affirmations about the person, powers and perfection of God.

The Works of God

I praise You, Father, Lord of heaven and earth, because You have hidden these things from the wise and learned, and revealed them to little children. Yes, Father, for this was well-pleasing in Your sight. You have delivered all things to Your Son Jesus. No one knows the Son except You, Father, and no one knows You except the Son and those to whom the Son chooses to reveal You. (Matthew 11:25–27; Luke 10:21–22)

Jesus, You preached the gospel of the kingdom of God and said, "The time is fulfilled, and the kingdom of God is at hand. Repent and believe the good news." (Mark 1:14–15)

Take a moment to consider the greatness of God's wonderful works.

My Relationship to God

Jesus, I believe that You are the Christ, the Son of God, and that by believing I have life in Your name. (John 20:31)

If I confess You with my mouth, Lord Jesus, and believe in my heart that God raised You from the dead, I will be saved.

For it is with my heart that I believe unto righteousness, and it is with my mouth that I confess unto salvation. As the Scripture says, "Whoever trusts in Him will not be put to shame." (Romans 10:9–11)

Pause to thank God for the relationship that you enjoy with Him in Jesus Christ.

The Character I Want to Cultivate

Let those who think they stand take heed lest they fall. (1 Corinthians 10:12)

I do not dare to classify or compare myself with other people, for it is unwise to measure or compare myself with others. I will not boast beyond proper limits but within the sphere of Your gospel, O Christ. "Let those who boast boast in the Lord." For it is not those who commend themselves who are approved, but those whom You commend, Lord. (2 Corinthians 10:12–14, 17–18)

Take a moment to ask the Lord for the grace to grow in godly character.

My Relationship to Others

I will remind others to be subject to rulers and authorities, to be obedient, to be ready for every good work, to slander no one, to be peaceable and gentle, and to show true humility toward all people. (Titus 3:1–2)

Young men should be submissive to those who are older, and all of us should clothe ourselves with humility toward one another, for You, O God, "oppose the proud but give grace to the humble." (1 Peter 5:5)

Pause to review your relationships with others and to commit them to the Lord.

The Attributes of God

Ah, Lord God!
You have made the heavens and the earth
    by Your great power and outstretched arm.
Nothing is too difficult for You.
You are the great and mighty God;
Your name is the Lord of hosts.
You are great in counsel and mighty in deed,
    and Your eyes see everything that we do;
You reward us according to our ways
    and according to the fruit of our deeds.
    (Jeremiah 32:17–19)

Your word, O God, is living and active and sharper than any double-edged sword, piercing even to the dividing of soul and spirit and of joints and marrow; it judges the thoughts and attitudes of the heart. And there is no creature hidden from Your sight, but everything is uncovered and laid bare before Your eyes—You to whom we must give account. (Hebrews 4:12–13)

Pause to reflect on these affirmations about the person, powers and perfection of God.

The Works of God

By Your word, O God, the heavens existed long ago and the earth was formed out of water and by water. By these waters also the world of that time was deluged and destroyed. And by Your word the present heavens and earth are reserved for fire, being kept for the day of judgment and the destruction of the ungodly. (2 Peter 3:5–7)

You are worthy, our Lord and God, to receive glory and honor and power, for You created all things, and by Your will they were created and have their being. (Revelation 4:11)

Take a moment to consider the greatness of God's wonderful works.

My Relationship to God

From everyone who has been given much, much will be required, and from the one who has been entrusted with much, much more will be asked. (Luke 12:48)

As Your servant, O Christ, and a steward of Your possessions, may I be found faithful. (1 Corinthians 4:1–2)

Pause to thank God for the relationship that you enjoy with Him in Jesus Christ.

The Character I Want to Cultivate

I will covet no one's money or possessions. (Acts 20:33)

Godliness with contentment is great gain. For I brought nothing into the world, and I can take nothing out of it. But if I have food and clothing, with these I will be content. (1 Timothy 6:6–8)

Take a moment to ask the Lord for the grace to grow in godly character.

My Relationship to Others

I will remember those who led me, who spoke Your word, O God, to me. I will consider the outcome of their way of life and imitate their faith. (Hebrews 13:7)

I will obey those who lead me and submit to them, for they keep watch over my soul as those who must give an account.

I will obey them, so that they may do this with joy and not with grief, for this would be unprofitable for me. (Hebrews 13:17)

Pause to review your relationships with others and to commit them to the Lord.

DAY 23

The Attributes of God

> O Lord of hosts, You are wonderful in counsel
>   and great in wisdom. (Isaiah 28:29)

In You, O Christ, are hidden all the treasures of wisdom and
knowledge. (Colossians 2:3)

*Pause to reflect on these affirmations about the person, powers
and perfection of God.*

The Works of God

O Lord, if we your people, who are called by Your name,
will humble ourselves and pray and seek Your face and turn
from our wicked ways, then You will hear from heaven and
will forgive our sin and heal our land. (2 Chronicles 7:14)

> Blessed is the nation whose God You are, O Lord,
>   the people whom You have chosen for Your
>   inheritance. (Psalm 33:12)

*Take a moment to consider the greatness of God's wonderful
works.*

My Relationship to God

I know that if my earthly house is destroyed, I have a building from You, O God, eternal in the heavens, a house not
made with hands. For in this house I groan, longing to be
clothed with my heavenly dwelling, because when I am
clothed, I will not be found naked. While I am in this house,
I groan, being burdened, because I do not want to be

unclothed but to be clothed, so that what is mortal may be swallowed up by life. Now it is You, O God, who have made me for this very purpose and have given me Your Spirit as a guarantee. (2 Corinthians 5:1–5)

Lord, I make it my ambition to please You whether I am at home in the body or away from it. For we must all appear before the judgment seat of Christ, that each one may receive what is due for the things done while in the body, whether good or bad. (2 Corinthians 5:9–10)

Pause to thank God for the relationship that you enjoy with Him in Jesus Christ.

The Character I Want to Cultivate

Lord, may I obey Your instruction to watch and pray so that I will not fall into temptation; the spirit is willing, but the flesh is weak. (Matthew 26:41)

I will devote myself to prayer, being watchful and thankful. (Colossians 4:2)

Take a moment to ask the Lord for the grace to grow in godly character.

My Relationship to Others

I will obey those who are in authority over me in all things, not with external service, as one who pleases people, but with a sincere heart, fearing You, Lord. Whatever I do, I will work at it with all my heart, as working for You, and not for people, knowing that I will receive the reward of the inheritance from You. It is You I am serving, Lord Jesus Christ. (Colossians 3:22–24)

I will provide those who serve under me with what is just and fair, knowing that I also have a Master in heaven. (Colossians 4:1)

Pause to review your relationships with others and to commit them to the Lord.

DAY 24

The Attributes of God

O Most High, You are sovereign over the kingdoms on earth and give them to whomever You wish and set over them the lowliest of people. I will bless You, Most High, and praise and honor You who live forever. Your dominion is an eternal dominion, and Your kingdom endures from generation to generation. You regard all the inhabitants of the earth as nothing and do as You please with the host of heaven and the inhabitants of the earth. No one can hold back Your hand or say to You: "What have You done?" I praise, exalt and honor You, King of heaven, for all Your works are true, and all Your ways are just, and You are able to humble those who walk in pride. (Daniel 4:17, 34–35, 37)

All authority in heaven and on earth has been given to You, Jesus Christ, who are the Son of God. (Matthew 28:18)

Pause to reflect on these affirmations about the person, powers and perfection of God.

The Works of God

Jesus, You who come from above are above all; he who is from the earth belongs to the earth and speaks as one from the earth. You who come from heaven are above all. You, whom God has sent, speak the words of God, for You give the Spirit without limit. (John 3:31, 34)

The Father judges no one, but has given all judgment to You, Jesus, His Son, that all may honor You just as they honor the Father. Those who do not honor You do not honor the Father who sent You. (John 5:22–23)

Take a moment to consider the greatness of God's wonderful works.

My Relationship to God

Your grace, O Lord, was poured out on me abundantly, along with the faith and love that are in Christ Jesus. (1 Timothy 1:14)

O God, You have saved me and called me with a holy calling, not according to my works but according to Your own purpose and grace. (2 Timothy 1:9)

Pause to thank God for the relationship that you enjoy with Him in Jesus Christ.

The Character I Want to Cultivate

I will consider it all joy whenever I fall into various trials, knowing that the testing of my faith produces endurance. And I will let endurance finish its work, so that I may be mature and complete, lacking in nothing. (James 1:2–4)

I am blessed when I persevere under trial, because when I have been approved, I will receive the crown of life that You, O God, have promised to those who love You. (James 1:12)

Take a moment to ask the Lord for the grace to grow in godly character.

My Relationship to Others

We are to put off falsehood and speak truthfully to our neighbors, for we are members of one another. (Ephesians 4:25)

We thank You, O God, for other believers, and we pray that their faith would grow more and more, and that their love for each other would increase. (2 Thessalonians 1:3)

Pause to review your relationships with others and to commit them to the Lord.

The Attributes of God

O Lord, You are good, a refuge in times of trouble;
You know those who trust in You. (Nahum 1:7)

You, O God, are light; in You there is no darkness at all.
(1 John 1:5)

*Pause to reflect on these affirmations about the person, powers
and perfection of God.*

The Works of God

Jesus, we thank You that You did not ask that the Father take
us out of the world, but that He protect us from the evil one
when You prayed: "Father, I desire those You have given Me
to be with Me where I am, that they may behold My glory,
the glory You have given Me because You loved Me before
the foundation of the world." (John 17:15, 24)

Lord, grant to us the power of the Spirit that you promised
the apostles when You told them, "You will receive power
when the Holy Spirit comes upon you; and you will be My
witnesses in Jerusalem, and in all Judea and Samaria, and to
the ends of the earth." (Acts 1:8)

Take a moment to consider the greatness of God's wonderful works.

My Relationship to God

Since I have been justified by Christ's blood, how much
more shall I be saved from Your wrath, O God, through
Him. For if, when I was Your enemy, I was reconciled to You
through the death of Your Son, how much more, having

been reconciled, shall I be saved through His life. And not only this, but I also rejoice in You through my Lord Jesus Christ, through whom I have now received the reconciliation. (Romans 5:9–11)

God, You made Him who knew no sin to be sin for me, so that in Him I might become Your righteousness. (2 Corinthians 5:21)

Pause to thank God for the relationship that you enjoy with Him in Jesus Christ.

The Character I Want to Cultivate

I will not seek to justify myself in other people's eyes; You, O God, know my heart, and what is highly esteemed among people is detestable in Your sight. (Luke 16:15)

I will not love praise from people more than praise from You, O God. (John 12:43)

Take a moment to ask the Lord for the grace to grow in godly character.

My Relationship to Others

I shall seek to keep Your commandments, O God: "You shall love the Lord your God with all your heart and with all your soul and with all your mind." This is the first and greatest commandment. And the second is like it: "You shall love your neighbor as yourself." All the Law and the Prophets hang on these two commandments. (Matthew 22:37–40)

This is Your commandment: that we believe in the name of Your Son Jesus Christ and love one another. (1 John 3:23)

Pause to review your relationships with others and to commit them to the Lord.

DAY 26

The Attributes of God

> You declare the end from the beginning and from
>   ancient times what is still to come, saying,
> "My purpose will stand, and I will do all My pleasure."
>   (Isaiah 46:10)

> The word that goes forth from Your mouth, O Lord,
>   will not return to You empty
>   but will accomplish what You desire
>   and achieve the purpose for which You sent it.
>   (Isaiah 55:11)

*Pause to reflect on these affirmations about the person, powers
and perfection of God.*

The Works of God

The law was added that the transgression might increase.
But where sin increased, grace abounded all the more, so
that just as sin reigned in death, so also grace might reign
through righteousness to bring eternal life through You,
Jesus Christ our Lord. (Romans 5:20–21)

O Christ, You have completed the law so that there may be
righteousness to everyone who believes. (Romans 10:4)

*Take a moment to consider the greatness of God's wonderful
works.*

My Relationship to God

Your love, O Christ, compels me, because I am convinced
that You are the One who died for all, and therefore all died.

And You died for all, that those who live should no longer live for themselves but for You who died for them and were raised again. (2 Corinthians 5:14–15)

God my Savior, when Your kindness and love appeared, You saved me, not by works of righteousness that I had done, but according to Your mercy. You saved me through the washing of regeneration and renewal by Your Holy Spirit, whom You poured out on me abundantly through Jesus Christ my Savior, so that having been justified by Your grace, I might become Your heir, having the hope of eternal life. (Titus 3:4–7)

Pause to thank God for the relationship that you enjoy with Him in Jesus Christ.

The Character I Want to Cultivate

There is a way that seems right to me,
but its end is the way of death. (Proverbs 14:12)

I will examine all things, hold fast to the good and abstain from every form of evil. (1 Thessalonians 5:21–22)

Take a moment to ask the Lord for the grace to grow in godly character.

My Relationship to Others

I will be hospitable to others without grumbling. (1 Peter 4:9)

As each of us has received a gift, we should use it to serve others, as good stewards of Your manifold grace, O God. (1 Peter 4:10)

Pause to review your relationships with others and to commit them to the Lord.

DAY 27

The Attributes of God

O Son of Man, You will come with the clouds of heaven. In the presence of the Ancient of Days, You will be given dominion and glory and a kingdom, so that people of every nation and language will worship You. Your dominion is an everlasting dominion that will not pass away, and Your kingdom is one that will never be destroyed. (Daniel 7:13–14)

To You, the only God our Savior, through Jesus Christ our Lord, be glory, majesty, dominion and authority, before all ages, now and forever. Amen. (Jude 25)

Pause to reflect on these affirmations about the person, powers and perfection of God.

The Works of God

Faith comes from hearing, and hearing by Your word, O Christ. (Romans 10:17)

The faith of Your chosen people, O God, and the knowledge of the truth that leads to godliness, is faith and knowledge resting in the hope of eternal life. It is an eternal life that You promised before the beginning of time—and You do not lie. At the appointed time You manifested Your word through the preaching entrusted to the apostles by Your command, O God our Savior. (Titus 1:1–3)

Take a moment to consider the greatness of God's wonderful works.

My Relationship to God

O God, You are rich in mercy; because of Your great love for me, You made me alive with Christ, even when I was dead in transgressions. It is by grace I have been saved. (Ephesians 2:4–5)

Once I was alienated from You, O God, and was an enemy in my mind because of my evil works. But now You have reconciled me, by Christ's fleshly body through death, to present me holy and blameless in Your sight and free from reproach. (Colossians 1:21–22)

Pause to thank God for the relationship that you enjoy with Him in Jesus Christ.

The Character I Want to Cultivate

I will not set my heart on evil things or be an idolater or commit sexual immorality. (1 Corinthians 10:6–8)

This is Your will, O God, that I be sanctified, that I abstain from immorality and learn to control my own body in holiness and honor. For You did not call me to be impure, but to live a holy life. (1 Thessalonians 4:3–4, 7)

Take a moment to ask the Lord for the grace to grow in godly character.

My Relationship to Others

I will not bring charges against others without cause,
    when they have done me no harm.
    (Proverbs 3:30)

I will not take revenge but leave room for Your wrath, O God, for You have said, "Vengeance is Mine; I will repay." I will not be overcome by evil, but overcome evil with good. (Romans 12:19, 21)

Pause to review your relationships with others and to commit them to the Lord.

DAY 28

The Attributes of God

> I will give thanks to You, Lord, for You are good;
> Your lovingkindness endures forever. (Psalm 118:1)

> Your testimonies, which You have commanded,
>   are righteous and trustworthy.
> Your righteousness is everlasting,
>   and Your law is truth. (Psalm 119:138, 142)

Pause to reflect on these affirmations about the person, powers and perfection of God.

The Works of God

No one can lay a foundation other than the one already laid; You are the foundation, O Jesus Christ. (1 Corinthians 3:11)

Jesus, You meet our needs as our high priest: You are holy, blameless, undefiled, set apart from sinners and exalted above the heavens. Unlike the other high priests, You do not need to offer sacrifices day after day, first for Your own sins, and then for the sins of the people, for You did this once for all when You offered up Yourself. (Hebrews 7:26–27)

Take a moment to consider the greatness of God's wonderful works.

My Relationship to God

O Father, You have qualified me to share in the inheritance of the saints in the light. For You have rescued me from the dominion of darkness and brought me into the kingdom of

Your beloved Son, in whom I have redemption, the forgiveness of sins. (Colossians 1:12–14)

I was not redeemed from an aimless way of life, O Christ, with perishable things, such as silver or gold, but with Your precious blood as of a lamb without blemish or defect. (1 Peter 1:18–19)

Pause to thank God for the relationship that you enjoy with Him in Jesus Christ.

The Character I Want to Cultivate

I will submit myself to You, O God, and resist the devil, and he will flee from me. I will humble myself before You, Lord, and You will exalt me. (James 4:7, 10)

I will humble myself under Your mighty hand, O God, that You may exalt me in due time; I will cast all my anxiety upon You, because You care for me. (1 Peter 5:6–7)

Take a moment to ask the Lord for the grace to grow in godly character.

My Relationship to Others

Wives should submit to their husbands, as is fitting in You, O Lord. (Colossians 3:18)

Husbands should love their wives and not be bitter toward them. (Colossians 3:19)

Pause to review your relationships with others and to commit them to the Lord.

DAY 29

The Attributes of God

Heaven and earth will pass away, but Your words, Lord Jesus, will never pass away. (Matthew 24:35; Luke 21:33)

To You—the King eternal, immortal, invisible, the only God—be honor and glory for ever and ever. (1 Timothy 1:17)

Pause to reflect on these affirmations about the person, powers and perfection of God.

The Works of God

O God, You were pleased to have all Your fullness dwell in Christ and through Him to reconcile all things to Yourself, whether things on earth or things in heaven, having made peace through the blood of His cross. (Colossians 1:19–20)

During the days You lived on earth, Jesus, You offered up prayers and petitions with loud cries and tears to the One who could save You from death, and You were heard because of Your reverent submission. Although You were a Son, You learned obedience by the things that You suffered; and being perfected, You became the source of eternal salvation for all who obey You, being designated by God as a high priest according to the order of Melchizedek. (Hebrews 5:7–10)

Take a moment to consider the greatness of God's wonderful works.

My Relationship to God

Those You foreknew, O God, You also predestined to be conformed to the likeness of Your Son, that He might be the firstborn among many brothers and sisters. And those You predestined, You also called; those You called, You also justified; those You justified, You also glorified. (Romans 8:29–30)

When I was dead in my trespasses and in the uncircumcision of my flesh, You made me alive with Christ, O God. You forgave me all my trespasses, having canceled the written code, with its regulations, that was against me and was contrary to me; You took it away, nailing it to the cross. And having disarmed the powers and authorities, You made a public spectacle of them, triumphing over them by the cross. (Colossians 2:13–15)

Pause to thank God for the relationship that you enjoy with Him in Jesus Christ.

The Character I Want to Cultivate

I greatly rejoice in my salvation, even though now for a little while, if necessary, I grieve because of various trials. They come so that my faith, though much more precious than gold, that perishes even though it is refined by fire, may be proved genuine and that it may result in praise, glory and honor when You are revealed, O Jesus Christ. (1 Peter 1:6–7)

I will be self-controlled and alert; my adversary the devil prowls around like a roaring lion looking for someone to devour. But I will resist him, standing firm in the faith, knowing that my brothers and sisters throughout the world are undergoing the same kind of sufferings. (1 Peter 5:8–9)

Take a moment to ask the Lord for the grace to grow in godly character.

My Relationship to Others

I will lay up Your words in my heart and in my soul and teach them to my children, talking about them when I sit in my house and when I walk along the way and when I lie down and when I rise up. (Deuteronomy 11:18–19)

> Those who are foolish despise their father's discipline,
>   but those who heed correction are prudent.
>   (Proverbs 15:5)

Pause to review your relationships with others and to commit them to the Lord.

DAY 30

The Attributes of God

> Before You formed me in the womb,
> You knew me, O Lord;
> Before I was born,
> You set me apart. (Jeremiah 1:5)

O God, You number even the very hairs of my head. (Matthew 10:30; Luke 12:7)

Pause to reflect on these affirmations about the person, powers and perfection of God.

The Works of God

Because You live forever, Lord Jesus, You have a permanent priesthood. Therefore You are also able to save us completely—we who come to God through You, since You always live to intercede for us. (Hebrews 7:24–25)

By the will of God, we have been sanctified through the offering of Your body, O Jesus Christ, once for all. And every priest stands daily ministering and offering again and again the same sacrifices, which can never take away sins. But when You had offered for all time one sacrifice for sins, You sat down at the right hand of God, waiting from that time for Your enemies to be made a footstool for Your feet. For by one offering, You have made perfect forever those who are being sanctified. (Hebrews 10:10–14)

Take a moment to consider the greatness of God's wonderful works.

My Relationship to God

I do not want to be conformed to the pattern of this world but transformed by the renewing of my mind, that I may be able to test and approve what Your will is, O God, and that it is good and pleasing and perfect. (Romans 12:2)

God of my Lord Jesus Christ, the Father of glory, may You give me a spirit of wisdom and of revelation in the full knowledge of You, and may the eyes of my heart be enlightened, in order that I may know the hope to which You have called me, the riches of Your glorious inheritance in the saints, and the incomparable greatness of Your power toward us who believe. (Ephesians 1:17–19)

Pause to thank God for the relationship that you enjoy with Him in Jesus Christ.

The Character I Want to Cultivate

Since Your day, O Lord, will come like a thief, I ought to conduct my life with holiness and godliness as I look forward to the coming of Your day. According to Your promise I am looking for a new heaven and a new earth, in which righteousness dwells. Therefore, since I am looking for these things, I will be diligent to be found at peace with You— pure and blameless before You. (2 Peter 3:10–14)

I will abide in You, Christ Jesus, so that when You appear, I may have confidence and not be ashamed before You at Your coming. (1 John 2:28)

Take a moment to ask the Lord for the grace to grow in godly character.

My Relationship to Others

> Better a meal of vegetables where there is love than a
> fattened calf with hatred. (Proverbs 15:17)

> If we erase a sin by forgiving it, we show love,
>   but if we repeat the matter, we come between close
>   friends. (Proverbs 17:9)

*Pause to review your relationships with others and to commit
them to the Lord.*

DAY 31

The Attributes of God

Long ago You ordained Your plan, O Lord,
   and now You are bringing it to pass.
      (2 Kings 19:25; Isaiah 37:26)

With You, Lord, one day is like a thousand years, and a thousand years are like one day. (2 Peter 3:8)

Pause to reflect on these affirmations about the person, powers and perfection of God.

The Works of God

Every good and perfect gift is from above, coming down from You, the Father of lights, with whom there is no variation or shifting shadow. Of Your own will You brought us forth by the word of truth, that we might be a kind of first-fruits of Your creatures. (James 1:17–18)

Christ Jesus, You died for sins once for all, the righteous for the unrighteous, to bring me to God. Having been put to death in the body but made alive by the Spirit, You have gone into heaven and are at God's right hand, after angels and authorities and powers were made subject to You. (1 Peter 3:18, 22)

Take a moment to consider the greatness of God's wonderful works.

My Relationship to God

I trusted in You, O Christ, when I heard the word of truth, the gospel of my salvation. Having believed, I was sealed in

You with the Holy Spirit of promise, who is a deposit guaranteeing my inheritance until the redemption of those who are God's possession—to the praise of Your glory. (Ephesians 1:13–14)

Since I have been raised with You, O Christ, I should seek the things above, where You are seated at the right hand of God. I will set my mind on the things above, not on the things on the earth, for I died, and my life is now hidden with You in God. When You who are my life appear, then I also will appear with You in glory. (Colossians 3:1–4)

Pause to thank God for the relationship that you enjoy with Him in Jesus Christ.

The Character I Want to Cultivate

I will work out my salvation with fear and trembling, for it is You, O God, who works in me to will and to act according to Your good purpose. (Philippians 2:12–13)

Whatever I do, whether in word or in deed, I will do all in Your name, Lord Jesus, giving thanks to God the Father through You. (Colossians 3:17)

Take a moment to ask the Lord for the grace to grow in godly character.

My Relationship to Others

All things are for our benefit, so that the grace that is reaching more and more people may cause thanksgiving to abound to Your glory, O God. (2 Corinthians 4:15)

I will offer petitions, prayers, intercession and thanksgiving on behalf of all people, for kings and all those who are in authority, that I may live a peaceful and quiet life in all godliness and reverence. This is good and acceptable in Your sight, O God our Savior, for You desire all people to be saved and to come to the knowledge of the truth. (1 Timothy 2:1–4)

Pause to review your relationships with others and to commit them to the Lord.

PART TWO

Topical Guide to
Renewal and Growth

THE ATTRIBUTES OF GOD

The Person of God

O God, You revealed Yourself to Moses as "I AM WHO I AM." (Exodus 3:14)

You are the Lord, the God of our fathers—the God of Abraham, the God of Isaac and the God of Jacob. This is Your name forever, the name by which You are to be remembered from generation to generation. (Exodus 3:15)

I will sing to You, Lord, for You are highly exalted. You, O Lord, are my strength and my song; You have become my salvation. You are my God, and I will praise You, my father's God, and I will exalt You. (Exodus 15:1–2)

I will proclaim Your name, O Lord, and praise Your greatness, O my God. (Deuteronomy 32:3)

O Sovereign Lord, You are God! Your words are true, and You have promised good things to Your servant. (2 Samuel 7:28)

You live, O Lord! Blessed are You, my Rock! You are exalted, O God, Rock of my salvation! (2 Samuel 22:47)

I will arise and bless You, Lord my God; You are from everlasting to everlasting. Blessed be Your glorious name, which is exalted above all blessing and praise! (Nehemiah 9:5)

O God, You are exalted beyond our understanding; the number of Your years is unsearchable. (Job 36:26)

O Lord, our Lord, how majestic is Your name in all the earth! You have set Your glory above the heavens! (Psalm 8:1)

I will be still and know that You are God. You will be exalted among the nations. You will be exalted in the earth. (Psalm 46:10)

You, O Lord Most High, are awesome, the great King over all the earth! You are the King of all the earth, and I will sing Your praise. You reign over the nations; You are seated on Your holy throne. (Psalm 47:2, 7–8)

Great are You, Lord, and most worthy of praise in Your city, O God, Your holy mountain. As is Your name, O God, so is Your praise to the ends of the earth; Your right hand is filled with righteousness. (Psalm 48:1, 10)

Your righteousness, O God, reaches to the heavens. You who have done great things, O God, who is like You? (Psalm 71:19)

Great are You, Lord, and most worthy of praise; You are to be feared above all gods, for all the gods of the nations are idols, but You made the heavens. Splendor and majesty are before You; strength and beauty are in Your sanctuary. I will ascribe to You, O Lord, glory and strength. I will ascribe to You the glory due Your name and worship You in the beauty of holiness. (Psalm 96:4–9)

My soul blesses You, O Lord my God; You are very great; You are clothed with splendor and majesty. (Psalm 104:1)

May you be blessed, O Lord, the God of Israel, from everlasting to everlasting. I will praise you. (Psalm 106:48)

You are my God, and I will give thanks to You; You are my God, and I will exalt You. I will give thanks to You, Lord, for You are good; Your loyal love endures forever. (Psalm 118:28–29)

Your name, O Lord, endures forever, Your renown, O Lord, through all generations. (Psalm 135:13)

I will exalt You, my God and King; I will bless Your name for ever and ever. Every day I will bless You, and I will praise Your name for ever and ever. Great are You, Lord, and most worthy of praise; Your greatness is unsearchable. (Psalm 145:1–3)

Holy, Holy, Holy are You, Lord of hosts; the whole earth is full of Your glory. (Isaiah 6:3)

I will trust in You forever, for in You, Yahweh, the Lord, I have an everlasting Rock. (Isaiah 26:4)

You are the Lord, and there is no other; apart from You there is no god. From the rising of the sun to its setting, we know there is none besides You. You are the Lord, and there is no other. (Isaiah 45:5–6)

You, Lord, alone have declared what is to come from the distant past. There is no god apart from You, a righteous God and a Savior. There is none besides You. You are God, and there is no other. (Isaiah 45:21–22)

My Redeemer, the Lord of hosts is Your name; You are the Holy One of Israel. (Isaiah 47:4)

You, O Lord, are the true God; You are the living God and the everlasting King. At Your wrath the earth trembles, and the nations cannot endure Your indignation. (Jeremiah 10:10)

You, O Lord, are in Your holy temple; let all the earth be silent before You. (Habakkuk 2:20)

Jesus is Your beloved Son, O God, in whom You are well pleased. (Matthew 3:17; Mark 1:11; Luke 3:22)

Jesus, You are the Christ, the Son of the living God. (Matthew 16:16)

Glory to You, O God, in the highest, and on earth peace to those on whom Your favor rests. (Luke 2:14)

The Word became flesh and dwelt among us. We have seen His glory, the glory of Your only begotten, O Father, full of grace and truth. (John 1:14)

Jesus, You are the Son of God; You are the King of Israel. (John 1:49)

No one has seen the Father except You, the One who is from God; only You have seen the Father. (John 6:46)

Lord Jesus Christ, Your works have proved that the Father is in You, and that You are in the Father. (John 10:38)

Jesus, You are the Christ, the Son of God, who came into the world. (John 11:27)

Jesus, You are the way and the truth and the life. No one comes to the Father except through You. (John 14:6)

Jesus, You are in the Father, and the Father is in You. You spoke the words of Your Father and did the works of Your Father who dwells in You. You claimed to be in the Father and the Father in You, and You proved it through Your works. (John 14:10–11)

Jesus, You are my Lord and my God. (John 20:28)

You are but one God, Father, from whom all things came and for whom I live; and there is but one Lord, Jesus Christ, through whom all things came and through whom I live. (1 Corinthians 8:6)

You, O Lord, are the Spirit, and where the Spirit of the Lord is, there is freedom. (2 Corinthians 3:17)

O God and Father of the Lord Jesus—You are blessed forever. (2 Corinthians 11:31)

You, O God, are the blessed and only Sovereign, the King of kings and Lord of lords. You alone have immortality and dwell in unapproachable light; no one has seen You or can see You. To You be honor and eternal dominion. (1 Timothy 6:15–16)

You, O Son of God, are the radiance of God's glory and the exact representation of His being, upholding all things by Your powerful word. After You cleansed our sins, You sat down at the right hand of the Majesty on high, having become as much superior to angels as the name You have inherited is more excellent than theirs. (Hebrews 1:3–4)

Jesus Christ, You are the same yesterday, today and forever. (Hebrews 13:8)

Lord Jesus Christ, You received honor and glory from God the Father when the voice came to You from the Majestic Glory, saying, "This is My beloved Son, with whom I am well pleased." (2 Peter 1:17)

Lord God, You are the Alpha and the Omega, who is, and who was, and who is to come, the Almighty. (Revelation 1:8)

You, Lord Jesus, are the first and the last, and the Living One; You were dead, and behold, You are alive forevermore and hold the keys of death and of Hades. (Revelation 1:17–18)

The Powers of God

Nothing is too difficult for You, O Lord. (Genesis 18:14)

You, O Lord, shall reign for ever and ever. (Exodus 15:18)

O Lord, You will be gracious to whom You will be gracious, and You will have compassion on whom You will have compassion. (Exodus 33:19)

No one can see You, Lord, and live. (Exodus 33:20)

O Lord God, You have shown Your servants Your greatness and Your strong hand, for what god is there in heaven or on earth who can do the works and mighty deeds You do? (Deuteronomy 3:24)

To You, Lord my God, belong the heavens, even the highest heavens, the earth and everything in it. (Deuteronomy 10:14)

You are the living God, and there is no god besides You. You put to death and You bring to life, You have wounded and You will heal, and no one can deliver from Your hand. (Deuteronomy 32:39)

Lord, You are the God of knowledge, and by You actions are weighed. (1 Samuel 2:3)

You, O Lord, will guard the feet of Your saints, but the wicked will be silenced in darkness. It is not by strength that one prevails; those who contend with You, Lord, will be shattered. You will thunder against them from heaven; You will judge the ends of the earth. You will give strength to Your king and exalt the horn of Your anointed. (1 Samuel 2:9–10)

You, Lord, do not see as people see. People look at the outward appearance, but You look at the heart. (1 Samuel 16:7)

O God, will You indeed dwell on earth? Heaven and the highest heaven cannot contain You. (1 Kings 8:27)

Lord, You are great and greatly to be praised; You are to be feared above all gods. For all the gods of the nations are idols, but You made the heavens. Splendor and majesty are before You; strength and joy are in Your place. I will ascribe to You, O Lord, glory and strength. I will ascribe to You the glory due Your name and worship You in the beauty of holiness. (1 Chronicles 16:25–29)

Yours, O Lord, is the greatness and the power and the glory and the victory and the majesty, for everything in heaven and earth is Yours. Yours, O Lord, is the kingdom, and You are exalted as head over all. Both riches and honor come from You, and You are the ruler of all things. In Your hand is power and might to exalt and to give strength to all. Therefore, my God, I give You thanks and praise Your glorious name. All things come from You, and I can only give You what comes from Your hand. (1 Chronicles 29:11–14)

O Lord, the God of our fathers, are You not the God who is in heaven? Are You not the ruler over all the kingdoms of the nations? Power and might are in Your hand, and no one is able to withstand You. (2 Chronicles 20:6)

You, O God, are wise in heart and mighty in strength. Who has resisted You without harm? (Job 9:4)

God, You reveal deep things out of darkness and bring the shadow of death into the light. You make nations great and destroy them; You enlarge nations and disperse them. (Job 12:22–23)

Your voice, O God, thunders in marvelous ways; You do great things which we cannot comprehend. (Job 37:5)

You, Almighty God, are beyond our reach; You are exalted in power, and in Your justice and great righteousness, You do not oppress. (Job 37:23)

I know that You can do all things and that no purpose of Yours can be thwarted. (Job 42:2)

You are in Your holy temple, O Lord; You are on Your heavenly throne. You observe all people; Your eyes examine them. (Psalm 11:4)

I will ascribe to You glory and strength, O Lord. I will ascribe to You the glory due Your name and worship You, Lord, in the beauty of holiness. (Psalm 29:1–2)

Your counsel, O Lord, stands firm forever, the plans of Your heart through all generations. (Psalm 33:11)

You have set our iniquities before You, our secret sins in the light of Your presence. (Psalm 90:8)

You reign, O Lord; You are clothed with majesty; You are robed in majesty and armed with strength. Indeed, the world is firmly established; it cannot be moved. Your throne is established from of old; You are from everlasting. Your testimonies stand firm; holiness adorns Your house, O Lord, forever. (Psalm 93:1–2, 5)

My days are like a lengthened shadow, and I wither away like grass. But You, O Lord, will endure forever, and the remembrance of Your name to all generations. In the beginning You laid the foundations of the earth, and the heavens are the work of Your hands. They will perish, but You will endure. They will all wear out like a garment; like clothing You will change them, and they will be discarded. But You are the same, and Your years will have no end. (Psalm 102:11–12, 25–27)

O Lord, you have established Your throne in heaven, and Your kingdom rules over all. (Psalm 103:19)

From the rising of the sun to its setting, Your name, O Lord, is to be praised. You are high above all nations; Your glory is above the heavens. Who is like You, O Lord our God, the One who is enthroned on high, You who humble Yourself to behold the things that are in the heavens and in the earth? (Psalm 113:3–6)

Lord, whatever pleases You, You do in the heavens and on the earth, in the seas and all their depths. (Psalm 135:6)

Though You are on high, Lord, You look upon the lowly, but the proud You know from afar. (Psalm 138:6)

Lord, You have searched me and You know me. You know when I sit down and when I rise up; You understand my thoughts from afar. You scrutinize my path and my lying down and are acquainted with all my ways. Before a word is on my tongue, O Lord, You know it completely. (Psalm 139:1–4)

Where can I go from Your Spirit? Or where can I flee from Your presence? If I ascend to heaven, You are there. If I make my bed in Sheol, You are there. If I take the wings of the dawn, if I dwell in the depths of the sea, even there Your hand will lead me. Your right hand will lay hold of me. If I say, "Surely the darkness will cover me," even the night will be light around me. The darkness is not dark to You, and the night shines as the day; darkness and light are alike to You. (Psalm 139:7–12)

All Your works will praise you, O Lord, and Your saints will bless You. They will speak of the glory of Your kingdom and talk of Your power, so that all people may know of Your mighty acts and the glorious majesty of Your kingdom. Your kingdom is an everlasting kingdom, and Your dominion endures through all generations. (Psalm 145:10–13)

In my heart I plan my way, but You, O Lord, determine my steps. (Proverbs 16:9)

Many are the plans in my heart, but it is Your counsel, O Lord, that will stand. (Proverbs 19:21)

Your lamp, O Lord, searches my spirit; it searches the inward depths of my being. (Proverbs 20:27)

All my ways are right in my own eyes, but You, Lord, weigh my heart. (Proverbs 21:2)

I know that whatever You do, O God, will remain forever; nothing can be added to it and nothing taken from it. You, O God, do it so that people will revere You. (Ecclesiastes 3:14)

Oh God, You will bring every work into judgment, including every hidden thing, whether it is good or evil. (Ecclesiastes 12:14)

Surely as You, O Lord of hosts, have thought, so it will be, and as You have purposed, so it will stand. For You, Lord of hosts, have purposed, and who can annul it? Your hand is stretched out, and who can turn it back? (Isaiah 14:24, 27)

O God, You sit enthroned above the circle of the earth, and its inhabitants are like grasshoppers. You stretch out the heavens like a curtain and spread them out like a tent to dwell in. You reduce rulers to nothing and make the judges of this world meaningless. (Isaiah 40:22–23)

You are the Lord, and there is no savior besides You. From ancient days You are He, and no one can deliver out of Your hand; You act, and who can reverse it? (Isaiah 43:11, 13)

You have sworn by Yourself; the word has gone out of Your mouth in righteousness and will not return. Every knee will bow before You, and every tongue will acknowledge You. (Isaiah 45:23)

You declare the end from the beginning, and from ancient times what is still to come, saying, "My purpose will stand, and I will do all My pleasure." (Isaiah 46:10)

The word that goes forth from Your mouth, O Lord, will not return to You empty but will accomplish what You desire and achieve the purpose for which You sent it. (Isaiah 55:11)

You are the high and lofty One who inhabits eternity, whose name is holy. You live in a high and holy place but also with those who are contrite and lowly in spirit, to revive the spirit of the lowly and to revive the heart of the contrite. (Isaiah 57:15)

Before You formed me in the womb, You knew me, O Lord; before I was born, You set me apart. (Jeremiah 1:5)

There is none like You, O Lord; You are great, and Your name is mighty in power. Who should not revere You, O King of the nations? It is Your rightful due. For among all the wise of the nations and in all their kingdoms, there is no one like You. (Jeremiah 10:6–7)

I know, O Lord, that my life is not my own; it is not for me to direct my steps. (Jeremiah 10:23)

You know me, O Lord; You see me and test my thoughts about You. (Jeremiah 12:3)

Are You a God nearby, and not a God far away? Can I hide in secret places so that You cannot see me? Do You not fill heaven and earth? (Jeremiah 23:23–24)

Ah, Lord God! You have made the heavens and the earth by Your great power and outstretched arm. Nothing is too difficult for You. You are the great and mighty God; Your name is the Lord of hosts. You are great in counsel and mighty in deed, and Your eyes see everything that we do; You reward us according to our ways and according to the fruit of our deeds. (Jeremiah 32:17–19)

You are the Lord, the God of all people. Nothing is too difficult for You. (Jeremiah 32:27)

Blessed be Your name, O God, for ever and ever, for wisdom and power belong to You. You change the times and the seasons; You raise up kings and depose them. You give wisdom to the wise and knowledge to those who have understanding. You reveal deep and hidden things; You know what is in the darkness, and light dwells with You. (Daniel 2:20–22)

How great are Your signs, O God, and how mighty are Your wonders! Your kingdom is an eternal kingdom; Your dominion endures from generation to generation. (Daniel 4:3)

I will be silent before You, Lord, for You have aroused Yourself from Your holy dwelling place. (Zechariah 2:13)

Where two or three come together in Your name, O Jesus, You are there in their midst. (Matthew 18:20)

Heaven and earth will pass away, but Your words, Lord Jesus, will never pass away. (Matthew 24:35; Luke 21:33)

All authority in heaven and on earth has been given to You, Jesus Christ, who are the Son of God. (Matthew 28:18)

Nothing is impossible with You, O God. (Luke 1:37)

It is easier for heaven and earth to disappear than for a stroke of a letter of Your law to fail, O God. (Luke 16:17)

Your love, O Christ, compels me, because I am convinced that You are the One who died for all, and therefore all died. And You died for all, that those who live should no longer live for themselves but for You who died for them and was raised again. (2 Corinthians 5:14–15)

To You—the King eternal, immortal, invisible, the only God—be honor and glory for ever and ever. (1 Timothy 1:17)

Your word, O God, is living and active and sharper than any double-edged sword, piercing even to the dividing of soul and spirit and of joints and marrow; it judges the thoughts and attitudes of the heart. And there is no creature hidden from Your sight, but everything is uncovered and laid bare before Your eyes—You to whom we must give account. (Hebrews 4:12–13)

With You, Lord, one day is like a thousand years, and a thousand years are like one day. (2 Peter 3:8)

To You, the only God our Savior, through Jesus Christ our Lord, be glory, majesty, dominion and authority, before all ages, now and forever. Amen. (Jude 25)

Lord Jesus, You are holy and true; You hold the key of David. What You open no one can shut, and what You shut no one can open. (Revelation 3:7)

The Perfection of God

Far be it from You to kill the righteous with the wicked, treating the righteous and the wicked alike. Far be it from You! Will not the Judge of all the earth do right? (Genesis 18:25)

Who is like You, O Lord? Who is like You—majestic in holiness, awesome in praises, working wonders? (Exodus 15:11)

O Lord, You are a jealous God, punishing the children for the sin of the fathers to the third and fourth generation of those who hate You, but showing lovingkindness to a thousand generations of those who love You and keep Your commandments. (Exodus 20:5–6; Deuteronomy 5:9–10)

O Lord, O Lord God, You are compassionate and gracious, slow to anger and abounding in lovingkindness and truth, maintaining love to thousands, and forgiving iniquity, transgression and sin. (Exodus 34:6–7)

I will not worship any other god, for Your name, O Lord, is Jealous; You are a jealous God. (Exodus 34:14)

You, O Lord my God, are a consuming fire, a jealous God. (Deuteronomy 4:24)

You, Lord God, are the faithful God; You keep Your covenant and Your lovingkindness to a thousand generations of those who love You and keep Your commands. (Deuteronomy 7:9)

You, O God, are the Rock; Your work is perfect, for all Your ways are just. You are a God of faithfulness and without injustice; upright and just are You. (Deuteronomy 32:4)

As for You, O God, Your way is perfect; Your word, O Lord, is proven. You are a shield for all who take refuge in You. For who are You, O God, besides the Lord? And who is the Rock except You, who are our God? (2 Samuel 22:31–32)

O Lord, God of Israel, there is no God like You in heaven above or on earth below; You keep Your covenant and mercy with Your servants who walk before You with all their heart. (1 Kings 8:23; 2 Chronicles 6:14)

I will give thanks to You, Lord, for You are good; Your love endures forever. (1 Chronicles 16:34)

O Lord, God of heaven, You are the great and awesome God, keeping Your covenant of loyal love with those who love You and obey Your commands. (Nehemiah 1:5)

You have been just in all that has happened to us; You have acted faithfully, while we did wrong. (Nehemiah 9:33)

To You, O God, belong wisdom and power; counsel and understanding are Yours. (Job 12:13)

You are not a God who takes pleasure in wickedness; evil cannot dwell with You. (Psalm 5:4)

I will give thanks to You, O Lord, because of Your righteousness. I will sing praise to Your name, O Lord Most High. (Psalm 7:17)

O Lord, You reign forever. You have established Your throne for judgment. You will judge the world in righteousness, and You will govern the peoples with justice. You, O Lord, will also be a refuge for the oppressed, a stronghold in times of trouble. Those who know Your name will trust in You, for You, Lord, have never forsaken those who seek You. (Psalm 9:7–10)

You, O Lord, are righteous; You love righteousness; the upright will see Your face. (Psalm 11:7)

As for You, O God, Your way is perfect; Your word, O Lord, is proven. You are a shield to all who take refuge in You. For who is God besides You, Lord? And who is the Rock except You, our God? (Psalm 18:30–31)

Your law, O Lord, is perfect, restoring the soul. Your testimony, O Lord, is sure, making wise the simple. Your precepts, O Lord, are right, rejoicing the heart. Your commandment, O Lord, is pure, enlightening the eyes. The fear of You, O Lord, is clean, enduring forever. Your judgments, O Lord, are true and altogether righteous. They are more desirable than gold, than much pure gold; they are sweeter than honey, than honey from the comb. Moreover, by them is Your servant warned; in keeping them there is great reward. (Psalm 19:7–11)

Good and upright are You, Lord; therefore You instruct sinners in Your ways. (Psalm 25:8)

Your lovingkindness, O Lord, reaches to the heavens, Your faithfulness to the skies. Your righteousness is like the mighty mountains; Your judgments are like the great deep. O Lord, You preserve people and beasts. How priceless is Your lovingkindness, O God! Both the high and low among people find refuge in the shadow of Your wings. For with You is the fountain of life; in Your light we see light. (Psalm 36:5–7, 9)

Be exalted, O God, above the heavens; let Your glory be over all the earth. For Your mercy reaches to the heavens, and Your faithfulness reaches to the clouds. (Psalm 57:5, 10)

One thing You have spoken, two things I have heard: That You, O God, are strong and that You, O Lord, are loving. For You reward us according to what we have done. (Psalm 62:11–12)

You, Lord, are good and ready to forgive and abundant in mercy to all who call upon You. (Psalm 86:5)

You, O Lord, are a compassionate and gracious God, slow to anger and abounding in lovingkindness and truth. (Psalm 86:15)

Righteousness and justice are the foundation of Your throne; lovingkindness and truth go before You. (Psalm 89:14)

It is good to give thanks to You, Lord, to sing praises to Your name, O Most High, to declare Your lovingkindness in the morning and Your faithfulness at night. (Psalm 92:1–2)

I will exalt You, Lord my God, and worship You, for You, Lord God, are holy. (Psalm 99:9)

I will enter Your gates, O Lord, with thanksgiving and Your courts with praise; I will give thanks to You and bless Your name. For You are good and Your lovingkindness endures forever; Your faithfulness continues through all generations. (Psalm 100:4–5)

O Lord, You execute righteousness and justice for all who are oppressed. You are compassionate and gracious, slow to anger and abounding in lovingkindness. (Psalm 103:6, 8)

I will give thanks to You, O Lord, for You are good; Your lovingkindness endures forever. I will give thanks to You, Lord, for Your unfailing love and Your wonderful acts to

Your people, for You satisfy the thirsty soul and fill the hungry soul with good things. (Psalm 107:1, 8–9)

Your merciful love is higher than the heavens, O Lord, and Your truth reaches to the skies. (Psalm 108:4)

Great are Your works, O Lord; they are pondered by all who delight in them. Splendid and majestic is Your work, and Your righteousness endures forever. You have caused Your wonderful acts to be remembered; You, Lord, are gracious and compassionate. (Psalm 111:2–4)

Your word is settled in heaven forever, O Lord. Your faithfulness continues through all generations. You established the earth, and it stands. Your laws continue to this day according to Your purposes, for all things serve You. (Psalm 119:89–91)

Your testimonies, which You have commanded, are righteous and trustworthy. Your righteousness is everlasting, and Your law is truth. (Psalm 119:138, 142)

How precious are Your thoughts to me, O God! How vast is the sum of them! If I should count them, they would outnumber the grains of sand. When I awake, I am still with You. (Psalm 139:17–18)

I know that You, Lord, will maintain the cause of the afflicted and justice for the poor. (Psalm 140:12)

I will express the memory of Your abundant goodness and joyfully sing of Your righteousness. You, O Lord, are gracious and compassionate, slow to anger and great in lovingkindness. You are good to all, and Your tender mercies are over all Your works. (Psalm 145:7–9)

You, O Lord of hosts, will be exalted in judgment; You, the holy God, will show Yourself holy in righteousness. (Isaiah 5:16)

Lord, You long to be gracious and rise to show compassion. For You, O Lord, are a God of justice; blessed are all those who wait for You! (Isaiah 30:18)

You, O Lord, are our judge, You are our lawgiver, You are our king; it is You who will save us. (Isaiah 33:22)

It pleased You, O Lord, for the sake of Your righteousness, to make Your law great and glorious. (Isaiah 42:21)

Only in You, Lord, are righteousness and strength. (Isaiah 45:24)

You, O Lord, have declared: "My thoughts are not your thoughts, neither are your ways My ways. As the heavens are higher than the earth, so are My ways higher than your ways, and My thoughts than your thoughts." (Isaiah 55:8–9)

Lord of hosts, You judge righteously and test my heart and mind. To You I have committed my cause. (Jeremiah 11:20)

I call this to mind, and therefore I have hope: Your mercies, O Lord, never cease, for Your compassions never fail. They are new every morning; great is Your faithfulness. (Lamentations 3:21–23)

I know that You are a gracious and compassionate God, slow to anger and abounding in lovingkindness, a God who relents from sending calamity. (Jonah 4:2)

O Lord, You are good, a refuge in times of trouble; You know those who trust in You. (Nahum 1:7)

Your eyes are too pure to look at evil; You cannot look on wickedness, my holy God. (Habakkuk 1:13)

My soul magnifies You, O Lord, and my spirit rejoices in You, God my Savior, for You, Mighty One, have done great things for me, and holy is Your name. Your mercy is on those who fear You, from generation to generation. (Luke 1:46–47, 49–50)

Oh, the depth of the riches of Your wisdom and knowledge, O God! How unsearchable are Your judgments and Your ways past finding out! For who has known Your mind, O Lord? Or who has been Your counselor? Or who has first given to You, that You should repay? For from You and through You and to You are all things. To You be the glory forever! Amen. (Romans 11:33–36)

Blessed are You, O God and Father of our Lord Jesus Christ, the Father of mercies and the God of all comfort. (2 Corinthians 1:3)

In You, O Christ, are hidden all the treasures of wisdom and knowledge. (Colossians 2:3)

O Lord, You are not slow concerning Your promise, as some count slowness, but are patient with us, not wanting anyone to perish, but for all to come to repentance. (2 Peter 3:9)

You, O God, are light; in You there is no darkness at all. (1 John 1:5)

Great and marvelous are Your works, Lord God Almighty! Righteous and true are Your ways, King of the nations! Who will not fear You, O Lord, and glorify Your name? For You alone are holy. All nations will come and worship before You, for Your righteous acts have been revealed. (Revelation 15:3–4)

Hallelujah! Salvation and glory and power belong to You, our God, because Your judgments are true and righteous. (Revelation 19:1–2)

THE WORKS OF GOD

Creation

In the beginning, O God, You created the heavens and the earth. Now the earth was formless and empty, and darkness was over the surface of the deep, and Your Spirit, O God, was hovering over the face of the waters. And, O God, You said, "Let there be light," and there was light. And You, O God, saw that the light was good, and You separated the light from the darkness. You called the light "day," and the darkness You called "night." So the evening and the morning were the first day. (Genesis 1:5–10)

O God, You said, "Let Us make man in Our image, in Our likeness, and let them rule over the fish of the sea and the birds of the air and over the livestock and over all the earth and over all the creatures that creep on the earth." So You created man in Your own image; in Your image, O God, You created him; male and female You created them. Then You blessed them and said to them, "Be fruitful and multiply; fill the earth and subdue it; and rule over the fish of the sea and the birds of the air and over every living creature that moves on the earth." Then You, O God, said, "Behold, I have given you every seed-bearing plant on the face of the whole earth and every tree that has fruit with seed in it; they will be yours for food. And to all the beasts of the earth and all the birds of the air and all the creatures that move on the ground, in which there is life, I have given every green plant for food"; and it was so. You, O God, saw all that You had made, and it was very good. So the evening and the morning were the sixth day. (Genesis 1:26–31)

O God, You completed the heavens and the earth in all their vast array. By the seventh day You finished the work that You had done, and You rested on the seventh day from all Your creative work. And You blessed the seventh day and sanctified it, because on it You rested from all the work of creating that You had done. (Genesis 2:1–3)

O Lord, in six days You made the heavens and the earth, the sea, and all that is in them, and rested on the seventh day. Therefore You blessed the Sabbath day and made it holy. (Exodus 20:11)

You alone are the Lord. You made the heavens, even the heaven of heavens, and all their starry host, the earth and all that is on it, the seas and all that is in them. You give life to all that is in them, and the host of heaven worships You. (Nehemiah 9:6)

When I consider Your heavens, the work of Your fingers, the moon and the stars, which You have set in place, what is man that You are mindful of him, and the son of man that You care for him? You made him a little lower than the heavenly beings and crowned him with glory and honor. You made human beings the rulers over the works of Your hands, and You put everything under their feet. (Psalm 8:3–6)

The heavens declare Your glory, O God, and the skies proclaim the work of Your hands. Day after day they pour forth speech; night after night they reveal knowledge. (Psalm 19:1–2)

The earth is Yours, O Lord, and everything in it, the world and all who dwell in it. For You founded it upon the seas and established it upon the waters. (Psalm 24:1–2)

O Mighty One, God, the Lord, You have spoken and summoned the earth from the rising of the sun to the place where it sets. (Psalm 50:1)

Every animal of the forest is Yours, and the cattle on a thousand hills, O God. You know every bird in the mountains, and everything that moves in the field is Yours. (Psalm 50:10–11)

You answer us with awesome deeds of righteousness, O God of our salvation, You who are the hope of all the ends of the earth and of the farthest seas. You formed the mountains by Your strength, having armed Yourself with power. You stilled the roaring of the seas, the roaring of their waves, and the tumult of the peoples. (Psalm 65:5–7)

The day is Yours, O God; the night also is Yours; You established the sun and moon. It was You who set all the boundaries of the earth; You made both summer and winter. (Psalm 74:16–17)

You, O Lord, are the great God, the great King above all gods. In Your hand are the depths of the earth; the summits of the mountains are Yours also. The sea is Yours, for You made it, and Your hands formed the dry land. You are our God and we are the people of Your pasture and the sheep under Your care. (Psalm 95:3–5, 7)

O Lord, You formed my inward parts. You wove me together in my mother's womb. I thank You because I am fearfully and wonderfully made. Your works are wonderful, and my soul knows it full well. My frame was not hidden from You when I was made in secret and skillfully wrought in the depths of the earth. Your eyes saw my embryo, and all the days ordained for me were written in Your book before one of them came to be. (Psalm 139:13–16)

By wisdom, O Lord, You founded the earth; by understanding You established the heavens; by Your knowledge the deeps were divided, and the clouds drop down the dew. (Proverbs 3:19–20)

O God, You have made everything beautiful in its time. You have also set eternity in our hearts; yet we cannot fathom what You have done from beginning to end. (Ecclesiastes 3:11)

It is You, O Lord, who measured the waters in the hollow of Your hand. You marked off the heavens with the breadth of Your hand. You have calculated the dust of the earth in a measure, and weighed the mountains in the balance and the hills in scales. (Isaiah 40:12)

You, O Holy One, have asked, "To whom will You compare Me? Or who is My equal?" We lift our eyes to the heavens and see who has created them. You bring out the starry host by number and call them each by name. Because of Your great might and the strength of Your power, not one of them is missing. Do we not know? Have we not heard? You are the everlasting God, the Lord, the Creator of the ends of the earth. You do not grow tired or weary. No one can fathom Your understanding. (Isaiah 40:25–26, 28)

You form the light and create darkness; You bring prosperity and create disaster; You, O Lord, do all these things. (Isaiah 45:7)

You are the Lord who created the heavens, You are God. You fashioned and made the earth and established it; You did not create it to be empty but formed it to be inhabited. You are the Lord, and there is no other. (Isaiah 45:18)

Your hand, O Lord, laid the foundations of the earth, and Your right hand spread out the heavens; when You summon them, they all stand up together. (Isaiah 48:13)

Heaven is Your throne, O Lord, and the earth is Your footstool. Your hand made all these things, and so they came into being. (Isaiah 66:1–2)

You, O Lord, give the sun for light by day and decree the moon and stars for light by night; You stir up the sea so that its waves roar—the Lord of hosts is Your name. (Jeremiah 31:35)

O Lord, You made the earth by Your power; You established the world by Your wisdom and stretched out the heavens by Your understanding. (Jeremiah 51:15)

O Lord God of hosts—You who touch the earth and it melts, and all who live in it mourn; You who build Your staircase in the heavens and lay its foundation over the earth; You who call for the waters of the sea and pour them out over the face of the earth—the Lord is Your name. (Amos 9:5–6)

Through You, O Christ, all things were made, and without You nothing was made that has been made. In You was life, and that life was a light for all people. (John 1:3–4)

God, You made the world and everything in it. You are Lord of heaven and earth; You do not dwell in temples built by hands. You are not served by human hands, as though You needed anything, since You Yourself give life and breath and everything else to all people. (Acts 17:24–25)

Since the creation of the world, Your invisible attributes, O God—Your eternal power and divine nature—have been clearly seen, revealed in what You have made, so that people are without excuse. (Romans 1:20)

You, O God, give life to the dead and call into being things that do not exist. (Romans 4:17)

The whole family in heaven and on earth derives its name from You, the God and Father of our Lord Jesus Christ. (Ephesians 3:14–15)

Christ, You are the image of the invisible God, the firstborn over all creation. For by You all things were created that are in heaven and on earth, visible and invisible, whether thrones or dominions or rulers or authorities; all things were created by You and for You. And You are before all things, and in You all things hold together. (Colossians 1:15–17)

Everything You created is good, O God, and I am to reject nothing but receive it with thanksgiving, because it is sanctified by Your word and prayer. (1 Timothy 4:4–5)

In the past, O God, You spoke to the fathers through the prophets at many times and in various ways, but in these last days You have spoken to us by Your Son, whom You appointed heir of all things, and through whom You made the universe. (Hebrews 1:1–2)

By faith I understand that the universe was formed by Your word, O God, so that what is seen was not made out of things which are visible. (Hebrews 11:3)

You are worthy, our Lord and God, to receive glory and honor and power, for You created all things, and by Your will they were created and have their being. (Revelation 4:11)

Redemption

Because Adam listened to the voice of his wife and ate from the tree about which You, O God commanded him, "You must not eat of it," the ground was cursed; through painful toil he ate of it all the days of his life. It produced thorns and thistles for him, and he ate the plants of the field. By the sweat of his brow he ate his food until he returned to the ground, because from it he was taken; "for dust you are and to dust you will return." (Genesis 3:17–19)

The earth became corrupt in Your sight, O God, and was filled with violence. You looked upon the earth and saw how corrupt it had become, for all the people on earth had corrupted their ways. (Genesis 6:11–12)

You, O God, blessed Noah and his sons, and told them to be fruitful and multiply and fill the earth. You established Your covenant with them and with their descendants after them and with every living creature that was with them—the birds, the livestock and all the beasts of the earth, all those that came out of the ark with them—every living creature on earth. You, O God, established Your covenant that never again will all life be cut off by the waters of a flood; never again will there be a flood to destroy the earth. The sign of Your covenant, O God, for all generations to come is the rainbow that You set in the clouds; whenever a rainbow appears in the clouds, You will remember Your everlasting covenant with humankind and every living creature of every kind on the earth. (Genesis 9:1, 9–16)

O Lord, You said to Abraham, "By Myself I have sworn, that because you have not withheld your son, your only son, I will surely bless you and make your descendants as numerous as the stars in the sky and as the sand on the seashore. Your descendants will take possession of the cities of their enemies, and through your offspring all nations on earth will be blessed, because you have obeyed My voice." (Genesis 22:16–18)

May my faith be like Joseph's when he said to his brothers, "Do not be grieved or angry with yourselves for selling me here, for God sent me before you to save lives. He sent me ahead of you to preserve for you a remnant on earth and to save your lives by a great deliverance. So it was not you who sent me here, but God." (Genesis 45:5, 7–8)

In Your unfailing love You led the people You redeemed. In Your strength You guided them to Your holy dwelling. You brought them in and planted them in the mountain of Your inheritance—the place, O Lord, You made for Your dwelling; the sanctuary, O Lord, Your hands established. (Exodus 15:13, 17)

The children of Israel were a people holy to You, the Lord their God. Lord God, You chose them out of all the peoples on the face of the earth to be Your people, Your treasured possession. Lord, You did not set Your love on them and choose them because they were more numerous than other peoples, for they were the fewest of all peoples. But it was because You loved them, Lord, and kept the oath You swore to their fathers that You brought them out with a mighty hand and redeemed them from the house of slavery, from the hand of Pharaoh of Egypt. (Deuteronomy 7:6–8)

Lord, You are our praise, and You are our God, who performed for the children of Israel those great and awesome wonders which they saw with their own eyes. (Deuteronomy 10:21)

You set before Your people life and prosperity, death and destruction; and You commanded them to love You, the Lord their God, to walk in Your ways, and to keep Your commandments, statutes, and judgments, so that they would live and multiply and that You would bless them in the land they were entering to possess. You called heaven and earth as witnesses against them that You set before them life and death, blessings and curses, and told them to choose life, so that they and their children would live by loving You, listening to Your voice, and holding fast to You. (Deuteronomy 30:15–16, 19–20)

Blessed are You, Lord, who have not left Your people without a kinsman-redeemer. (Ruth 4:14)

You, O Lord, do not save by sword or by spear, for the battle is Yours. (1 Samuel 17:47)

With the kind You show Yourself kind; with the blameless You show Yourself blameless; with the pure You show Yourself pure; but to the crooked You show Yourself shrewd. You save the humble, but Your eyes are on the haughty to bring them low. (2 Samuel 22:26–28)

O Lord, if we your people, who are called by Your name, will humble ourselves and pray and seek Your face and turn from our wicked ways, then You will hear from heaven and will forgive our sin and heal our land. (2 Chronicles 7:14)

Your eyes, O Lord, move to and fro throughout the whole earth to strengthen those whose hearts are fully committed to You. (2 Chronicles 16:9)

Lord, You save the humble but bring low those whose eyes are haughty. (Psalm 18:27)

Lord, You guide the humble in what is right and teach the humble Your way. (Psalm 25:9)

Blessed is the nation whose God is You, Lord, the people whom You have chosen for Your inheritance. (Psalm 33:12)

I will praise You forever for what You have done; I will hope in Your name, for it is good. I will praise You in the presence of Your saints. (Psalm 52:9)

Be blessed, Lord God, the God of Israel; You alone do wonderful things. (Psalm 72:18)

I will remember Your works, O Lord; surely I will remember Your wonders of long ago. I will meditate on all Your works and consider all Your mighty deeds. Your way, O God, is holy. What god is so great as You? You are the God who works wonders; You have revealed Your strength among the peoples. You redeemed your people with Your power, the descendants of Jacob and Joseph. (Psalm 77:11–15)

One generation shall praise Your works to another, O Lord, and shall declare Your mighty acts. I will meditate on the glorious splendor of Your majesty and on Your wonderful works.

Many shall speak of the might of Your awesome works, and I will proclaim Your great deeds. (Psalm 145:4–6)

O Lord, You uphold all who fall and lift up all who are bowed down. The eyes of all look to You, and You give them their food at the proper time. You open Your hand and satisfy the desire of every living thing. (Psalm 145:14–16)

You, O Lord, are near to all who call upon You, to all who call upon You in truth. You fulfill the desires of those who fear You; You hear their cry and save them. You preserve all who love You, but all the wicked You will destroy. (Psalm 145:18–20)

You, O Lord, watch over the strangers; You sustain the orphan and the widow, but You thwart the way of the wicked. (Psalm 146:9)

We praise You, Jesus, that God's word is fulfilled in You:

You will come forth a Shoot from the stump of Jesse; from his roots a Branch will bear fruit. The Spirit of the Lord will rest on You—the Spirit of wisdom and of understanding, the Spirit of counsel and of power, the Spirit of knowledge and of the fear of the Lord—and You will delight in the fear of the Lord. You will not judge by what You see with Your eyes, or decide by what You hear with Your ears, but with righteousness You will judge the poor and decide with fairness for the meek of the earth, and You will strike the earth with the rod of Your mouth; with the breath of Your lips You will slay the wicked. Righteousness will be Your belt and faithfulness the sash around Your waist. (Isaiah 11:1–5)

O God, You give strength to the weary and increase the power of the weak. Even youths grow tired and weary, and young men stumble and fall; but we who wait for You, O Lord, will renew our strength. We will mount up with wings like eagles; we will run and not grow weary; we will walk and not be faint. (Isaiah 40:29–31)

Shout for joy, O heavens! Rejoice, O earth! Break out into singing, O mountains! For You, O Lord, have comforted Your people and will have compassion on Your afflicted. (Isaiah 49:13)

Lord, You have bared Your holy arm in the sight of all the nations, and all the ends of the earth will see Your salvation, O God. (Isaiah 52:10)

O Servant of God, people despised and rejected You; You were a man of sorrows and acquainted with grief. And like one from whom people hide their faces, You were despised, and we did not esteem You. Surely You have borne our infirmities and carried our sorrows, yet we considered You stricken, smitten by God and afflicted. But You were pierced for our transgressions; You were crushed for our iniquities. The punishment that brought us peace was upon You, and by Your wounds we are healed. All of us like sheep have gone astray, all of us have turned to our own way, and the Lord has laid on You the iniquity of us all. (Isaiah 53:3–6)

Surely Your hand, O Lord, is not too short to save, nor Your ear too dull to hear. But our iniquities have separated us from You, our God. Our sins have hidden Your face from us, so that You will not hear. Yet You, Lord, saw that there was no one to intervene; so Your own arm worked salvation for You, and Your righteousness sustained You. You put on righteousness as Your breastplate, and the helmet of salvation on Your head. You put on the garments of vengeance and wrapped Yourself in zeal as a cloak. From the west, many will fear Your name, O Lord, and from the rising of the sun, they will revere Your glory. For You will come like a flood that Your breath drives along. (Isaiah 59:1–2, 16–19)

Nations will come to Your light and kings to the brightness of your dawning. (Isaiah 60:3)

As the earth brings forth its sprouts and as a garden causes that which is sown to spring up, so You, Lord God, will make righteousness and praise spring up before all nations. (Isaiah 61:11)

I will tell of Your lovingkindnesses, O Lord, Your praises, according to all You have done for us, and Your great goodness toward the house of Israel, which You have bestowed on them according to Your mercies and according to the multitude of Your lovingkindnesses. (Isaiah 63:7)

I will sing to You, Lord, and give praise to You, Lord, for You have rescued the life of the needy from the hands of evildoers. (Jeremiah 20:13)

Lord, thank You for Your promise to us:

"I will put My law within you and write it on your hearts. I will be your God, and you will be My people. No longer will you teach your neighbor, nor will you teach a friend, saying, 'Know the Lord,' because You shall all know Me, from the least of you to the greatest. For I will forgive your iniquity and will remember your sins no more." (Jeremiah 31:33–34)

You, Lord God, take no pleasure in the death of the wicked but are pleased when the wicked turn from their ways and live. (Ezekiel 18:23; 33:11)

O Lord, You led Your people with cords of human kindness, with bands of love; You lifted the yoke from their neck and bent down to feed them. (Hosea 11:4)

Who is a God like You, who pardons iniquity and forgives the transgression of the remnant of Your inheritance? You do not stay angry forever but delight to show mercy. You will have compassion on Your people; You will tread their iniquities underfoot and hurl all their sins into the depths of the sea. (Micah 7:18–19)

Lord, I have heard of Your fame, and I stand in awe of Your deeds. O Lord, revive Your work in the midst of the years, in our time make them known; in wrath remember mercy. (Habakkuk 3:2)

For those who revere Your name, O Lord Almighty, the sun of righteousness will rise with healing in his wings. And they will go out and leap like calves released from the stall. (Malachi 4:2)

Behold, a virgin was with child and gave birth to a son, and they called You Immanuel, which means, "God with us." (Matthew 1:23)

After Your baptism and temptation, Jesus, You began to preach and say, "Repent, for the kingdom of heaven is at hand." (Matthew 4:17)

You, O Son of Man, have authority on earth to forgive sins. (Matthew 9:6)

Jesus, wherever You went, the blind received sight, the lame walked, the lepers were cured, the deaf heard, the dead were raised and the good news was preached to the poor. (Matthew 11:5)

We can come to You, Lord Jesus Christ, for to all of us who are weary and burdened, You will give rest. We can take up Your yoke and learn from You, for You are gentle and humble in heart, and we will find rest for our souls. For Your yoke is easy, and Your burden is light. (Matthew 11:28–30)

Jesus, You who are the Son of Man, did not come to be served, but to serve, and to give Your life as a ransom for many. (Matthew 20:28)

Jesus, we praise You that You taught us to remember You—You took bread, gave thanks, broke it, and gave it to Your disciples, saying, "Take and eat; this is My body." You took the cup, gave thanks and offered it to them, saying, "Drink from it, all of you. This is My blood of the new covenant, which is poured out for many for the forgiveness of sins." (Matthew 26:26–28)

It is not the healthy who need a physician, but the sick. You, Jesus, have not come to call the righteous, but sinners. (Mark 2:17)

Jesus, You did all things well. You made the deaf hear and the mute speak. (Mark 7:37)

If I am ashamed of You and Your words in this adulterous and sinful generation, O Son of Man, You will be ashamed of me when You come in the glory of Your Father with the holy angels. (Mark 8:38)

You, O Son of Man, did not come to be served, but to serve, and to give Your life as a ransom for many. (Mark 10:45)

You, O Lord, have performed mighty deeds with Your arm; You have scattered those who are proud in the thoughts of their heart. You have brought down rulers from their thrones and have lifted up the humble. (Luke 1:51–52)

Blessed are You, O Lord, God of Israel, because You have visited us and have redeemed Your people. You have raised up a horn of salvation for us in the house of Your servant David (as You spoke by the mouth of Your holy prophets of long ago), salvation from our enemies and from the hand of all who hate us—to show mercy to our fathers and to remember Your holy covenant, the oath You swore to our father Abraham: to rescue us from the hand of our enemies, and to enable us to serve You without fear in holiness and righteousness before You all our days. (Luke 1:68–75)

John was called Your prophet, O Most High; for he went on before You to prepare the way for You, and to give Your people the knowledge of salvation through the forgiveness of their sins because of Your tender mercy, O God, with which the sunrise from on high came from heaven to shine on those living in darkness and in the shadow of death, to guide their feet into the path of peace. (Luke 1:76–79)

The angel said to the shepherds, "Do not be afraid. I bring you good news of great joy that will be for all the people. For today in the city of David a Savior has been born to you, who is Christ the Lord." (Luke 2:10–11)

You, O Jesus, cured many who had diseases, sicknesses, and evil spirits, and gave sight to many who were blind. So You replied to the messengers sent from John the Baptist, "Go back and report to John what you have seen and heard: The blind receive sight, the lame walk, the lepers are cured, the deaf hear, the dead are raised, and the good news is preached to the poor. And blessed is he who does not fall away on account of Me." (Luke 7:21–23)

You, Jesus, the Son of Man, came to seek and to save that which was lost. (Luke 19:10)

Blessed are You, O King, who come in the name of the Lord! Peace in heaven and glory in the highest! (Luke 19:38)

The Scriptures predicted that You, Christ Jesus, would suffer and rise from the dead on the third day, and that repentance and forgiveness of sins would be preached in Your name to all nations, beginning at Jerusalem. (Luke 24:46–47)

O Christ, You were in the world, and the world was made through You, and the world did not know You. You came to Your own, but Your own did not receive You. (John 1:10–11)

From Your fullness, O Christ, we have all received grace upon grace. For the law was given through Moses; grace and truth came through You, Jesus Christ. (John 1:16–17)

Jesus, You are the Lamb of God, who takes away the sin of the world. (John 1:29)

God so loved the world that He gave You, Jesus, His only begotten Son, that whoever believes in You should not perish but have eternal life. For God did not send You into the world to condemn the world, but to save the world through You. (John 3:16–17)

You who come from above are above all; he who is from the earth belongs to the earth and speaks as one from the earth. You who come from heaven are above all. You, whom God has sent, speak the words of God, for You give the Spirit without limit. (John 3:31, 34)

Just as the Father raises the dead and gives them life, even so You, the Son, give life to whom You wish. (John 5:21)

All these testified that You, Jesus, are the Son of God: John the Baptist, the works that You did, the Father and the Scriptures. (John 5:31–39)

It is the Spirit who gives life; the flesh counts for nothing. The words You spoke, Jesus, are spirit and are life. (John 6:63)

While You were in the world, Jesus, You were the light of the world. For judgment You came into this world, that those who do not see may see, and that those who see may become blind. (John 9:5, 39)

You are the good Shepherd, Lord Jesus; You lay down Your life for the sheep. You are the good Shepherd; You know Your sheep and Your sheep know You—just as the Father knows You and You know the Father—and You lay down Your life for the sheep. (John 10:11, 14–15)

Lord Jesus, You are the resurrection and the life. Those who believe in You will live, even though they die, and those who live and believe in You will never die. (John 11:25–26)

You, Jesus, have come as a light into the world, that whoever believes in You should not stay in darkness. You do not judge those who hear Your words but do not keep them, for You did not come to judge the world, but to save the world. (John 12:46–47)

Now are You glorified, O Son of Man, and God is glorified in You. If God is glorified in You, God will glorify You, the Son, in Himself and will glorify You immediately. (John 13:31–32)

In Your Father's house are many dwellings, Lord Jesus; if it were not so, You would have told us. You went there to prepare a place for us. And as You went to prepare a place for us, You will come again and receive us to Yourself, that we also may be where You are. (John 14:2–3)

Holy Spirit, You convict the world concerning sin and righteousness and judgment. (John 16:8)

Jesus, You came from the Father and entered the world; now You have left the world and gone back to the Father. (John 16:28)

The Father granted You, the Son, authority over all people that You might give eternal life to as many as He has given You. (John 17:2)

Jesus, we thank You that You did not ask that the Father take us out of the world but that He protect us from the evil one when You prayed: "Father, I desire those You have given Me to be with Me where I am, that they may behold My glory, the glory You have given Me because You loved Me before the foundation of the world." (John 17:15, 24)

Lord, grant to us the power of the Spirit that you promised the apostles when You told them: "You will receive power when the Holy Spirit comes upon you; and you will be My witnesses in Jerusalem, and in all Judea and Samaria, and to the ends of the earth." (Acts 1:8)

Jesus, You are the stone that was rejected by the builders, but that has become the chief cornerstone. Salvation is found in no one else, for there is no other name under heaven given to us by which we can be saved. (Acts 4:11–12)

You, O God of our fathers, raised up Jesus who was killed by hanging on a tree. You exalted Him to Your own right hand as Prince and Savior, that He might give repentance and forgiveness of sins to Israel. (Acts 5:30–31)

God, You do not show favoritism but accept those from every nation who fear You and do what is right. (Acts 10:34–35)

God, You sent Your word to the children of Israel, telling the good news of peace through Jesus Christ, who is Lord of all. Jesus commanded the apostles to preach to the people and to testify that He is the One whom You appointed as judge of the living and the dead. To Him all the prophets witness that, through His name, everyone who believes in Him receives forgiveness of sins. (Acts 10:36, 42–43)

As the gospel spread to the Gentiles, many rejoiced and glorified Your word, O Lord, and all who were appointed for eternal life believed. (Acts 13:48)

In the past, O God, You overlooked the times of ignorance, but now You command all people everywhere to repent. For You have set a day when You will judge the world with justice by the Man You have appointed. You have given assurance of this to all people by raising Him from the dead. (Acts 17:30–31)

God, You promised the gospel beforehand through Your prophets in the Holy Scriptures concerning Your Son—who was a descendant of David according to the flesh, and who was declared with power to be Your Son, according to the Spirit of holiness, by Your resurrection from the dead—Jesus Christ our Lord. (Romans 1:2–4)

We know that whatever the law says, it says to those who are under the law, that every mouth may be silenced, and the whole world held accountable to You, O God, because no one will be justified in Your sight by the works of the law, for through the law comes the knowledge of sin. (Romans 3:19–20)

Apart from the law, Your righteousness, O God, has been made known, being witnessed by the Law and the Prophets, even Your righteousness through faith in Jesus Christ to all who believe. For there is no difference, for all have sinned and fall short of Your glory, O God, being justified freely by Your grace through the redemption that is in Christ Jesus. (Romans 3:21–24)

O God, our Father, You presented Christ as a sacrifice of atonement through faith in His blood. You did this to demonstrate Your righteousness at the present time, because in Your mercy, You passed over the sins committed before Jesus died. You did it to demonstrate Your righteousness in the present time, that You might be just and the justifier of those who have faith in Jesus. (Romans 3:25–26)

You, O God, will impute righteousness to us who believe in You who raised Jesus our Lord from the dead. Jesus was delivered over to death because of our sins and was raised in order to make us right with You. (Romans 4:24–25)

At the right time, when we were helpless, Christ died for the ungodly. For rarely will anyone die for one who is righteous, though perhaps for a good person someone might even dare to die. But You, O God, demonstrate Your own love for us in that while we were still sinners, Christ died for us. (Romans 5:6–8)

If by the trespass of the one man, death reigned through that one man, much more will we, who receive the abundance of grace and of the gift of righteousness, reign in life through You, the one Man, Jesus Christ. Consequently, just as the result of one trespass was condemnation for all of us, so also the result of one act of righteousness was justification that brings life for all of us. For just as through the disobedience of the one man the many were made sinners, so also through Your obedience, O Son of Man, many will be made righteous. (Romans 5:17–19)

The wages of sin is death, but Your gift, O God, is eternal life in Christ Jesus our Lord. (Romans 6:23)

Everything You have created, O God, eagerly waits in expectation of the time when Your children will appear in their full and final glory. (Romans 8:19)

You, O God, will have mercy on whom You have mercy, and You will have compassion on whom You have compassion. It does not depend on human desire or effort, but on Your mercy. (Romans 9:15–16)

You, O Christ, died and returned to life, that You might be the Lord of both the dead and the living. (Romans 14:9)

Your foolishness, O God, is wiser than human wisdom, and Your weakness is stronger than human strength. But You chose the foolish things of the world to shame the wise, and You chose the weak things of the world to shame the strong;

the lowly things of this world and the despised things You have chosen, and the things that are not, to nullify the things that are, so that no one may boast before You. (1 Corinthians 1:25, 27–29)

No one can lay a foundation other than the one already laid; You are the foundation, O Jesus Christ. (1 Corinthians 3:11)

You, O Christ, our Passover lamb, have been sacrificed for us. (1 Corinthians 5:7)

You died for our sins, O Christ, according to the Scriptures; You were buried, and You were raised on the third day according to the Scriptures. (1 Corinthians 15:3–4)

We know Your grace, O Lord Jesus Christ, that though You were rich, yet for our sakes You became poor, that we, through Your poverty, might become rich. (2 Corinthians 8:9)

Thanks be to You, O God, for Your indescribable gift! (2 Corinthians 9:15)

Clearly no one is justified before You, O God, by the law, for "The righteous will live by faith." (Galatians 3:11)

When the fullness of time had come, You, O God, sent forth Your Son, born of a woman, born under law, to redeem those under law, that we might receive the adoption as sons. (Galatians 4:4–5)

Your power, O God, toward us who believe is power according to the working of Your mighty strength, which You exerted in Christ when You raised Him from the dead and seated Him at Your right hand in the heavenly realms, far above all rule and authority, power and dominion, and every title that can be given, not only in the present age but also in the one to come. (Ephesians 1:19–21)

God placed all things under Your feet, O Christ, and appointed You to be head over all things for the church, which is Your body, the fullness of You who fill all in all. (Ephesians 1:22–23)

You are able to do immeasurably more than all that we ask or think, O God, according to Your power that is at work within us. To You be glory in the church and in Christ Jesus throughout all generations, for ever and ever. (Ephesians 3:20–21)

There is one body and one Spirit, just as we were called in one hope of our calling in You—one Lord, one faith, one baptism, one God and Father of all. You are over all and through all and in all. (Ephesians 4:4–6)

My attitude should be the same as Yours, Christ Jesus; though You are in Your very nature God, You did not consider equality with God something to be grasped, but emptied Yourself, taking the nature of a servant and being made in human form. And appearing as a human being, You humbled Yourself and became obedient to death, even death on a cross. (Philippians 2:5–8)

Christ, You are the head of the body, the church; You are the beginning and the firstborn from among the dead, so that in everything You might have the supremacy. (Colossians 1:18)

O God, You were pleased to have all Your fullness dwell in Christ and through Him to reconcile all things to Yourself, whether things on earth or things in heaven, having made peace through the blood of His cross. (Colossians 1:19–20)

The mystery that has been kept hidden for ages and generations is now disclosed to the saints. You, Lord God, have chosen to make known among the Gentiles the glorious riches of this mystery, which is Christ in us, the hope of glory. (Colossians 1:26–27)

In You, O Christ, there is no Greek or Jew, circumcised or uncircumcised, barbarian, Scythian, slave or free, but You, O Christ, are all and in all. (Colossians 3:11)

You, O Lord, are one God, and there is only one Mediator between You and people, the Man Christ Jesus, who gave Himself as a ransom for all—the testimony given in its proper time. (1 Timothy 2:5–6)

God's grace was given to us in You, Christ Jesus, before the beginning of time and has now been revealed through Your appearing, O Savior; You abolished death and brought life and immortality to light through the gospel. (2 Timothy 1:9–10)

The faith of Your chosen, O God, and the knowledge of the truth that leads to godliness, is faith and knowledge resting in the hope of eternal life. It is an eternal life that You promised before the beginning of time—and You do not lie. At the appointed time You manifested Your word through the preaching entrusted to the apostles by Your command, O God our Savior. (Titus 1:1–3)

How shall we escape if we ignore Your great salvation? This salvation, which was first announced by the Lord, was confirmed by those who heard Him. You, O God, also bore witness to it by signs and wonders and various miracles and gifts of the Holy Spirit distributed according to Your will. (Hebrews 2:3–4)

We see You, Jesus, the One who was made a little lower than the angels—now crowned with glory and honor because You suffered death, so that by the grace of God You might taste death for everyone. In bringing many of us to glory, it was fitting that God, for whom and through whom everything exists, should make You—the author of our salvation—perfect through suffering. (Hebrews 2:9–10)

Since the children God has given You, Jesus, have bodies made of flesh and blood, You shared in their humanity so that by Your death You might destroy him who holds the power of death—that is, the devil—and free those who all their lives were held in slavery by their fear of death. (Hebrews 2:14–15)

We thank You, O Christ, that You were made like Your brothers and sisters in every way, in order that You might become a merciful and faithful high priest in things pertaining to God, to make propitiation for our sins. Because You Yourself suffered when You were tempted, You are able to help us who are being tempted. (Hebrews 2:17–18)

Because You live forever, Lord Jesus, You have a permanent priesthood. Therefore You are also able to save us completely—we who come to God through You, since You always live to intercede for us. (Hebrews 7:24–25)

You, O Christ, are the mediator of a new covenant, because You died as a ransom to set free those who are called from the transgressions committed under the first covenant, that they may receive the promise of the eternal inheritance. (Hebrews 9:15)

By the will of God, I have been sanctified through the offering of Your body, O Jesus Christ, once for all. And every priest stands daily ministering and offering again and again the same sacrifices, which can never take away sins. But when You had offered for all time one sacrifice for sins, You sat down at the right hand of God, waiting from that time for Your enemies to be made a footstool for Your feet. For by one offering, You have made perfect forever those who are being sanctified. (Hebrews 10:10–14)

I have come to Mount Zion, to the heavenly Jerusalem, Your city, O living God. I have come to myriad angels, and to the assembly and church of the firstborn who are enrolled in heaven. I have come to You, the Judge of all people, to the spirits of the righteous made perfect, to Jesus the mediator of a new covenant, and to the sprinkled blood that speaks of better things than the blood of Abel. (Hebrews 12:22–24)

Every good and perfect gift is from above, coming down from You, the Father of lights, with whom there is no variation, or shifting shadow. Of Your own will You brought us forth by the word of truth, that we might be a kind of first-fruits of Your creatures. (James 1:17–18)

As living stones, we are being built into a spiritual house to be a holy priesthood, offering spiritual sacrifices acceptable to You, O God, through Jesus Christ. We are a chosen people, a royal priesthood, a holy nation, a people for Your own possession, O God, that we may declare Your praises; You called us out of darkness into Your marvelous light. (1 Peter 2:5, 9)

O Christ, You suffered for me, leaving me an example that I should follow in Your steps. "He committed no sin, and no deceit was found in his mouth." When You were reviled, You did not retaliate; when You suffered, You made no threats, but entrusted Yourself to Him who judges righteously; and You Yourself bore my sins in Your body on the tree, so that I might die to sins and live for righteousness; by Your wounds I have been healed. For I was like a sheep going astray, but now I have returned to You, the Shepherd and Overseer of my soul. (1 Peter 2:21–25)

By this Your love, O God, was manifested to us, that You have sent Your only begotten Son into the world that we might live through Him. In this is love, not that we loved You, O God, but that You loved us and sent Your Son to be the propitiation for our sins. (1 John 4:9–10)

You, Father, have sent the Son to be the Savior of the world. If I confess that Jesus is Your Son, O God, You abide in me and I in You. (1 John 4:14–15)

Jesus Christ, You are the faithful witness, the firstborn from the dead, and the ruler of the kings of the earth. To You—who love us and have freed us from our sins by Your blood and have made us to be a kingdom and priests to serve Your God and Father—be glory and power for ever and ever. (Revelation 1:5–6)

Lord, thank you for the invitation you extended to me when You said, "Behold, I stand at the door and knock. If you hear My voice and open the door, I will come in to you and dine with you, and you with Me. To you who overcome, I will give the right to sit with Me on My throne, just as I overcame and sat down with My Father on His throne." (Revelation 3:20–21)

Lamb of God, You are worthy to take the scroll and to open its seals, because You were slain, and with Your blood You purchased us for God from every tribe and language and people and nation. You have made us to be a kingdom and priests to serve our God, and we will reign on the earth. (Revelation 5:9–10)

A great multitude, which no one could number, from all nations and tribes and peoples and languages will stand before the throne and before You, the Lamb, clothed with white robes with palm branches in their hands, and they will cry out with a loud voice, "Salvation belongs to our God, who sits on the throne, and to the Lamb!" (Revelation 7:9–10)

Consummation

To us a child was born, to us a son was given, and the government is on Your shoulders. And You are called Wonderful

Counselor, Mighty God, Everlasting Father, Prince of Peace. Of the increase of Your government and peace there will be no end. You reign on the throne of David and over his kingdom, establishing and upholding it with justice and righteousness from this time on and forever. Your zeal, O Lord of hosts, will accomplish this. (Isaiah 9:6–7)

Lord, we look forward to the day when Your kingdom will come in all its fullness: The wolf will dwell with the lamb, and the leopard will lie down with the goat, and the calf and the lion and the yearling together, and a little child will lead them. The cow will feed with the bear; their young will lie down together, and the lion will eat straw like the ox. The infant will play near the hole of the cobra, and the young child will put his hand into the viper's hole. They will neither harm nor destroy on all Your holy mountain, for the earth will be full of the knowledge of You, O Lord, as the waters cover the sea. (Isaiah 11:6–9)

You, O Lord of hosts, have planned it, to bring low the pride of all glory and to humble all who are renowned on the earth. (Isaiah 23:9)

You, Lord God, will swallow up death forever, and You will wipe away the tears from every face; You will remove the reproach of Your people from all the earth. For You, the Lord, have spoken. And it will be said in that day, "Behold, this is our God; we have waited for Him, and He will save us. This is the Lord; we have trusted in Him. Let us rejoice and be glad in His salvation." (Isaiah 25:8–9)

Behold, You will come with power, Lord God, and Your arm will rule for You. Behold, Your reward is with You, and Your recompense accompanies You. You will feed Your flock like a shepherd; You will gather the lambs in Your arms and carry them close to Your heart; You will gently lead those that have young. (Isaiah 40:10–11)

The heavens will vanish like smoke; the earth will wear out like a garment, and its inhabitants will die in the same way. But Your salvation, O Lord, will last forever, and Your righteousness will never fail. (Isaiah 51:6)

You will create a new heavens and a new earth, O Sovereign Lord. The former things will not be remembered, nor will they come to mind. (Isaiah 65:17)

The wolf and the lamb will feed together, and the lion will eat straw like the ox, and dust will be the serpent's food. They will neither harm nor destroy in all Your holy mountain. (Isaiah 65:25)

You, O Lord, will come with fire, and with Your chariots like a whirlwind; You will render Your anger with fury and Your rebuke with flames of fire. (Isaiah 66:15)

You, O God, are jealous and You, O Lord, avenge; You take vengeance and are filled with wrath. You take vengeance on Your adversaries, and You reserve wrath against Your enemies. You, O Lord, are slow to anger and great in power and will not leave the guilty unpunished. Your way is in the whirlwind and the storm, and clouds are the dust of Your feet. (Nahum 1:2–3)

The earth will be filled with the knowledge of Your glory, O Lord, as the waters cover the sea. (Habakkuk 2:14)

From the rising to the setting of the sun, Your name will be great among the nations. In every place incense and pure offerings will be brought to Your name, for Your name will be great among the nations. (Malachi 1:11)

Son of Man, You will come in the glory of Your Father with Your angels, and then You will reward everyone according to their works. (Matthew 16:27)

As the lightning comes from the east and flashes to the west, so will be Your coming, O Son of Man. Your sign will appear in the sky, and all the nations of the earth will mourn, and they will see You coming on the clouds of the sky with power and great glory. (Matthew 24:27, 30)

I must be ready, for You, Jesus, the Son of Man, will come at an hour when I do not expect You. (Matthew 24:44; Luke 12:40)

You, Jesus, will be great and will be called the Son of the Most High. The Lord God will give You the throne of Your father David, and You will reign over the house of Jacob forever, and Your kingdom will never end. (Luke 1:32–33)

If I am ashamed of You and Your words, Jesus, then You, O Son of Man, will be ashamed of me when You come in Your glory and in the glory of Your Father and of the holy angels. (Luke 9:26)

The children of this age marry and are given in marriage, but those who are considered worthy of taking part in that age and the resurrection from the dead will neither marry nor be given in marriage. They can no longer die, for they are like the angels and are Your children, O God, being children of the resurrection. (Luke 20:34–36)

An hour is coming, and now is, when the dead will hear Your voice, O Son of God, and those who hear will live. For as the Father has life in Himself, so He has granted You to have life in Yourself, and He has given You authority to execute judgment because You are the Son of Man. (John 5:25–27)

An hour is coming when all who are in the graves will hear Your voice, O Son of Man, and will come out—those who have done good will rise to a resurrection of life, and those who have done evil will rise to a resurrection of judgment. (John 5:28–29)

You, O God, will judge people's secret thoughts through Jesus Christ, according to the gospel. (Romans 2:16)

We will all stand before Your judgment seat, O Lord. For You have said, "As I live, every knee will bow before Me, and every tongue will confess to God." So then, each of us will give an account of himself to You. (Romans 14:10–12)

The first man was of the dust of the earth; You, Jesus Christ, the second Man, are from heaven. As was the earthly man, so are those who are of the earth; and as You, the Man from heaven are, so also are those who are of heaven. And just as we have borne the image of the earthly man, so shall we bear Your likeness—You who are the heavenly Man. (1 Corinthians 15:47–49)

We will not all sleep, but we will all be changed in a moment—in the twinkling of an eye—at the last trumpet. For the trumpet will sound, and the dead will be raised imperishable, and we shall be changed. For this perishable must clothe itself with the imperishable, and this mortal with immortality. (1 Corinthians 15:51–53)

God highly exalted You, Christ Jesus, and gave You the name that is above every name, that at Your name, Jesus, every knee should bow, in heaven and on earth and under the earth, and every tongue should confess that You are Lord, to the glory of God the Father. (Philippians 2:9–11)

We are not to be ignorant about those who fall asleep or grieve like other people, who have no hope. For if we believe that You, Jesus, died and rose again, even so the Father will bring with You those who have fallen asleep in You. According to Your own word, we who are alive and remain until Your coming will not precede those who have fallen asleep. For You Yourself will come down from heaven with a loud command, with the voice of the archangel, and with the trumpet of God, and the dead in You will rise first. Then we who are alive and remain will be caught up together with them in the clouds to meet You in the air. And so we will be with You forever. (1 Thessalonians 4:13–17)

We are looking for the blessed hope of Your glorious appearing, Christ Jesus, our great God and Savior. You gave Yourself for us to redeem us from all iniquity and to purify for Yourself a people for Your own possession, zealous for good works. (Titus 2:13–14)

Since Your day, O Lord, will come like a thief, I ought to conduct my life with holiness and godliness as I look forward to the coming of Your day. According to Your promise, I am looking for a new heaven and a new earth, in which righteousness dwell. Therefore, since I am looking for these things, I will be diligent to be found at peace with You— pure and blameless before You. (2 Peter 3:10–14)

Jesus Christ, You are coming with the clouds, and every eye will see You, even those who pierced You; and all the peoples of the earth will mourn because of You. Even so, Amen. (Revelation 1:7)

The kingdom of the world has become Your kingdom, O God, and of Your Christ, and You will reign for ever and ever. (Revelation 11:15)

Blessed are those who die in You, Lord, from now on. They will rest from their labor, for their works will follow them. (Revelation 14:13)

Like the roar of rushing waters and like loud peals of thunder, a great multitude will shout, "Hallelujah! For the Lord God Almighty reigns. Let us rejoice and be glad and give Him glory! For Your marriage, O Lamb, has come, and Your bride has made herself ready." Blessed are those who are invited to Your marriage supper, O Lamb. (Revelation 19:6–7, 9)

We praise You, O Jesus, our Messiah, for the vision we have from John: He saw heaven opened, and there before him was a white horse. You are its rider, called Faithful and True; and in righteousness You judge and make war. Your eyes are like a flame of fire, and on Your head are many crowns. You have a name written on You that no one knows except Yourself. You are clothed in a robe dipped in blood, and Your name is the Word of God. The armies of heaven, riding on white horses and dressed in fine linen, white and clean, are following You. Out of Your mouth goes a sharp sword with which You will strike down the nations. And You will rule them with a rod of iron. You tread the winepress of the fury of the wrath of God Almighty. And on Your robe and on Your thigh You have a name written: KING OF KINGS AND LORD OF LORDS. (Revelation 19:11–16)

There will be a new heaven and a new earth, for the first heaven and the first earth will pass away, and there will no longer be any sea. (Revelation 21:1)

Your Holy City, the new Jerusalem, O God, will come down out of heaven from You, prepared as a bride adorned for her husband. A loud voice from the throne will say, "Behold, the tabernacle of God is with people, and He will dwell with them, and they will be His people, and God Himself will be with them and be their God, and He will wipe every tear from their eyes. There will be no more death or mourning or crying or pain, for the first things have passed away." You, O God, who are seated on the throne will say, "Behold, I make all things new." (Revelation 21:2–5)

Lord Jesus, You are the Alpha and the Omega, the Beginning and the End. To anyone who is thirsty, You will give to drink without cost from the spring of the water of life. Those who overcome will inherit all this, and You will be their God and they will be Your children. (Revelation 21:6–7)

There will be no temple in the new Jerusalem, because You, Lord God Almighty, and the Lamb are its temple. The city will not need the sun or the moon to shine on it, for Your glory, O God, gives it light, and the Lamb is its lamp. The nations will walk by the city's light, and the kings of the earth will bring their splendor into it. And its gates will never be shut by day, for there will be no night there. (Revelation 21:22–25)

You, Lord Jesus, are coming quickly. Your reward is with You, and You will give to everyone according to what they have done. You are the Alpha and the Omega, the First and the Last, the Beginning and the End. Yes, You are coming quickly. Amen. Come, Lord Jesus. (Revelation 22:12–13, 20)

MY RELATIONSHIP TO GOD

God's Grace and Love

I am unworthy of all the lovingkindness and faithfulness You have shown Your servant. (Genesis 32:10)

O Lord, bless us and keep us; O Lord, make Your face shine upon us and be gracious to us; O Lord, turn Your face toward us and give us peace. (Numbers 6:24–26)

You, O Lord, are a shield around me; You bestow glory on me and lift up my head. (Psalm 3:3)

I will be glad and rejoice in Your love, for You saw my affliction and have known the anguish of my soul. (Psalm 31:7)

How great is Your goodness, O Lord, which You have stored up for those who fear You, which You have prepared for those who take refuge in You in the sight of others! (Psalm 31:19)

Many are the sorrows of the wicked, but Your lovingkindness shall surround those who trust in You, O Lord. (Psalm 32:10)

Your eye, O Lord, is on those who fear You, on those whose hope is in Your unfailing love. (Psalm 33:18)

O Lord my God, many are the wonders You have done, and Your thoughts toward us no one can recount to You; were I to speak and tell of them, they would be too many to declare. (Psalm 40:5)

Blessed is the one You choose and bring near to live in Your courts. We will be satisfied with the goodness of Your house, of Your holy temple. (Psalm 65:4)

In the day of my trouble I will call upon You, for You will answer me. You are great and do wondrous deeds; You alone are God. (Psalm 86:7, 10)

Because I love You, You will deliver me; You will protect me, for I acknowledge Your name. I will call upon You, and You will answer me; You will be with me in trouble, You will deliver me and honor me. (Psalm 91:14–15)

May Your merciful kindness be my comfort, according to Your promise to Your servant. (Psalm 119:76)

You, O Lord, will judge Your people and have compassion on Your servants. (Psalm 135:14)

You have loved me with an everlasting love; You have drawn me with lovingkindness. (Jeremiah 31:3)

I believe that it is through Your grace, our Lord Jesus, that I am saved. (Acts 15:11)

I have been set apart for the gospel of God—I am among those who are called to belong to You, Jesus Christ. (Romans 1:1, 6)

You have loved me, O God, and called me to be a saint; You, O God my Father, and the Lord Jesus Christ have given me grace and peace. (Romans 1:7)

Having been justified by faith, I have peace with You, O God, through the Lord Jesus Christ, through whom I have gained access by faith into this grace in which I stand; and I rejoice in the hope of Your glory. (Romans 5:1–2)

I am convinced that neither death nor life, nor angels nor principalities, nor things present nor things to come, nor powers, nor height nor depth, nor anything else in all creation, will be able to separate me from Your love, O God, that is in Christ Jesus my Lord. (Romans 8:38–39)

I thank You, God, because of Your grace in Christ Jesus. In Him we have been enriched in every way, in all speech and in all knowledge. We do not lack any spiritual gift as we eagerly wait for the revelation of our Lord Jesus Christ. (1 Corinthians 1:4–5, 7)

O God, I know that You will keep me strong to the end, so that I will be blameless on the day of our Lord Jesus Christ. You are faithful; through You I was called into fellowship with Your Son, Jesus Christ our Lord. (1 Corinthians 1:8–9)

Thanks be to You, O God, who always lead us in triumph in Christ and through us spread everywhere the fragrance of the knowledge of You. (2 Corinthians 2:14)

You, O God, set me apart from my mother's womb and called me through Your grace. (Galatians 1:15)

O God, You chose me in Christ before the foundation of the world to be holy and blameless in Your sight. In love You predestined me to be adopted as Your child through Jesus Christ, according to the good pleasure of Your will, to the praise of the glory of Your grace, which You bestowed upon me in the One You love. (Ephesians 1:4–6)

In You, O Christ, I have obtained an inheritance, having been predestined according to the plan of Him who works all things according to the counsel of His will, that I who have trusted in You should be to the praise of His glory. (Ephesians 1:11–12)

By grace I have been saved through faith, and this not of myself; it is Your gift, O God, and not of works, so that I cannot boast. (Ephesians 2:8–9)

I am confident of this, that You who began a good work in me will carry it on to completion until Your day, Christ Jesus. (Philippians 1:6)

Your grace, O Lord Jesus Christ, is with my spirit. (Philippians 4:23)

Your grace, O Lord, was poured out on me abundantly, along with the faith and love that are in Christ Jesus. (1 Timothy 1:14)

God, You have saved me and called me with a holy calling, not according to my works but according to Your own purpose and grace. (2 Timothy 1:9)

In Your great grace, O God, You called me to Your eternal glory in Christ. After I have suffered a little while, You Yourself will perfect, confirm, strengthen and establish me. (1 Peter 5:10)

We have known and have believed the love You, O God, have for us. God, You are love, and those who abide in love abide in You, and You in them. In this way, love has been perfected among us so that we may have confidence in the day of judgment; because as You are, so are we in this world. There is no fear in love, but perfect love casts out fear, because fear involves punishment, and those who fear have not been perfected in love. (1 John 4:16–18)

I have been called, having been loved by You, God the Father, and kept by Jesus Christ. (Jude 1)

God's Salvation and Forgiveness

Lord, You are close to the brokenhearted and save those who are crushed in spirit. (Psalm 34:18)

The salvation of the righteous comes from You, the Lord; You are their stronghold in time of trouble. You, O Lord, help them and deliver them; You deliver them from the wicked and save them, because they take refuge in You. (Psalm 37:39–40)

You lifted me out of the slimy pit, O God, out of the mud and mire; You set my feet on a rock and gave me a firm place to stand. You put a new song in my mouth, a hymn of praise to You, my God. Many will see and fear and put their trust in You, O Lord. (Psalm 40:2–3)

Your sacrifices, O God, are a broken spirit; a broken and contrite heart, O God, You will not despise. (Psalm 51:17)

Have mercy on me, O God, have mercy on me, for in You my soul takes refuge. I will take refuge in the shadow of Your wings until destruction passes by. I cry out to You, O God Most High, to You who fulfill Your purpose for me. (Psalm 57:1–2)

My soul silently waits for You alone, O God; my salvation comes from You. You alone are my rock and my salvation; You are my stronghold; I will never be shaken. (Psalm 62:1–2)

My mouth will tell of Your righteousness and of Your salvation all day long, though I know not its measure. I will come in Your strength, O Lord God; I will proclaim Your righteousness, Yours alone. Since my youth, O God, You have taught me, and to this day I declare Your wondrous deeds. (Psalm 71:15–17)

Surely Your salvation is near to those who fear You. (Psalm 85:9)

You, O God, will not always strive with us, nor will You harbor Your anger forever. You do not treat us as our sins deserve or repay us according to our iniquities. For as high as the heavens are above the earth, so great is Your love for us who fear You; as far as the east is from the west, so far have You removed our transgressions from us. As a father has compassion on his children, so You, O Lord, have compassion on us. (Psalm 103:9–13)

I love You, Lord, because You have heard my voice and my supplications. Because You turned Your ear to me, I will call on You as long as I live. (Psalm 116:1–2)

You, O Lord, are my strength and my song; You have become my salvation. (Psalm 118:14)

There is not a righteous person on earth who continually does good and never sins. (Ecclesiastes 7:20)

Surely You are my salvation; I will trust and not be afraid. You, the Lord God, are my strength and my song, and You have become my salvation. (Isaiah 12:2)

Let the wicked forsake their ways and the unrighteous their thoughts; let them return to You, Lord, and You will have mercy on them, and to You, our God, for You will abundantly pardon. (Isaiah 55:7)

I will greatly rejoice in You, Lord; my soul will be joyful in You, my God. For You have clothed me with garments of salvation and arrayed me in a robe of righteousness, as a bridegroom decks himself with ornaments, and as a bride adorns herself with her jewels. (Isaiah 61:10)

All of us have become like those who are unclean, and all our righteous acts are like filthy rags. We all shrivel up like leaves, and our iniquities, like the wind, sweep us away. But now, O Lord, You are our Father. We are the clay; You are the potter; we are all the work of Your hand. (Isaiah 64:6, 8)

Heal me, O Lord, and I will be healed; save me, and I will be saved, for You are my praise. (Jeremiah 17:14)

Why should any of us complain when punished for our sins? Let us search out and examine our ways, and let us return to You, Lord. (Lamentations 3:39–40)

You have declared to us, O Lord, "Even now, return to Me with all your heart, with fasting and weeping and mourning."

So we will rend our hearts and not our garments. We will return to You, O Lord our God, for You are gracious and compassionate, slow to anger and abounding in lovingkindness, and You relent from sending calamity. (Joel 2:12–13)

I give You thanks that to all who receive You, Lord Jesus Christ, and believe in Your name, You give the right to become children of God—children born not of natural descent, nor of human decision or a husband's will, but born of God. (John 1:12–13)

If we drink ordinary water, we will be thirsty again; but if we drink the water You give, Jesus, we will never thirst. Indeed, the water You give becomes in us a spring of water welling up to eternal life. (John 4:13–14)

I should not work for the food that perishes, but for the food that endures to eternal life, which You, O Son of Man, give me, for God the Father has set His seal on You. (John 6:27)

Lord Jesus, all those the Father gives You will come to You, and whoever comes to You, You will never cast out. For You have come down from heaven, not to do Your own will, but the will of Him who sent You. And this is the will of Him who sent You, that You will lose none of all those He has given You, but raise them up at the last day. For Your Father's will is that those who look to You and believe in You may have eternal life, and You will raise them up at the last day. (John 6:37–40)

I shall know the truth, and the truth shall set me free. Everyone who commits sin is a slave of sin. And a slave has no permanent place in the family, but a child belongs to it forever. So if You, the Son of God, set me free, I shall be free indeed. (John 8:32, 34–36)

Jesus, You are the door; whoever enters through You will be saved and will come in and go out and find pasture. The thief comes only to steal and kill and destroy; You have come that we may have life and have it abundantly. (John 10:9–10)

Blessed are those who have not seen You, Jesus, and yet have believed in You. (John 20:29)

Since I have been justified by Christ's blood, how much more shall I be saved from Your wrath, O God, through Him. For if, when I was Your enemy, I was reconciled to You through the death of Your Son, how much more, having been reconciled, shall I be saved through His life. And not only this, but I also rejoice in You through my Lord Jesus Christ, through whom I have now received reconciliation. (Romans 5:9–11)

Sin shall not be my master, because I am not under law, but under grace. I have been set free from sin and have become a slave of righteousness. (Romans 6:14, 18)

Those You foreknew, O God, You also predestined to be conformed to the likeness of Your Son, that He might be the firstborn among many brothers and sisters. And those You predestined, You also called; those You called, You also justified; those You justified, You also glorified. (Romans 8:29–30)

I was washed, I was sanctified, I was justified in Your name, O Lord Jesus Christ, and by the Spirit of our God. (1 Corinthians 6:11)

I must not receive Your grace in vain. For You say, "In the acceptable time I heard you, and in the day of salvation I helped you." Now is the time of Your favor, O God; now is the day of salvation. (2 Corinthians 6:1–2)

In You, O Christ, I have redemption through Your blood, the forgiveness of sins, in accordance with the riches of God's grace that He lavished on me with all wisdom and understanding. (Ephesians 1:7–8)

O God, You are rich in mercy; because of Your great love for me, You made me alive with Christ, even when I was dead in transgressions. It is by grace I have been saved. (Ephesians 2:4–5)

I am no longer a stranger and alien, but a fellow citizen with Your people, O God, and a member of Your household, built on the foundation of the apostles and prophets, with Christ Jesus Himself as the chief cornerstone. (Ephesians 2:19–20)

O Father, You have qualified me to share in the inheritance of the saints in the light. For You have rescued me from the dominion of darkness and brought me into the kingdom of Your beloved Son, in whom I have redemption, the forgiveness of sins. (Colossians 1:12–14)

Once I was alienated from You, O God, and was an enemy in my mind because of my evil works. But now You have reconciled me, by Christ's fleshly body through death, to present me holy and blameless in Your sight and free from reproach. (Colossians 1:21–22)

God did not appoint me to suffer wrath but to obtain salvation through You, my Lord Jesus Christ. You died for me, so that, whether I am awake or asleep, I may live together with You. (1 Thessalonians 5:9–10)

From the beginning, God, You chose me for salvation through sanctification by the Spirit and through belief in the truth. You called me to this through the gospel, that I might obtain the glory of my Lord Jesus Christ. (2 Thessalonians 2:13–14)

It is a trustworthy saying, that deserves full acceptance, that You, Christ Jesus, came into the world to save sinners. I obtained mercy as the worst of sinners, so that You, O Christ Jesus, might display Your unlimited patience as an example for those who would believe on You for eternal life. (1 Timothy 1:15–16)

God my Savior, when Your kindness and love appeared, You saved me, not by works of righteousness that I had done, but according to Your mercy. You saved me through the washing of regeneration and renewal by Your Holy Spirit, whom You poured out on me abundantly through Jesus Christ my Savior, so that having been justified by Your grace, I might become Your heir, having the hope of eternal life. (Titus 3:4–7)

If I claim to be without sin, I deceive myself, and the truth is not in me. If I confess my sins, You are faithful and just and will forgive me my sins and purify me from all unrighteousness. If I claim I have not sinned, I make You a liar and Your word is not in me. (1 John 1:8–10)

God's Care, Guidance and Provision

Blessed are You, the Lord, the God of Abraham, who have not abandoned Your lovingkindness and Your truth. (Genesis 24:27)

O Lord, I claim Your promise to Jacob: "Behold, I am with you and will watch over you wherever you go; I will not leave you until I have done what I have promised you." (Genesis 28:15)

I have waited for Your salvation, O Lord. (Genesis 49:18)

Others may intend evil, but You, O God, can use it for good to accomplish Your loving purposes. (Genesis 50:20)

Your presence will go with me, and You will give me rest. (Exodus 33:14)

The secret things belong to You, Lord our God, but the things revealed belong to us and to our children forever, that we may observe Your words. (Deuteronomy 29:29)

O Lord, You Yourself go before me and will be with me; You will never leave me nor forsake me. I will not be afraid or be dismayed. (Deuteronomy 31:8)

O Lord, You are my rock and my fortress and my deliverer; O God, You are my rock; I will take refuge in You. You are my shield and the horn of my salvation, my stronghold and my refuge—my Savior; You save me from violence. I call on You, Lord; You are worthy of praise, and I am saved from my enemies. (2 Samuel 22:2–4)

O God, You are my strong fortress, and You set the blameless free in Your way. You make my feet like the feet of a deer; You enable me to stand on the heights. You train my hands for battle, so that my arms can bend a bow of bronze. You give me Your shield of victory; You stoop down to make me great. You broaden the path beneath me, and my feet have not slipped. (2 Samuel 22:33–37)

Oh, that You would bless me and enlarge my territory! Let Your hand be with me and keep me from evil, so it may not grieve me. (1 Chronicles 4:10)

Lord, there is no one besides You to help the powerless against the mighty. Help us, O Lord our God, for we rest in You. O Lord, You are our God; do not let people prevail against You. (2 Chronicles 14:11)

You will light my lamp; You, O Lord my God, will make my darkness light. O God, You arm me with strength and make my way perfect. (Psalm 18:28, 32)

You, O Lord, are my shepherd; I shall not be in want. You make me lie down in green pastures. You lead me beside quiet waters. You restore my soul. You guide me in the paths of righteousness for Your name's sake. Even though I walk through the valley of the shadow of death, I will fear no evil, for You are with me. Your rod and Your staff, they comfort me. You prepare a table before me in the presence of my enemies. You anoint my head with oil; my cup overflows. Surely goodness and mercy will follow me all the days of my life, and I will dwell in Your house, O Lord, forever. (Psalm 23:1–6)

In You, O Lord, I have taken refuge; let me never be ashamed; deliver me in Your righteousness. Since You are my rock and my fortress, for Your name's sake lead me and guide me. Into Your hands I commit my spirit; redeem me, O Lord, God of truth. (Psalm 31:1, 3, 5)

My times are in Your hand; deliver me from the hand of my enemies and from those who pursue me. (Psalm 31:15)

You are my hiding place; You will preserve me from trouble and surround me with songs of deliverance. (Psalm 32:7)

O God, You are my refuge and strength, an ever-present help in trouble. Therefore I will not fear, though the earth give way and the mountains slip into the heart of the sea. (Psalm 46:1–2)

I will call upon You in the day of trouble, and You will deliver me, and I will honor You. (Psalm 50:15)

Surely You, O God, are my helper; You, O Lord, are the One who sustains my soul. (Psalm 54:4)

I am continually with You; You hold me by my right hand. You guide me with Your counsel, and afterward You will take me to glory. (Psalm 73:23–24)

Blessed are those You discipline, O Lord, the people You teach from Your word. (Psalm 94:12)

I lift up my eyes to the hills—where does my help come from? My help comes from You, O Lord, who made heaven and earth. You will not allow my foot to slip; You who watch over me will not slumber. You are my keeper; You, Lord, are my shade at my right hand. The sun will not harm me by day, nor the moon by night. You will keep me from all evil; You will preserve my soul. You will watch over my coming and going from this time forth and forever. (Psalm 121:1–3, 5–8)

I will not despise Your discipline, O Lord, nor resent Your correction; for You discipline those You love, as a father the son he delights in. (Proverbs 3:11–12)

I will not fear, for You are with me; I will not be dismayed, for You are my God. You will strengthen me and help me; You will uphold me with Your righteous right hand. For You are the Lord my God, who takes hold of my right hand and says to me, "Do not fear; I will help you." (Isaiah 41:10, 13)

Even to my old age, You are the same, O Lord, and even when my hair is gray, You will carry me. You have made me, and You will bear me. You will sustain me, and You will deliver me. (Isaiah 46:4)

O Lord, my Redeemer, the Holy One of Israel, You are the Lord our God, who teaches us to profit, who leads us in the way we should go. (Isaiah 48:17)

You, O Lord God, have given me the tongue of the learned, to know the word that sustains the weary. You awaken me morning by morning; You awaken my ear to hear as the learned. (Isaiah 50:4)

I called to You, Lord, in my distress, and You answered me. From the depths of the grave, I called for help, and You heard my voice. (Jonah 2:2)

Holy Spirit, help me in my weakness, for I do not know what I ought to pray for, but You Yourself intercede for me with groans that words cannot express. And He who searches my heart knows Your mind, O Spirit, because You intercede for the saints according to the will of God. (Romans 8:26–27)

If You, O God, are for me, who can be against me? You who did not spare Your own Son, but delivered Him up for us all, how will You not also, with Him, freely give us all things? (Romans 8:31–32)

No temptation has overtaken me except what is common to all people. And You, O God, are faithful; You will not let me be tempted beyond what I am able, but with the temptation You will also provide a way out, so that I may be able to endure it. (1 Corinthians 10:13)

As Your sufferings, O Christ, abound in me, so also my comfort abounds through You, O Christ. (2 Corinthians 1:5)

Lord of peace, may You Yourself give me peace always and in every way. O Lord, be with all of us. (2 Thessalonians 3:16)

May You, O God of peace—who through the blood of the eternal covenant brought back from the dead our Lord Jesus, our great Shepherd of the sheep—equip me with every good thing to do Your will, and may You work in me what is pleasing in Your sight, through Jesus Christ, to whom be glory forever and ever. (Hebrews 13:20–21)

Your divine power, O God, has given me all things that pertain to life and godliness, through the knowledge of You who called me by Your own glory and virtue. Through these You have given me Your very great and precious promises, so that through them I may be a partaker of the divine nature, having escaped the corruption that is in the world by lust. (2 Peter 1:3–4)

Knowing and Loving God

If I have found grace in Your sight, teach me Your ways, so I may know You and continue to find favor with You. (Exodus 33:13)

When I seek You, Lord my God, I will find You if I seek You with all my heart and with all my soul. (Deuteronomy 4:29)

O Lord my God, You are one. I want to love You, Lord my God, with all my heart and with all my soul and with all my strength. (Deuteronomy 6:4–5)

I want to love You, Lord my God, and to serve You with all my heart and with all my soul. (Deuteronomy 11:13)

I will carefully observe the commandment to love You, Lord my God, to walk in all Your ways and to hold fast to You. (Deuteronomy 11:22)

I want to know You, O God, and serve You with a whole heart and with a willing mind; for You search my heart and understand every motive behind my thoughts. (1 Chronicles 28:9)

It is the breath of Your spirit in me, Almighty God, that gives me understanding. (Job 32:8)

I have set You always before me, O Lord; because You are at my right hand, I will not be shaken. Therefore my heart is glad, and my tongue rejoices; my body also will rest in hope. You will make known to me the path of life; in Your presence is fullness of joy; in Your right hand are pleasures forever. (Psalm 16:8–9, 11)

As the deer pants for the water brooks, so my soul pants for You, O God. My soul thirsts for You, for the living God. When shall I come and appear before You? (Psalm 42:1–2)

God, You are my God. Earnestly I seek You; my soul thirsts for You. My body longs for You in a dry and weary land where there is no water. (Psalm 63:1)

Those who are far from You will perish; You have cut off all who are unfaithful to You. But as for me, it is good to be near You, O God. I have made You my refuge, Lord God, that I may tell of all Your works. (Psalm 73:25–28)

How lovely are Your dwellings, O Lord of hosts! My soul longs and even faints for Your courts, O Lord; my heart and my flesh cry out for You, the living God. (Psalm 84:1–2)

Better is one day in Your courts than a thousand elsewhere, O Lord Almighty. I would rather be a doorkeeper in Your house, my God, than dwell in the tents of the wicked. For You, Lord God, are a sun and shield. You will give grace and glory; no good thing do You withhold from those who walk in integrity. O Lord of hosts, blessed are those who trust in You! (Psalm 84:10–12)

Teach me Your way, O Lord; I will walk in Your truth; unite my heart to fear Your name. (Psalm 86:11)

Let those who love You, Lord, hate evil. You preserve the souls of Your saints and deliver them from the hand of the wicked. Light is sown for the righteous and gladness for the upright in heart. (Psalm 97:10–11)

I will give You my heart and let my eyes delight in Your ways. (Proverbs 23:26)

Walking in the way of Your laws, O Lord, I wait for You; Your name and Your memory are the desire of my soul. (Isaiah 26:8)

My soul yearns for You in the night; my spirit within me diligently seeks You. When Your judgments come upon the earth, the inhabitants of the world learn righteousness. (Isaiah 26:9)

I will seek You, Lord, while You may be found and call upon You while You are near. (Isaiah 55:6)

I will call upon You and come and pray to You, and You will listen to me. I will seek You and find You when I search for You with all my heart. (Jeremiah 29:12–13)

Father in heaven, hallowed be Your name. Your kingdom come; Your will be done on earth as it is in heaven. (Matthew 6:9–10)

I will not be afraid of those who kill the body and after that can do no more. But I will fear You, the One who, after killing, has authority to cast into hell. (Luke 12:4–5)

Whoever acknowledges You before others, O Son of Man, You will also acknowledge before the angels of God. But whoever disowns You before others will be denied before the angels of God. (Luke 12:8–9)

As the Father has loved You, Jesus, You also have loved me. I must abide in Your love. If I keep Your commandments, I will abide in Your love, just as You kept Your Father's commandments and abide in His love. You have told me this so that Your joy may be in me and that my joy may be full. (John 15:9–11)

We are Your friends if we do what You command. No longer do You call us servants, because a servant does not know what his master is doing. Instead, You have called us friends, for everything that You learned from Your Father, You have made known to us. We did not choose You, but You chose us and appointed us to go and bear fruit—fruit that will last. Then whatever we ask the Father in Your name, He may give to us. (John 15:14–16)

Father, You Yourself love me because I have loved Jesus and have believed that He came forth from You. (John 16:27)

This is eternal life: that I may know You, the only true God, and Jesus Christ, whom You have sent. (John 17:3)

I do not want to be conformed to the pattern of this world but to be transformed by the renewing of my mind, that I may be able to test and approve what Your will is, O God, and that it is good and pleasing and perfect. (Romans 12:2)

You, O God, made known to us the mystery of Your will according to Your good pleasure, which You purposed in Christ, to be put in effect in the fullness of the times, that You might gather together all things—things in the heavens and things upon the earth—in Christ. (Ephesians 1:9–10)

God of my Lord Jesus Christ, the Father of glory, may You give me a spirit of wisdom and of revelation in the full knowledge of You, and may the eyes of my heart be enlightened, in order that I may know the hope to which You have called me, the riches of Your glorious inheritance in the saints, and the incomparable greatness of Your power toward us who believe. (Ephesians 1:17–19)

O God, grant that I, according to the riches of Your glory, may be strengthened with power through Your Spirit in my inner being, so that Christ may dwell in my heart through faith. And may I, being rooted and grounded in love, be able to comprehend with all the saints what is the width and length and height and depth of the love of Christ, and to know this love that surpasses knowledge, that I may be filled to all Your fullness, O God. (Ephesians 3:16–19)

Grace be with all who love You, our Lord Jesus Christ, with an incorruptible love. (Ephesians 6:24)

May my love abound more and more in full knowledge and depth of insight, so that I may be able to approve the things that are excellent, in order to be sincere and blameless until Your day, O Christ—having been filled with the fruit of righteousness that comes through You, to the glory and praise of God. (Philippians 1:9–11)

O God, may You fill me with the knowledge of Your will through all spiritual wisdom and understanding, so that I may walk worthy of You, Lord, and please You in every way, bearing fruit in every good work, and growing in the knowledge of You; strengthened with all power according to Your glorious might, so that I may have great endurance and patience with joy. (Colossians 1:9–11)

O Lord, direct my heart into the love of God and into Your patience, O Christ. (2 Thessalonians 3:5)

As one who shares in the heavenly calling, I should fix my thoughts on You, Jesus, the Apostle and High Priest of my confession. (Hebrews 3:1)

Though I have not seen You, Jesus, I love You; and though I do not see You now but believe in You, I rejoice with joy inexpressible and full of glory, for I am receiving the end of my faith, the salvation of my soul. (1 Peter 1:8–9)

If I obey Your commandments, O Christ, I abide in You, and You in me. And this is how I know that You abide in me: by the Spirit whom You have given me. (1 John 3:24)

I know that I abide in You, Christ, and You in me, because You have given me of Your Spirit. (1 John 4:13)

Praising and Thanking God

My heart rejoices in You, Lord; my horn is exalted in You, Lord. My mouth boasts over my enemies, for I delight in Your salvation. (1 Samuel 2:1)

I will give thanks to You, Lord, call upon Your name and make known to others what You have done. I will sing to You, sing praises to You, and tell of all Your wonderful acts. (1 Chronicles 16:8–9)

I glory in Your holy name, O Lord. Let the hearts of those who seek You rejoice. I will seek You, O Lord, and Your strength; I will seek Your face always. I will remember the wonderful works You have done, the miracles and the judgments You pronounced. (1 Chronicles 16:10–12)

I trust in Your loyal love; my heart rejoices in Your salvation. I will sing to You, O Lord, for You have dealt bountifully with me. (Psalm 13:5–6)

I will bless You, Lord, at all times; Your praise will always be in my mouth. (Psalm 34:1)

I will sing of Your strength, yes, I will sing of Your mercy in the morning, for You have been my stronghold, my refuge in times of trouble. To You, O my Strength, I will sing praises, for You are my fortress, my loving God. (Psalm 59:16–17)

Because Your lovingkindness is better than life, my lips will praise You. So I will bless You as long as I live; I will lift up my hands in Your name. (Psalm 63:3–4)

I will praise Your name in song, O God, and magnify You with thanksgiving. (Psalm 69:30)

My soul will bless You, Lord, and not forget all Your benefits. You forgive all my iniquities and heal all my diseases. You redeem my life from the pit and crown me with love and compassion. You satisfy my desires with good things, so that my youth is renewed like the eagle's. (Psalm 103:2–5)

I will sing to You, Lord, as long as I live; I will sing praise to You, my God, while I have my being. May my meditation be pleasing to You; I will be glad in You, Lord. (Psalm 104:33–34)

My mouth will speak Your praise, O Lord, and every creature will bless Your holy name for ever and ever. (Psalm 145:21)

I will praise You, Lord, while I live; I will sing praises to You, my God, while I have my being. (Psalm 146:2)

I will exult in You, Lord; I will rejoice in You, O God of my salvation. You, Lord God, are my strength; You make my feet like the feet of a deer and enable me to go on the heights. (Habakkuk 3:18–19)

We should not get drunk on wine, for that is dissipation. Instead, we should be filled with the Spirit, speaking to one another with psalms, hymns, and spiritual songs; singing and making music in our hearts to You, always giving thanks to You, Father, for everything, in the name of our Lord Jesus Christ. (Ephesians 5:18–20)

I will rejoice in You always, Lord. (Philippians 4:4)

God, I will rejoice always, pray without ceasing, and give thanks in all circumstances, for this is Your will for us in Christ Jesus. (1 Thessalonians 5:16–18)

Since I am receiving a kingdom that cannot be shaken, I will be thankful and so worship You acceptably, my God, with reverence and awe, for You are a consuming fire. (Hebrews 12:28–29)

I will fear You, God, and give You glory, because the hour of Your judgment has come. I will worship You who made the heavens and the earth, the sea and the springs of water. (Revelation 14:7)

Identity and Life in Christ

I am the salt of the earth, but if the salt loses its flavor, how can it be made salty again? It is no longer good for anything, except to be thrown out and trampled underfoot. I am the light of the world. A city set on a hill cannot be hidden. Neither do people light a lamp and put it under a basket, but on a lampstand, and it gives light to all who are in the house. In the same way, may I let my light shine before all people, that they may see my good deeds and praise You, my Father in heaven. (Matthew 5:13–16)

Jesus, You have asked the Father, and He has given me another Comforter to be with me forever, even the Spirit of truth, whom the world cannot receive, because it neither sees Him nor knows Him. But I know Him, for He lives in me. (John 14:16–17)

Lord Jesus, You are in Your Father, and I am in You, and You are in me. (John 14:20)

I died to sin; how can I live in it any longer? (Romans 6:2)

If I have been united with You, O Christ, in the likeness of Your death, I will certainly also be united with You in the likeness of Your resurrection. (Romans 6:5)

I know that my old self was crucified with You, O Christ, so that the body of sin might be done away with, that I should no longer be a slave to sin; for anyone who has died has been freed from sin. (Romans 6:6–7)

I have become dead to the law through Your body, O Christ, that I might belong to another, to You who were raised from the dead, in order that I might bear fruit to God. But now, by dying to what once bound me, I have been released from the law so that I serve in newness of the Spirit and not in the old way of the letter. (Romans 7:4, 6)

I delight in Your law, O God, in my inner being. (Romans 7:22)

There is now no condemnation for those who are in You, Christ Jesus, because the law of the Spirit of life in You has set us free from the law of sin and death. (Romans 8:1–2)

I am not in the flesh but in the Spirit, since the Spirit, O God, lives in me. And whoever does not have the Spirit of Christ does not belong to Him. (Romans 8:9)

If You, O Christ, are in me, my body is dead because of sin, yet my spirit is alive because of righteousness. And if the

Spirit of Him who raised You, Jesus, from the dead is living in me, He who raised You, Christ, from the dead will also give life to my mortal body through His Spirit, who lives in me. (Romans 8:10–11)

I did not receive a spirit of slavery again to fear, but I received Your Spirit of adoption by whom I cry, "Abba, Father." The Spirit Himself testifies with my spirit that I am Your child, O God. (Romans 8:15–16)

We do not live for ourselves alone, nor do we die for ourselves alone. If we live, we live to You, Lord; and if we die, we die to You, Lord. So, whether we live or die, we belong to You, Lord. (Romans 14:7–8)

I have been sanctified in You, Christ Jesus, and called to be a saint, together with all those everywhere who call on Your name, O Lord Jesus Christ—their Lord and mine. (1 Corinthians 1:2)

It is because of You, O God, that I am in Christ Jesus, who has become for me wisdom from You—that is, my righteousness, sanctification and redemption. (1 Corinthians 1:30)

We are Your temple, O God, and Your Spirit lives in us. (1 Corinthians 3:16)

If we are joined to You, O Lord, we are one with You in spirit. (1 Corinthians 6:17)

You make me stand firm in Christ and You anointed me; You are God, who also sealed me and gave me the Spirit in my heart as a deposit. (2 Corinthians 1:21–22)

We are an epistle from Christ, written not with ink, but with You, O Spirit of the living God, not on tablets of stone, but on tablets of human hearts. (2 Corinthians 3:3)

I am not competent to claim anything for myself, but my competence comes from You, God. You have made me competent as a minister of a new covenant, not of the letter, but of the Spirit; for the letter kills, but the Spirit gives life. (2 Corinthians 3:5–6)

We all—with unveiled faces beholding Your glory, O Lord, as in a mirror—are being transformed into the same image from glory to glory, which comes from You, Lord, who are the Spirit. (2 Corinthians 3:18)

You, God, who said "Let light shine out of darkness," made Your light shine in my heart to give me the light of the knowledge of Your glory, O God, in the face of Christ. But I have this treasure in an earthen vessel to show that this all-surpassing power is from You, God, and not from me. (2 Corinthians 4:6–7)

Those who are in You, O Christ, are new creations; the old things have passed away; behold, they have become new. (2 Corinthians 5:17)

You, O Christ, are not weak in dealing with us, but are powerful among us. For though You were crucified in weakness, yet You live by the power of God. For we are weak in You, yet by the power of God, we will live with You to serve others. (2 Corinthians 13:3–4)

We are all children of God through faith in You, Christ Jesus, for all of us who were baptized into You, Christ, have clothed ourselves with Christ. (Galatians 3:26–27)

Because I am a child, God, You have sent the Spirit of Your Son into my heart, crying, "Abba, Father." So I am no longer a slave, but a child; and if a child, then an heir through You, O God. (Galatians 4:6–7)

It is for freedom that You, O Christ, have set me free. I should stand firm, therefore, and not let myself be burdened again by a yoke of slavery. (Galatians 5:1)

May I never boast except in Your cross, our Lord Jesus Christ, through which the world has been crucified to me, and I to the world. (Galatians 6:14)

May You be blessed, O God and Father of our Lord Jesus Christ—You who have blessed me with every spiritual blessing in the heavenly realms in Christ. (Ephesians 1:3)

I trusted in You, O Christ, when I heard the word of truth, the gospel of my salvation. Having believed, I was sealed in You with the Holy Spirit of promise, who is a deposit guaranteeing my inheritance until the redemption of those who are God's possession—to the praise of Your glory. (Ephesians 1:13–14)

You, O God, raised me up with Christ Jesus and seated me with You in the heavenly realms in Christ Jesus, in order that, in the coming ages, You might show the surpassing riches of Your grace in kindness toward me in Christ Jesus. (Ephesians 2:6–7)

I am Your workmanship, O God, created in Christ Jesus for good works, which You prepared beforehand for me to do. (Ephesians 2:10)

I do not want to grieve You, Holy Spirit of God, with whom I was sealed for the day of redemption. (Ephesians 4:30)

It has been granted to us on behalf of You, O Christ, not only to believe in You, but also to suffer for You. (Philippians 1:29)

Whatever was gain to me I now consider loss for Your sake, O Christ. What is more, I consider all things loss compared to the surpassing greatness of knowing You as my Lord; for Your sake I suffer the loss of all things and consider them rubbish, that I may gain You and be found in You, not having a righteousness of my own that comes from the law, but that which is through faith in You—the righteousness that comes from God on the basis of faith. (Philippians 3:7–9)

I want to know You, O Christ, and the power of Your resurrection and the fellowship of Your sufferings, being conformed to Your death, that I may attain to the resurrection from the dead. (Philippians 3:10–11)

I have been made complete in You, Christ, who are the head over all rule and authority. (Colossians 2:10)

Since I have been raised with You, O Christ, I should seek the things above, where You are seated at the right hand of God. I will set my mind on the things above, not on the things on the earth, for I died, and my life is now hidden with You in God. When You who are my life appear, then I also will appear with You in glory. (Colossians 3:1–4)

I have put off the old self with its practices and have put on the new self, which is being renewed in full knowledge according to the image of You, my Creator. (Colossians 3:9–10)

I have been chosen according to Your foreknowledge, O God my Father, in sanctification of the Spirit for obedience to Jesus Christ and sprinkling of His blood; grace and peace are mine in abundance. (1 Peter 1:2)

How great is the love You, O Father, have lavished on me, that I should be called Your child, O God—and I am! Therefore the world does not know me, because it did not know You. (1 John 3:1)

I am from You, O God, and I am one who overcomes, because You who are in me are greater than he who is in the world. (1 John 4:4)

O God, You have given me eternal life, and this life is in Your Son. Those who have Your Son have life; those who do not

Having the firstfruits of Your Spirit, O Lord, I groan inwardly as I wait eagerly for my adoption, the redemption of my body. For in hope I have been saved, but hope that I can see is not hope; for who hopes for what is already there? But if I hope for what I do not yet have, I eagerly wait for it with patience. (Romans 8:23–25)

Whatever things were written in the past were written for our learning, so that through endurance and the encouragement of the Scriptures we might have hope. (Romans 15:4)

God of hope, You will fill me with all joy and peace as I trust in You, so that I may overflow with hope by the power of Your Holy Spirit. (Romans 15:13)

I will judge nothing before the time when You come O Lord,; You will bring to light what is hidden in darkness and will expose the motives of people's hearts; and then each one will receive praise from God. (1 Corinthians 4:5)

Now I see dimly, as in a mirror, but then I shall see face to face. Now I know in part, but then I shall know fully, even as I am fully known. (1 Corinthians 13:12)

Since You, O God, have made me adequate as a minister of the new covenant, I do not lose heart. (2 Corinthians 3:6, 4:1)

I will not lose heart; even though my outward self is perishing, yet my inner self is being renewed day by day. For this light affliction, which is momentary, is working for me a far more exceeding and eternal weight of glory. So I do not look at the things that are seen but at the things that are unseen. For the things that are seen are temporary, but the things that are unseen are eternal. (2 Corinthians 4:16–18)

Lord, I make it my ambition to please You whether I am at home in the body or away from it. For we must all appear before the judgment seat of Christ, that we all may receive what is due us for the things done while in the body, whether good or bad. (2 Corinthians 5:9–10)

I have not been made perfect, but I press on to lay hold of that for which You, O Christ Jesus, also laid hold of me. I do not consider myself yet to have attained it, but one thing I do: forgetting what is behind and stretching forward to what is ahead, I press on toward the goal to win the prize of the upward call of God in You, Christ Jesus. (Philippians 3:12–14)

My citizenship is in heaven; from there I also eagerly await You, my Savior, Lord Jesus Christ. You will transform my lowly body and conform it to Your glorious body by the power that enables You to subject all things to Yourself. (Philippians 3:20–21)

My faith in You, Christ Jesus, and my love for all the saints spring from the hope that is stored up for me in heaven and that I have heard about in the word of truth, the gospel. (Colossians 1:4–5)

I desire that You Yourself, O God of peace, will sanctify me completely, and that my whole spirit, soul and body will be preserved blameless at the coming of my Lord Jesus Christ. You who call me are faithful; You also will do it. (1 Thessalonians 5:23–24)

Those who are rich in this present world should not be arrogant or set their hope on the uncertainty of riches but on You, O God, who richly provides us with everything for our enjoyment. They should do good, be rich in good works, and be generous and willing to share. In this way they will lay up treasure for themselves as a firm foundation for the future, so that they may lay hold of true life. (1 Timothy 6:17–19)

You, O Lord, will deliver me from every evil work and will bring me safely to Your heavenly kingdom. To You be glory forever and ever. (2 Timothy 4:18)

My hope in You, O God, is an anchor for my soul, both sure and steadfast, and it enters the inner sanctuary behind the veil, where Jesus the forerunner has entered on my behalf, having become a high priest forever, according to the order of Melchizedek. (Hebrews 6:19–20)

By Your grace, O God, I want to live to the end in faith, knowing that I will not receive the promises on earth, but see them and welcome them from a distance; I confess that I am a stranger and a pilgrim on the earth. Instead, I long for a better country, a heavenly one. In this way, You, O God, will not be ashamed to be called my God, for You have prepared a city for me. Like Moses, I esteem reproach for the sake of Christ as of greater value than the treasures of this world, because I am looking to the reward. (Hebrews 11:13, 16, 26)

May You be blessed, O God and Father of my Lord Jesus Christ. According to Your great mercy, You have given me new birth into a living hope through the resurrection of Jesus Christ from the dead, and into an inheritance that is incorruptible and undefiled and unfading, reserved in heaven for me. (1 Peter 1:3–4)

Now I am Your child, O God, and what I shall be has not yet been revealed. I know that when You are revealed, I shall be like You, for I shall see You as You are. And those who have this hope in You purify themselves, just as You are pure. (1 John 3:2–3)

You, O God, are able to keep me from falling and to present me before Your glorious presence faultless and with great joy. (Jude 24)

THE CHARACTER
I WANT TO CULTIVATE

Godliness and Reverence

Like Noah, I want to be a righteous person, blameless among the people of my time, and one who walks with You, O God. (Genesis 6:9)

I will be careful not to forget You, O Lord my God, by failing to observe Your commandments, Your ordinances and Your statutes. (Deuteronomy 8:11)

O Lord, You reward each person for righteousness and faithfulness. (1 Samuel 26:23)

You, the God of Israel, spoke; You, the Rock of Israel said to me: "Those who rule over others in righteousness, who rule in the fear of God, are like the light of morning when the sun rises, a morning without clouds, like the tender grass springing out of the earth through the sunshine after rain." (2 Samuel 23:3–4)

Like Hezekiah, I want to do what is good and right and true before You, Lord my God, by seeking You with all my heart. (2 Chronicles 31:20–21)

You know the way that I take; when You have tested me, I shall come forth as gold. My feet have held fast to Your steps; I have kept to Your way without turning aside. (Job 23:10–11)

I know that You, O Lord, have set apart the godly for Yourself; You, O Lord, hear when I call to You. (Psalm 4:3)

Who may ascend Your hill, O Lord? Who may stand in Your holy place? Those who have clean hands and pure hearts, who have not lifted up their souls to idols or sworn by what is false. (Psalm 24:3–4)

I will teach my children to fear You, O Lord: Who are they who love life and desire many days that they may see good? They are to keep their tongues from evil and their lips from speaking guile; they are to depart from evil and do good, to seek peace and pursue it. Your eyes, O Lord, are on the righteous, and Your ears are attentive to their cry. (Psalm 34:11–15)

I will not be like those who do not make You their strength, O God, but trust in the abundance of their wealth and strengthen themselves in evil desires. (Psalm 52:7)

I will be careful to lead a blameless life. I will walk in the integrity of my heart in the midst of my house. I will set no wicked thing before my eyes. I hate the work of those who fall away; it will not cling to me. A perverse heart shall depart from me; I will not know evil. Those who slander a neighbor in secret, I will silence; I will not endure those who have haughty eyes and proud hearts. My eyes will be on the faithful in the land, that they may dwell with me; the one whose walk is blameless will minister to me. No one who practices deceit will dwell in my house; no one who speaks falsely will stand in my presence. (Psalm 101:2–7)

I have sought You with my whole heart; do not let me stray from Your commands. (Psalm 119:10)

Trouble and anguish have come upon me, but Your commands are my delight. (Psalm 119:143)

I rejoice at Your word as one who finds great spoil. I hate and abhor falsehood, but I love Your law. Great peace have they who love Your law, and nothing causes them to stumble. O Lord, I hope for Your salvation, and I follow Your commands. My soul keeps Your testimonies, for I love them greatly. I keep Your precepts and Your testimonies, for all my ways are known to You. (Psalm 119:162–163, 165–168)

Unless You, O Lord, build the house, its builders labor in vain. Unless You, O Lord, guard the city, the watchmen stay awake in vain. (Psalm 127:1)

Surely the righteous will give thanks to Your name; the upright will dwell in Your presence. (Psalm 140:13)

I will honor You, Lord, with my wealth and with the first-fruits of all my increase. (Proverbs 3:9)

My ways are before Your eyes, O Lord, and You examine all my paths. (Proverbs 5:21)

Righteousness exalts a nation, but sin is a disgrace to any people. (Proverbs 14:34)

O Lord, You are far from the wicked, but You hear the prayer of the righteous. (Proverbs 15:29)

All my ways are pure in my own eyes, but You, O Lord, weigh my motives. (Proverbs 16:2)

I will commit my works to You, O Lord, and my plans will be established. (Proverbs 16:3)

Your name, O Lord, is a strong tower; the righteous run to it and are safe. (Proverbs 18:10)

Blessed are those who always fear You, O God, but those who harden their hearts fall into trouble. (Proverbs 28:14)

If I am afraid of people, fear will trap me. But if I trust in You, O Lord, You will keep me safe. (Proverbs 29:25)

I will fear You, O God, and keep Your commandments, for this applies to every person. (Ecclesiastes 12:13)

Who among us fears You, Lord, and obeys the word of Your Servant? Let those who walk in darkness and have no light trust in Your name, O Lord, and rely upon You, their God. (Isaiah 50:10)

As one who knows righteousness, who has Your law in my heart, I will not fear the reproach of others or be terrified when they revile me. (Isaiah 51:7)

I know and see that it is evil and bitter to forsake You, Lord my God, and to have no fear of You. (Jeremiah 2:19)

Cursed is the one who trusts in people, who depends on human strength and whose heart turns away from You, O Lord. But blessed is the one who trusts in You, whose confidence is in You. (Jeremiah 17:5, 7)

I want to let justice roll down like a river, and righteousness like an ever-flowing stream. (Amos 5:24)

You have shown me what is good, O Lord; and what do You require of me but to act justly and to love mercy and to walk humbly with You, my God? (Micah 6:8)

Blessed are those who hunger and thirst for righteousness, for they shall be satisfied. (Matthew 5:6)

I will take heed not to practice my righteousness before others to be seen by them. Otherwise, I will have no reward from You, my Father in heaven. (Matthew 6:1)

I will not fear those who kill the body but cannot kill the soul, but rather, I will fear You, the One who is able to destroy both soul and body in hell. (Matthew 10:28)

I will not seek to justify myself in other people's eyes; You, O God, know my heart, and what is highly esteemed among people is detestable in Your sight. (Luke 16:15)

I will not love praise from people more than praise from You, O God. (John 12:43)

Like Barnabas, I want to be a good person, filled with You, O Holy Spirit, and with faith. (Acts 11:24)

I will not be lacking in zeal, but I will stay fervent in spirit, serving You, O Lord. (Romans 12:11)

The hour has come for me to wake up from sleep, for my salvation is nearer now than when I first believed. The night is nearly over; the day is almost here. Therefore I will cast off the works of darkness and put on the armor of light. (Romans 13:11–12)

Your kingdom, O God, is not a matter of eating and drinking, but of righteousness and peace and joy in Your Holy Spirit. (Romans 14:17)

Whatever I do, I should do all to Your glory, O God. (1 Corinthians 10:31)

I want my conscience to testify that I have conducted myself in the world in the holiness and sincerity that are from You, not in fleshly wisdom but in Your grace, O God, especially in my relationships with others. (2 Corinthians 1:12)

Since I have Your promises, O God, I will cleanse myself from all pollution of body and spirit, perfecting holiness out of reverence for You. (2 Corinthians 7:1)

I am not trying to win the approval of other people; I want to win Your approval, O God. If I were still trying to please people, I would not be a servant of Christ. (Galatians 1:10)

You, O God, are not mocked, for whatever we sow, this we will also reap. The one who sows to please the flesh will reap corruption; the one who sows to please the Spirit will, from the Spirit, reap eternal life. (Galatians 6:7–8)

I will conduct myself in a manner worthy of Your gospel, O Christ, standing firm in one spirit with other believers, with one mind striving together for the faith of the gospel. (Philippians 1:27)

I will work out my salvation with fear and trembling, for it is You, O God, who work in me to will and to act according to Your good purpose. (Philippians 2:12–13)

I will seek Your interests, Christ Jesus, and not my own. (Philippians 2:21)

Whatever I do, whether in word or in deed, I will do all in Your name, Lord Jesus, giving thanks to God the Father through You. (Colossians 3:17)

As I have been instructed how I ought to walk and to please You, O God, I want to follow Paul's exhortation in the Lord Jesus to do this more and more. (1 Thessalonians 4:1)

Physical exercise profits a little, but godliness is profitable for all things, since it holds promise for both the present life and the life to come. (1 Timothy 4:8)

I want to be an example for other believers in speech, in behavior, in love, in faith and in purity. (1 Timothy 4:12)

I will flee youthful lusts and pursue righteousness, faith, love and peace, with those who call on You, Lord, out of a pure heart. (2 Timothy 2:22)

As one who has believed in You, O God, I want to be careful to devote myself to doing what is good. These things are good and profitable for everyone. (Titus 3:8)

I will pursue peace with all people and sanctification, without which no one will see You, O Lord. (Hebrews 12:14)

If I know the good I ought to do and do not do it, to me it is sin. (James 4:17)

Since I call on You, Father, who judge everyone's work impartially, I should conduct myself in reverent fear during the time of my sojourn on earth. (1 Peter 1:17)

I should live as one who is free, not using my freedom as a cloak for evil, but as Your servant, O God. (1 Peter 2:16)

I will be diligent to add to my faith, virtue; and to virtue, knowledge; and to knowledge, self-control; and to self-control, perseverance; and to perseverance, godliness; and to godliness, brotherly kindness; and to brotherly kindness, love. For if these qualities are mine in increasing measure, they will keep me from being barren and unfruitful in the full knowledge of You, our Lord Jesus Christ. (2 Peter 1:5–8)

If I say that I have fellowship with You, O God, and yet walk in the darkness, I lie and do not practice the truth. But if I walk in the light, as You are in the light, we have fellowship with one another, and the blood of Jesus, Your Son, purifies me from all sin. (1 John 1:6–7)

My desire is to continue to walk in the truth and to take pleasure when others do the same. (3 John 3–4)

I will not imitate what is evil but what is good. The one who does good is from You, O God; the one who does evil has not seen You. (3 John 11)

Love and Compassion

I will not let love and truth leave me; I will bind them around my neck and write them on the tablet of my heart. (Proverbs 3:3)

Those who are righteous have regard for the needs of their animals, but the mercies of the wicked are cruel. (Proverbs 12:10)

Through love and truth iniquity is atoned for; by the fear of You, O Lord, one turns aside from evil. When our ways are pleasing to You, Lord, You make even our enemies live at peace with us. (Proverbs 16:6–7)

If we pursue righteousness and love, we will find life, righteousness and honor. (Proverbs 21:21)

I will sow righteousness, reap the fruit of unfailing love, and break up my fallow ground; for it is time to seek You, Lord, until You come and rain righteousness on me. (Hosea 10:12)

Show me how to love, O Lord, for if I speak in human language and the language of angels, but have not love, I am only a resounding gong or a clanging cymbal. And if I have the gift of prophecy and understand all mysteries and all knowledge, and if I have all faith so as to remove mountains, but have not love, I am nothing. And if I give all my possessions to the poor, and if I deliver my body to be burned, but have not love, it profits me nothing. (1 Corinthians 13:1–3)

The love we have from You, O Lord, is patient, it is kind, it does not envy; love does not boast, it is not arrogant, it does not behave rudely; it does not seek its own, it is not provoked, it keeps no record of wrongs; it does not rejoice in unrighteousness but rejoices with the truth; it bears all things, believes all things, hopes all things, endures all things. Love never fails. (1 Corinthians 13:4–8)

I want everything I do to be done in love. (1 Corinthians 16:14)

I want to abound in faith, in speech, in knowledge, in all diligence, in love and in the grace of giving. (2 Corinthians 8:7)

I will imitate You, O God, as Your beloved child, and I will walk in love, just as Christ loved me and gave Himself up for me as a fragrant offering and sacrifice to You. (Ephesians 5:1–2)

As one of Your chosen people, O God, holy and beloved, I will put on a heart of compassion, kindness, humility, gentleness and patience, bearing with others and forgiving others even as You, Lord, forgave me; and above all these things I will put on love, which is the bond of perfection. (Colossians 3:12–14)

The goal of the instruction of Your Word, O Lord, is love that comes from a pure heart and a good conscience and a sincere faith. (1 Timothy 1:5)

I will keep the pattern of sound teaching that I have heard, in faith and love which are in You, Christ Jesus. (2 Timothy 1:13)

I will not love with words or tongue but will strive to love in deed and in truth. By this I will know that I am of the truth and my heart will be assured before You; for if my heart condemns me, You, O God, are greater than my heart, and You know all things. If my heart does not condemn me, I have confidence before You and receive from You whatever I ask, because I keep Your commandments and do the things that are pleasing in Your sight. (1 John 3:18–22)

This is love: that I walk in obedience to Your commandments, O God. And this is the commandment that I have heard from the beginning: I should walk in love. (2 John 6)

Wisdom, Discernment and Understanding

I ask for a wise and understanding heart to discern between good and evil. (1 Kings 3:9, 12)

Lord, make me to know my end and what is the measure of my days; let me know how fleeting my life is. (Psalm 39:4)

Teach me to number my days, that I may gain a heart of wisdom. (Psalm 90:12)

If I am wise, I will consider Your lovingkindness, O Lord. (Psalm 107:43)

To fear You, Lord, is the beginning of wisdom; all who practice Your commandments have good understanding. Your praise endures forever. (Psalm 111:10)

The entrance of Your words gives light; it gives understanding to the simple. (Psalm 119:130)

Lord, You give wisdom; from Your mouth come knowledge and understanding. You store up sound wisdom for the upright; You are a shield to those who walk in integrity, guarding the paths of the just and protecting the way of Your saints. Then I will understand righteousness and justice and honesty—every good path. For wisdom will enter my heart, and knowledge will be pleasant to my soul; discretion will protect me, and understanding will guard me. (Proverbs 2:6–11)

I will preserve sound wisdom and discretion, not letting them out of my sight; they will be life to my soul. (Proverbs 3:21–22)

Wisdom is foremost; therefore I will get wisdom, and though it cost all I have, I will get understanding. I will esteem her, and she will exalt me; I will embrace her, and she will honor me. (Proverbs 4:7–8)

I will guard my heart with all diligence, for out of it flow the issues of life. (Proverbs 4:23)

Wisdom is better than jewels, and all desirable things cannot be compared with her. Wisdom dwells together with prudence and finds knowledge and discretion. (Proverbs 8:11–12)

Blessed are those who listen to wisdom, watching daily at her gates, waiting at her doorposts. For whoever finds wisdom finds life and obtains favor from the Lord. But those who fail to find her injure their own souls; all who hate her love death. (Proverbs 8:34–36)

To fear You, O Lord, is the beginning of wisdom, and to know You, O Holy One, is understanding. (Proverbs 9:10)

The fruit of the righteous is a tree of life, and those who win souls are wise. (Proverbs 11:30)

There is a way that may seem right to me, but its end is the way of death. (Proverbs 14:12)

The fear of You, O Lord, is a fountain of life to turn one away from the snares of death. (Proverbs 14:27)

If I trust in my own heart, I am foolish, but if I walk in wisdom, I will be delivered. (Proverbs 28:26)

There is a time for everything, and a season for every activity under heaven. (Ecclesiastes 3:1)

The words of the wise are like goads and like nails driven by the masters who collect them; they are given by You, the one Shepherd. (Ecclesiastes 12:11)

You are the stability of our times, a wealth of salvation, wisdom, and knowledge; to fear You, Lord, is the key to this treasure. (Isaiah 33:6)

Whoever is wise understands these things; whoever is discerning knows them. Your ways, O Lord, are right; the righteous will walk in them, but transgressors will stumble in them. (Hosea 14:9)

In my obedience, I want to be wise about what is good and innocent about what is evil. (Romans 16:19)

I will not be unequally yoked together with unbelievers. For what does righteousness share with wickedness? Or what fellowship does light have with darkness? (2 Corinthians 6:14)

Though I walk in the flesh, I do not war according to the flesh. The weapons of my warfare are not fleshly, but divinely powerful to overthrow strongholds, casting down arguments and every pretension that sets itself up against the knowledge of You, O God, and taking every thought captive to the obedience of Christ. (2 Corinthians 10:3–5)

I will watch carefully how I walk, not as unwise but as wise, making the most of every opportunity, because the days are evil. I will not be foolish, but understand what Your will is, O Lord. (Ephesians 5:15–17)

Whatever is true, whatever is noble, whatever is right, whatever is pure, whatever is lovely, whatever is of good report—if anything is excellent or praiseworthy—I will think about such things. The things I have learned and received and heard and seen in those who walk with Christ, I will practice, and You, O God of peace, will be with me. (Philippians 4:8–9)

I will see to it that no one takes me captive through deceptive philosophy, which is based on human tradition and the basic principles of this world, rather than on You, O Christ. (Colossians 2:8)

I will examine all things, hold fast to the good and abstain from every form of evil. (1 Thessalonians 5:21–22)

If I lack wisdom, I should ask You, O God, who gives generously to all without reproach, and it will be given to me. (James 1:5)

Those who are wise and understanding will show it by their good conduct and works done in the humility that comes from wisdom. If I harbor bitter envy and selfish ambition in my heart, I should not boast and lie against the truth. This wisdom does not come down from above, but is earthly, natural, demonic. For where there is envy and selfish ambition, there is disorder and every evil practice. (James 3:13–16)

The wisdom that comes from above is first pure, then peaceable, gentle, submissive, full of mercy and good fruits, without partiality and hypocrisy. And the fruit of righteousness is sown in peace by those who make peace. (James 3:17–18)

Moral Integrity and Honesty

I shall not murder. (Exodus 20:13; Deuteronomy 5:17)

I shall not commit adultery. (Exodus 20:14; Deuteronomy 5:18)

I shall not steal. (Exodus 20:15; Deuteronomy 5:19)

I will not follow the crowd in doing wrong. (Exodus 23:2)

I will not accept a bribe, for a bribe blinds those who see and perverts the words of the righteous. (Exodus 23:8)

I will not steal, nor deal falsely, nor deceive others. (Leviticus 19:11)

I will not be dishonest in judgment, in measurement of weight or quantity. I will be honest and just in my business affairs. (Leviticus 19:35–36)

I will not show partiality in judgment; I will hear both small and great alike. I will not be afraid of anyone, for judgment belongs to You, O God. (Deuteronomy 1:17)

I know, my God, that You test my heart and are pleased with integrity. (1 Chronicles 29:17)

May those who hope in You not be ashamed because of me, O Lord God of hosts.

May those who seek You not be dishonored because of me, O God of Israel. (Psalm 69:6)

Blessed am I if I maintain justice, if I do righteousness at all times. (Psalm 106:3)

I will not enter the path of the wicked or walk in the way of evil people. (Proverbs 4:14)

To fear You, O Lord, is to hate evil; wisdom hates pride and arrogance and the evil way and the perverse mouth. (Proverbs 8:13)

If I walk in integrity, I walk securely, but those who pervert their ways will be found out. (Proverbs 10:9)

If I gain wealth by dishonesty, it will dwindle, but if I gather it by labor, it will increase. (Proverbs 13:11)

Those who walk in uprightness fear You, Lord, but those who are devious in their ways despise You. (Proverbs 14:2)

The one who justifies the wicked and the one who condemns the just—both of them are detestable to You, Lord. (Proverbs 17:15)

A good name is more desirable than great riches; favor is better than silver or gold. (Proverbs 22:1)

Whoever is faithful with very little is also faithful with much, and whoever is dishonest with very little will also be dishonest with much. If I am not faithful in handling worldly wealth, who will trust me with true riches? And if I am not faithful with someone else's property, who will give me property of my own? (Luke 16:10–12)

I will walk properly as in the daytime, not in partying and drunkenness, not in sexual immorality and evil conduct, not in dissension and jealousy. Instead I will put on You, Lord

Jesus Christ, like clothing, rather than thinking about how to satisfy my fleshly lusts. (Romans 13:13–14)

I will keep Your feast, O Christ, my Passover, not with old leaven, or with the leaven of malice and wickedness, but with the unleavened bread of sincerity and truth. (1 Corinthians 5:7–8)

I do not want even a hint of immorality, or any impurity or greed in my life, as these are improper for a saint. Nor will I give myself over to obscenity, foolish talk or coarse joking which are not fitting, but rather I will give myself to thanksgiving. (Ephesians 5:3–4)

I will consider the parts of my earthly body as dead to immorality, impurity, passion, evil desires and greed, which is idolatry. Because of these, O God, Your wrath is coming. I used to walk in these ways in the life I once lived. (Colossians 3:5–7)

This is Your will, O God, that I be sanctified, that I abstain from immorality and learn to control my own body in holiness and honor. For You did not call me to be impure, but to live a holy life. (1 Thessalonians 4:3–4, 7)

I desire to have a clear conscience and to live honorably in all things. (Hebrews 13:18)

I will not say when I am tempted, "I am being tempted by God"; for You, O God, cannot be tempted by evil, nor do You tempt anyone. But we are tempted when we are drawn away and enticed by our own lust. Then, after lust has conceived, it gives birth to sin; and sin, when it is full-grown, gives birth to death. (James 1:13–15)

I have been born again, not of perishable seed, but of imperishable, through Your living and abiding word, O God. Therefore, I will put away all malice and all guile and hypocrisy and envy and all slander. (1 Peter 1:23; 2:1)

Truthfulness and Prudence

I shall not bear false witness against my neighbor. (Exodus 20:16; Deuteronomy 5:20)

I will not go about spreading slander among people, nor will I do anything that endangers the life of my neighbor. (Leviticus 19:16)

I will put away perversity from my mouth and keep corrupt talk far from my lips. (Proverbs 4:24)

The mouth of the righteous is a fountain of life, but violence covers the mouth of the wicked. (Proverbs 10:11)

In a multitude of words, transgression does not cease, but if I restrain my lips, I am wise. (Proverbs 10:19)

A talebearer reveals secrets, but the person who is trustworthy conceals a matter. (Proverbs 11:13)

I will be satisfied with good from the fruit of my mouth, and the deeds of my hands will return to me. (Proverbs 12:14)

Reckless words pierce like a sword, but the tongue of the wise brings healing. (Proverbs 12:18)

Lying lips are hateful to You, Lord, but You delight in those who deal faithfully. (Proverbs 12:22)

A gentle answer turns away wrath, but a harsh word stirs up anger. The tongue of the wise uses knowledge rightly, but the mouth of the fool pours out folly. (Proverbs 15:1–2)

The tongue that brings healing is a tree of life, but perverseness in it crushes the spirit. (Proverbs 15:4)

Joy is found in giving an apt reply—and how good is a timely word! (Proverbs 15:23)

Fools have no delight in understanding but only in airing their own opinions. (Proverbs 18:2)

The words of a gossip are like choice morsels; they go down into the innermost parts of the body. (Proverbs 18:8)

The one who answers a matter before listening is foolish and shameful. (Proverbs 18:13)

Faithful are the wounds of a friend, but the kisses of an enemy are deceitful. (Proverbs 27:6)

These are the things I shall do: speak the truth to others, and judge with truth and justice for peace. I shall not plot evil against my neighbor, nor love a false oath, for these things You hate, O Lord. (Zechariah 8:16–17)

I will not let any corrupt word come out of my mouth, but only what is helpful for building others up according to their needs, that it may impart grace to those who hear. (Ephesians 4:29)

I will put away all of these things: anger, wrath, malice, slander and abusive language from my mouth. (Colossians 3:8)

I should be quick to hear, slow to speak, and slow to anger, for human anger does not produce Your righteousness, O God. (James 1:19–20)

The tongue is a small part of the body, but it makes great boasts. I will consider what a great forest is set on fire by a small spark. The tongue also is a fire, a world of evil that is set among the parts of the body, that corrupts the whole body, and sets the whole course of our life on fire and is set on fire by hell. (James 3:5–6)

People have tamed all kinds of animals, birds, reptiles, and creatures of the sea and they are still being tamed, but no one can tame the tongue. It is a restless evil, full of deadly poison. With the tongue we praise You, our Lord and Father, and with it we curse the ones who have been made in Your likeness, O God; out of the same mouth come blessing and cursing, and this should not be. (James 3:7–10)

Humility

When I am blessed with abundance, I will beware lest my heart become proud, and I forget You, O Lord my God, who provide all good things—lest I think that it was my power and the strength of my hand that brought this wealth. (Deuteronomy 8:12–14, 17)

When pride comes, then comes dishonor, but with humility comes wisdom. (Proverbs 11:2)

To fear You, Lord, is instruction for wisdom, and humility comes before honor. (Proverbs 15:33)

It is better to be of a humble spirit with the lowly than to divide the spoil with the proud. (Proverbs 16:19)

Before my downfall my heart is haughty, but humility comes before honor. (Proverbs 18:12)

Haughty eyes and a proud heart, the lamp of the wicked, are sin. (Proverbs 21:4)

Humility and the fear of You, O Lord, bring wealth and honor and life. (Proverbs 22:4)

I will not boast about tomorrow, for I do not know what that day may bring. (Proverbs 27:1)

I will let another praise me, and not my own mouth; a stranger, and not my own lips. (Proverbs 27:2)

If I am proud, it will bring me low, but if I am humble of spirit, I will gain honor. (Proverbs 29:23)

The proud will be humbled and the lofty will be brought low; You alone, O Lord, will be exalted. (Isaiah 2:11)

The one You esteem is humble and contrite of spirit and trembles at Your word. (Isaiah 66:2)

Should I seek great things for myself? I will seek them not. (Jeremiah 45:5)

You have called the humble of the earth, who have upheld Your justice, to seek You, Lord, to seek righteousness and to seek humility. (Zephaniah 2:3)

Blessed are the poor in spirit, for theirs is the kingdom of heaven. Blessed are those who mourn, for they will be comforted. Blessed are the meek, for they will inherit the earth. (Matthew 5:3–5)

I will not trust in myself or in my own righteousness, nor will I view others with contempt. (Luke 18:9)

I will be of the same mind with others; I will not be haughty in mind or wise in my own estimation, but I will associate with the humble. (Romans 12:16)

Who makes me different from anyone else? And what do I have that I did not receive? And if I did receive it, why should I boast as though I had not received it? (1 Corinthians 4:7)

I do not dare to classify or compare myself with other people, for it is unwise to measure or compare myself with others. I will not boast beyond proper limits but within the sphere of the gospel of Christ. "Let those who boast boast in the Lord." For it is not those who commend themselves who are approved, but the ones whom You, Lord, commend. (2 Corinthians 10:12–14, 17–18)

If I think I am something when I am nothing, I deceive myself. (Galatians 6:3)

I want to walk in a way that is worthy of the calling with which I was called, with all humility and meekness and patience. (Ephesians 4:1–2)

I should let my gentleness be evident to all people; O Lord, You are near. (Philippians 4:5)

I will submit myself to You, O God, and resist the devil, and he will flee from me. I will humble myself before You, O Lord, and You will exalt me. (James 4:7, 10)

I should not say, "Today or tomorrow I will go to this or that city, spend a year there, carry on business, and make a profit." For I do not even know what my life will be tomorrow. I am a vapor that appears for a little while and then vanishes away. Instead I ought to say, "If the Lord wills, I will live and do this or that." Otherwise, I boast in my arrogance, and all such boasting is evil. (James 4:13–16)

I will humble myself under Your mighty hand, O God, that You may exalt me in due time; I will cast all my anxiety upon You, because You care for me. (1 Peter 5:6–7)

Teachability

Before I was afflicted, I went astray, O Lord, but now I keep Your word. It was good for me to be afflicted, so that I might learn Your statutes. (Psalm 119:67, 71)

Your commandment is a lamp, O Lord; Your teaching is a light, and Your reproofs of discipline are the way to life. (Proverbs 6:23)

If I heed instruction, I am on the path of life, but if I refuse correction, I will go astray. (Proverbs 10:17)

If I listen to a life-giving rebuke, I will be at home among the wise. If I refuse instruction, I despise myself, but if I heed correction, I will gain understanding. (Proverbs 15:31–32)

If I heed the word, I will prosper, and I will be blessed if I trust in You, O Lord. (Proverbs 16:20)

I will listen to counsel and accept instruction, that I may be wise in my latter days. (Proverbs 19:20)

All Scripture is God-breathed and is useful for teaching, for reproof, for correction and for training in righteousness, that we, Your people, may be thoroughly equipped for every good work. (2 Timothy 3:16–17)

I will not despise Your discipline, O Lord, nor lose heart when You rebuke me, for whom You love You discipline, and You chastise every child whom You receive. (Hebrews 12:5–6)

I will endure discipline, for You, O God, are treating me as Your child. For what child is not disciplined by its father? If I am without discipline (and we all undergo discipline), then I am an illegitimate child and not a true child. Moreover, we have all had human fathers who disciplined us, and we respected them; how much more should I be disciplined by You, the Father of my spirit, and live? (Hebrews 12:7–9)

Contentment, Single-mindedness and Peace

I shall not covet my neighbor's house, my neighbor's wife, his manservant or maidservant, his ox or donkey, or anything that belongs to my neighbor. (Exodus 20:17; Deuteronomy 5:21)

This is the day that You, O Lord, have made; I will rejoice and be glad in it. (Psalm 118:24)

A heart at peace gives life to the body, but envy is rottenness to the bones. (Proverbs 14:30)

Better a little with the fear of You, O Lord, than great wealth with turmoil. (Proverbs 15:16)

Better is a little with righteousness than great income with injustice. (Proverbs 16:8)

I will have the understanding to cease. I will not set my desire on what flies away, for wealth surely sprouts wings and flies into the heavens like an eagle. (Proverbs 23:4–5)

I will eat and drink and see good in all my labor—it is Your gift, O God. (Ecclesiastes 3:13)

Blessed are the pure in heart, for they shall see You, O God. Blessed are the peacemakers, for they shall be called Your children, O God. (Matthew 5:8–9)

I will not lay up for myself treasures on earth, where moth and rust destroy and where thieves break in and steal. But I will lay up for myself treasures in heaven, where moth and rust do not destroy and where thieves do not break in and steal. For where my treasure is, there my heart will be also. (Matthew 6:19–21; Luke 12:34)

I cannot serve two masters; for either I will hate the one and love the other, or I will be devoted to the one and despise the other. I cannot serve You, God, and wealth. (Matthew 6:24; Luke 16:13)

I will not worry about my life, what I will eat or what I will drink; or about my body, what I will wear. Life is more than food, and the body more than clothes. The birds of the air do not sow or reap or gather into barns, and yet You, my heavenly Father, feed them. Am I not much more valuable than they? Can I add a single hour to my life by worrying? And why do I worry about clothes? I will consider how the lilies of the field grow; they neither labor nor spin, yet not even Solomon in all his splendor was dressed like one of these. But if You, O God, so clothe the grass of the field, which is here today and tomorrow is thrown into the fire, will You not much more clothe me? So I will not worry, saying, "What shall I eat?" or "What shall I drink?" or "What shall I wear?" For the pagans run after all these things, and You, my heavenly

Father, know that I need them. But I will seek first Your kingdom and Your righteousness, and all these things will be added to me. (Matthew 6:25–33; Luke 12:22–31)

I will not worry about tomorrow, for tomorrow will worry about itself. Each day has enough trouble of its own. (Matthew 6:34)

I do not want to be worried and troubled about many things; only one thing is needed. Like Mary, I want to choose what is better, that which will not be taken away from me. (Luke 10:41–42)

I will be on my guard against all covetousness, for my life does not consist in the abundance of my possessions. (Luke 12:15)

I do not want to lay up treasure for myself without being rich toward You, O God. (Luke 12:21)

I will be anxious for nothing, but in everything, by prayer and petition with thanksgiving, I will let my requests be known to You, O God. And Your peace, O God, which transcends all understanding, will guard my heart and my mind in Christ Jesus. (Philippians 4:6–7)

I want to learn to be content in whatever circumstances I am. Whether I am abased or in abundance, whether I am filled or hungry, I want to learn the secret of being content in any and every situation. I can do all things through You who strengthen me. (Philippians 4:11–13)

I will let Your peace, O Christ, to which I was called as a member of one body, rule in my heart, and I will be thankful. (Colossians 3:15)

Godliness with contentment is great gain. For I brought nothing into the world, and I can take nothing out of it. But if I have food and clothing, with these I will be content. (1 Timothy 6:6–8)

I will keep my life free from the love of money and be content with what I have, for You have said, "I will never leave you, nor will I forsake you." (Hebrews 13:5)

I want to be a person of faith, who does not doubt Your promises, O God, and not one who is double-minded and unstable in my ways. (James 1:6, 8)

I know that friendship with the world is enmity toward You, God. Those who want to be friends of the world makes themselves Your enemies, O God. (James 4:4)

I will not love the world or the things in the world. If I love the world, Your love, O Father, is not in me. For all that is in the world—the lust of the flesh, the lust of the eyes and the pride of life—is not of You, Father, but of the world. And the world and its lusts are passing away, but the one who does Your will, O God, abides forever. (1 John 2:15–17)

Discipline and Self-control

Like Ezra, I want to set my heart to study Your word, O Lord, and to do it, and to teach it to others. (Ezra 7:10)

How can young people keep their way pure? By keeping it according to Your word. (Psalm 119:9)

I have hidden Your word in my heart that I might not sin against You. (Psalm 119:11)

O Lord, You are my portion; I have promised to keep Your words. I considered my ways and turned my steps to Your testimonies. (Psalm 119:57, 59)

I have kept my feet from every evil path that I might keep Your word. I gain understanding from Your precepts; therefore I hate every false way. (Psalm 119:101, 104)

Your word is a lamp to my feet and a light to my path. I have inclined my heart to perform Your statutes to the very end. (Psalm 119:105, 112)

The wise fear and depart from evil, but fools are arrogant and bold. Those who are quick-tempered act foolishly, and those who plot evil are hated. (Proverbs 14:16–17)

A hot-tempered person stirs up dissension, but the one who is slow to anger calms a quarrel. (Proverbs 15:18)

Laziness casts one into a deep sleep, and an idle person will be hungry. (Proverbs 19:15)

I will not be quickly provoked in my spirit, for anger rests in the bosom of fools. (Ecclesiastes 7:9)

In my anger I will not sin; I will not let the sun go down while I am still angry, and I will not give the devil a foothold. (Ephesians 4:26–27)

I will devote myself to prayer, being watchful in it with thanksgiving. (Colossians 4:2)

I will make it my ambition to lead a quiet life, to mind my own business, and to work with my own hands, so that my walk will win the respect of those who are outside and I will lack nothing. (1 Thessalonians 4:11–12)

We are all children of the light and children of the day. We do not belong to the night or to the darkness. So then, let us not be like others who are asleep, but let us be alert and self-controlled. (1 Thessalonians 5:5–6)

Since I belong to the day, I will be self-controlled, putting on faith and love as a breastplate and the hope of salvation as a helmet. (1 Thessalonians 5:8)

I want to be above reproach, temperate, sensible, respectable, hospitable, able to teach, not given to drunkenness, not violent but gentle, not quarrelsome, not a lover of money. I want to manage my family well and keep my children under control with proper respect. And I want a good reputation with outsiders, so that I will not fall into disgrace and the snare of the devil. (1 Timothy 3:2–4, 7)

I want to be worthy of respect, not double-tongued, not addicted to wine, not fond of dishonest gain, but holding the mystery of the faith with a clear conscience. (1 Timothy 3:8–9)

I will not neglect my spiritual gifts. (1 Timothy 4:14)

You, O God, have not given me a spirit of timidity, but a spirit of power, of love and of self-control. (2 Timothy 1:7)

O God, I will be diligent to present myself to You as one approved, a worker who does not need to be ashamed and who correctly handles the word of truth. (2 Timothy 2:15)

Your grace, O God, has appeared, bringing salvation to all people, teaching us to deny ungodliness and worldly passions and to live sensibly, righteously, and godly in the present age. (Titus 2:11–12)

I will prepare my mind for action and be self-controlled, setting my hope fully on the grace to be given to me at Your revelation, Christ Jesus. (1 Peter 1:13)

The end of all things is near; therefore I will be clear minded and self-controlled for prayer. (1 Peter 4:7)

I will be self-controlled and alert; my adversary the devil prowls around like a roaring lion looking for someone to devour. But I will resist him, standing firm in the faith, knowing that my brothers and sisters throughout the world are undergoing the same kind of sufferings. (1 Peter 5:8–9)

Courage and Perseverance

I will be strong and courageous, being careful to obey Your word, O Lord; I will not turn from it to the right or to the left, that I may act wisely wherever I go. (Joshua 1:7)

I will be strong and courageous; I will not be afraid or discouraged, for You, Lord my God, will be with me wherever I go. (Joshua 1:9)

I will be strong and courageous and act. I will not be afraid or discouraged, for You, Lord God, are with me. You will not fail me or forsake me. (1 Chronicles 28:20)

I will not be afraid of my adversaries, but I will remember You, Lord, who are great and awesome. (Nehemiah 4:14)

I will take courage and not be afraid, for You, Lord Jesus, are with me. (Mark 6:50)

I will rejoice in hope, persevere in affliction and continue steadfastly in prayer. (Romans 12:12)

Thanks be to You, O God, the One who gives me the victory through our Lord Jesus Christ. Therefore I will be steadfast, immovable, abounding in Your work, Lord, knowing that my labor in You is not in vain. (1 Corinthians 15:57–58)

I will be on my guard, stand firm in the faith, act with courage, and be strong. (1 Corinthians 16:13)

I am hard pressed on every side, but not crushed; perplexed, but not in despair; persecuted, but not forsaken; struck down, but not destroyed; always carrying about in my body Your death, O Jesus, so that Your life may also be revealed in my body. For we who live are always being delivered over to death for Your sake, Jesus, so that Your life may be revealed in our mortal bodies. (2 Corinthians 4:8–11)

I will not become weary in doing good, for at the proper time I will reap a harvest if I do not give up. (Galatians 6:9)

I ask You, Lord, to establish my heart as blameless and holy before our God and Father at Your coming, our Lord Jesus, with all Your saints. (1 Thessalonians 3:13)

May You Yourself, our Lord Jesus Christ, and God our Father, who have loved us and have given us eternal consolation and good hope by grace, comfort our hearts and strengthen us in every good work and word. (2 Thessalonians 2:16–17)

I do not want to grow weary in doing what is right. (2 Thessalonians 3:13)

I will fight the good fight of faith and lay hold of the eternal life to which I was called when I made the good confession in the presence of many witnesses. In Your sight, O God, who gives life to all things, and in the sight of Christ Jesus, who testified the good confession before Pontius Pilate, I want to keep this command without blemish or reproach until the appearing of our Lord Jesus Christ, which You will bring about in Your own time. (1 Timothy 6:12–15)

I will be self-controlled in all things, endure hardship, do the work of an evangelist and fulfill my ministry. (2 Timothy 4:5)

I will fight the good fight, finish the race, and keep the faith, so that there will be laid up for me the crown of righteousness, which You, Lord, the righteous Judge, will award to me on that day; and not only to me, but also to all who have longed for Your appearing. (2 Timothy 4:7–8)

Since I have a great cloud of witnesses surrounding me, I want to lay aside every impediment and the sin that so easily entangles, and run with endurance the race that is set

before me, fixing my eyes on You, Jesus, the author and perfecter of my faith, who for the joy set before You endured
the cross, despising the shame, and sat down at the right
hand of the throne of God. I will consider You who endured
such hostility from sinners, so that I will not grow weary and
lose heart. (Hebrews 12:1–3)

I will consider it all joy whenever I fall into various trials,
knowing that the testing of my faith produces endurance.
And I will let endurance finish its work, so that I may be
mature and complete, lacking in nothing. (James 1:2–4)

I will be blessed if I persevere under trial, because when I
have been approved, I will receive the crown of life that You,
O God, have promised to those who love You. (James 1:12)

I greatly rejoice in my salvation, though now for a little
while, if necessary, I have been grieved by various trials, so
that my faith, being much more precious than gold, that perishes even though refined by fire, may be proved genuine
and may result in praise, glory and honor when You, O Jesus
Christ, are revealed. (1 Peter 1:6–7)

Who is going to harm me if I am eager to do good? But even
if I should suffer for what is right, I am blessed, and I will
not fear what they fear or be intimidated. (1 Peter 3:13–14)

Since Your day, O Lord, will come like a thief, what kind of
person should I be in conduct and life as I look forward to the
coming of Your day? According to Your promise, I am looking for a new heaven and a new earth, in which righteousness
dwells. Therefore, since I am looking for these things, I will be
diligent so that You find me in peace—spotless and blameless, living a holy and godly life. (2 Peter 3:10–14)

I will abide in You, O Christ, so that when You appear, I
may have confidence and not be ashamed before You at Your
coming. (1 John 2:28)

Being built up in the most holy faith and praying in the Holy Spirit, I want to keep myself in Your love, O God, as I wait for the mercy of our Lord Jesus Christ to bring me to eternal life. (Jude 20–21)

MY RELATIONSHIP
TO OTHERS

Love and Acceptance

I will not hate my brother or sister in my heart. (Leviticus 19:17)

I will not take vengeance or bear a grudge against others, but I will love my neighbor as myself. (Leviticus 19:18)

If we erase a sin by forgiving it, we show love. But if we repeat the matter, we come between close friends. (Proverbs 17:9)

If I forgive others for their transgressions, You, my heavenly Father, will also forgive me. (Matthew 6:14)

I will not judge, so that I will not be judged. For in the same way I judge others, I will be judged; and with the measure I use, it will be measured to me. (Matthew 7:1–2)

I shall seek to keep Your commandments, O God: "You shall love the Lord your God with all your heart and with all your soul and with all your mind." This is the first and greatest commandment. And the second is like it: "You shall love your neighbor as yourself." All the Law and the Prophets hang on these two commandments. (Matthew 22:37–40)

I will love my enemies, do good to those who hate me, bless those who curse me, and pray for those who mistreat me. I will do to others as I would have them do to me. (Luke 6:27–28, 31)

I will love my enemies, do good to them and lend to them, expecting nothing in return. Then my reward will be great, and I will be Your child, O Most High; for You are kind to the ungrateful and evil. I will be merciful just as You, Father, are merciful. (Luke 6:35–36)

If I do not judge, I will not be judged; if I do not condemn, I will not be condemned; if I forgive, I will be forgiven. (Luke 6:37)

O Lord, You have given us a new commandment: to love one another even as You have loved us, so we must love one another. By this all people will know that we are Your disciples, if we have love for one another. (John 13:34)

My love must be sincere. I will hate what is evil and cling to what is good. (Romans 12:9)

We must be devoted to one another in love, honoring one another above ourselves. (Romans 12:10)

I will bless those who persecute me; I will bless and not curse. (Romans 12:14)

I will rejoice with those who rejoice and weep with those who weep. (Romans 12:15)

I will accept those whose faith is weak, without passing judgment on their opinions. Who am I to judge another's servant? Whether or not they stand or fall is their master's concern, and they will stand, for You, Lord, are able to make them stand. (Romans 14:1, 4)

I will not judge my brothers and sisters or regard them with contempt. Instead of judging them, I will resolve not to put a stumbling block or obstacle in their way. (Romans 14:10, 13)

I will accept others just as You, O Jesus Christ, accepted me to the glory of God. (Romans 15:7)

I was called to freedom, but I will not use my freedom to indulge the flesh but through love I will serve others. For the whole law is summed up in this word: "You shall love your neighbor as yourself." (Galatians 5:13–14)

I will put away all bitterness and anger and wrath and shouting and slander, along with all malice. And I will be kind and compassionate to others, forgiving them just as You, O God, in Christ also forgave me. (Ephesians 4:31–32)

I will bear with others and forgive whatever complaints I have against them; I will forgive just as You, O Lord, forgave me. (Colossians 3:13)

I ask that You, O Lord, make me increase and abound in my love for believers and for unbelievers. (1 Thessalonians 3:12)

Concerning our love for our brothers and sisters: You have taught us, O God, to love each other, and You, Lord, urge us to increase our love more and more. (1 Thessalonians 4:9–10)

We must continue to love as brothers and sisters. (Hebrews 13:1)

I will not slander other believers. Anyone who slanders his brother or sister or judges them slanders the law and judges the law. When I judge the law, I am not a doer of the law, but a judge. You are the only Lawgiver and Judge, the One who is able to save and to destroy. Who am I to judge my neighbor? (James 4:11–12)

Above all, I will have a fervent love for others, because love covers a multitude of sins. (1 Peter 4:8)

This is the message we heard from the beginning: that we should love one another. We know that we have passed out of death into life, because we love our brothers and sisters. The one who does not love abides in death. By this we know love, that You, O Christ, laid down Your life for us, and we ought to lay down our lives for our brothers and sisters. (1 John 3:11, 14, 16)

We should love one another, for love is from You, O God, and everyone who loves has been born of You, and knows You. Whoever does not love does not know You, for You, O God, are love. (1 John 4:7–8)

In this is love, not that we loved You, God, but that You loved us and sent Your Son to be the propitiation for our sins. Since You, O God, so loved us, we also ought to love one another. No one has ever seen You, O God; but if we love one another, You, O God, abide in us, and Your love is perfected in us. (1 John 4:10–12)

Giving and Serving

I will give generously to others without a grudging heart. (Deuteronomy 15:10)

I will not withhold good from those to whom it is due, when it is within my power to act. (Proverbs 3:27)

If I am generous, I will prosper; if I water others, I will myself be refreshed. (Proverbs 11:25)

If we oppress the poor, we reproach You, our Maker, but if we are kind to the needy, we honor You. (Proverbs 14:31)

Those who are generous will be blessed, for they share their food with the poor. (Proverbs 22:9)

I will learn to do good, seek justice, remove the oppressor, defend the orphan and plead for the widow. (Isaiah 1:17)

Is this not the fast You have chosen: to loose the bonds of wickedness, to undo the cords of the yoke, and to let the oppressed go free and break every yoke? Is it not to share our food with the hungry and to provide the poor wanderer with shelter; when we see the naked, to clothe them, and not to turn away from our own flesh? Then our light will break forth like the dawn, and our healing will quickly appear, and our righteousness will go before us; Your glory, O Lord, will be our rear guard. Then we will call, and You will answer; we will cry, and You will say, "Here I am." If we put away the yoke from our midst, the pointing of the finger and malicious talk, and if we extend our souls to the hungry and satisfy the afflicted soul, then our light will rise in the darkness, and our gloom will become like the noonday. (Isaiah 58:6–10)

If I give another a cup of water to drink in Your name as Your follower, O Christ, I will by no means lose my reward. (Mark 9:41)

When I give, it will be given to me; good measure, pressed down, shaken together, running over, will be poured into my lap. For with the measure I use, it will be measured back to me. (Luke 6:38)

If I invite the poor, the crippled, the lame and the blind when I give a reception, I will be blessed, because they cannot repay me; I will be repaid at the resurrection of the righteous. (Luke 14:13–14)

I will contribute to the needs of the saints and practice hospitality. (Romans 12:13)

Those who sow sparingly will also reap sparingly, and those who sow bountifully will also reap bountifully. We should give as we have decided in our hearts, not reluctantly or under compulsion; for You, O God, love a cheerful giver. And You are able to make all grace abound to us, so that always having all sufficiency in everything, we may abound in every good work. As it is written: "He has scattered abroad His gifts to the poor; His righteousness endures forever." Now You, the One who supplies seed to the sower and bread for food, will also supply and increase our seed and will increase the fruits of our righteousness. (2 Corinthians 9:6–10)

Because of our ministry of supplying the needs of the saints, they will glorify You, O God, for the obedience that accompanies our confession of the gospel of Christ, and for our liberality of sharing with them and with everyone else. (2 Corinthians 9:13)

I will not forget to show hospitality to strangers, for by so doing some have entertained angels without knowing it. (Hebrews 13:2)

I will remember those in prison as though bound with them, and those who are mistreated, since I myself am also in the body. (Hebrews 13:3)

This is pure and undefiled religion before You, my God and Father: to visit orphans and widows in their affliction and to keep oneself unspotted by the world. (James 1:27)

As each of us has received a gift, we should use it to serve others, as good stewards of Your manifold grace, O God. (1 Peter 4:10)

General Affirmations

I will not defraud my neighbors or rob them. (Leviticus 19:13)

I will do no injustice in judgment, nor show partiality to the poor or favoritism to the great, but I will judge my neighbor fairly. (Leviticus 19:15)

I will not hate my brother or sister in my heart, but I will reprove my neighbors frankly and not incur sin because of them. (Leviticus 19:17)

I will not mistreat my neighbors, but I will fear You, God; for You are the Lord my God. (Leviticus 25:17)

I will trust in You enough to honor You, O Lord, as holy in the sight of others. (Numbers 20:12)

Far be it from me that I should sin against You, Lord, by ceasing to pray for others. (1 Samuel 12:23)

I will not plan evil against my neighbors, since they live trustfully by me. (Proverbs 3:29)

I will not bring charges against others without cause, if they have done me no harm. (Proverbs 3:30)

I will stay away from foolish people, for I will not find knowledge on their lips. (Proverbs 14:7)

Starting a quarrel is like breaching a dam, so I will stop a quarrel before it breaks out. (Proverbs 17:14)

I will not make friends with hot-tempered people or associate with those easily angered, lest I learn their ways and set a snare for my soul. (Proverbs 22:24–25)

I will not repay anyone evil for evil, but I will seek to do what is right in the sight of all. (Romans 12:17)

If it is possible, I will live at peace with all people, as far as it depends on me. (Romans 12:18)

I will not take revenge but leave room for Your wrath, O God, for You have said: "Vengeance is Mine; I will repay." I will not be overcome by evil, but overcome evil with good. (Romans 12:19, 21)

I will give to all what they are due: taxes to whom taxes are due, custom to whom custom, respect to whom respect, honor to whom honor. (Romans 13:7)

O God, You comfort us in all our afflictions, so that we can comfort those in any affliction with the comfort we ourselves have received from You, O God. (2 Corinthians 1:4)

I will not give cause for offense in anything, so that my ministry will not be discredited. (2 Corinthians 6:3)

I will not become conceited, provoking others and envying others. (Galatians 5:26)

May I obey those who are in authority over me with fear and trembling and with sincerity of heart, as I would obey Christ, not with external service as one who wants to please people, but as a slave of Christ, doing Your will, O God, from my heart. With good will may I serve as if I were serving you, O Lord, and not people, knowing that I will receive back from You whatever good I do. (Ephesians 6:5–8)

I will treat subordinates with respect, not threatening them, knowing that You, O Lord, are both their Master and mine and that You are in heaven, and there is no partiality with You. (Ephesians 6:9)

I will do all things without complaining or arguing, so that I may become blameless and pure—Your child, O God, without fault in the midst of a crooked and perverse generation, among whom I shine as a light in the world, holding out the word of life. (Philippians 2:14–16)

I will obey those who are in authority over me in all things, not with external service, as one who pleases people, but with a sincere heart, fearing You, Lord. Whatever I do, I will work at it with all my heart, as working for You, and not for people, knowing that I will receive the reward of the inheritance from You. It is You I am serving, Lord Jesus Christ. (Colossians 3:22–24)

I will provide my subordinates with what is just and fair, knowing that I also have a master—You, my Master in heaven. (Colossians 4:1)

I will not repay evil for evil to anyone, but I will pursue what is good for others. (1 Thessalonians 5:15)

I am to provide for my own, and especially for my family, so I do not deny the faith and become worse than an unbeliever. (1 Timothy 5:8)

I will avoid foolish and ignorant disputes, knowing that they produce quarrels. As Your servant, Lord, I must not quarrel but be gentle toward all, able to teach and patient. (2 Timothy 2:23–24)

I will hold firmly to the faithful word as I have been taught, so that I can exhort others by sound doctrine and refute those who oppose it. (Titus 1:9)

I will remind others to be subject to rulers and authorities, to be obedient, to be ready for every good work, to slander no one, to be peaceable and gentle, and to show true humility toward all men. (Titus 3:1–2)

I will submit myself for Your sake, O Lord, to every human authority, whether to a king as being supreme, or to governors sent by him to punish evildoers and to praise those who do right; for it is Your will, O God, that by doing good I may silence the ignorance of the foolish. (1 Peter 2:13–15)

I will honor all people, love the community of believers, fear You, O God, and honor the king. (1 Peter 2:17)

I will not return evil for evil or insult for insult, but blessing instead, because to this I was called, that I may inherit a blessing. (1 Peter 3:9)

Husband or Wife

A virtuous wife is the crown of her husband, but she who causes shame is like decay in his bones. (Proverbs 12:4)

Houses and wealth are inherited from fathers, but a prudent wife is from You, Lord. (Proverbs 19:14)

Who can find a virtuous wife? She is worth far more than jewels. The heart of her husband trusts in her so that he has no lack of gain. She brings him good, not harm, all the days of her life. (Proverbs 31:10–12)

Love is as strong as death; its jealousy is as cruel as the grave; its flames are a blazing fire from You, O Lord. Many waters cannot quench love, nor can rivers overflow it. If a man were to give all the wealth of his house for love, it would be utterly scorned. (Song of Songs 8:6–7)

A husband should not break his promises to the wife of his youth, because she is a companion and a wife by covenant. Lord God of hosts, You seek a godly offspring and hate divorce; therefore we must take heed to our spirit and not break faith. (Malachi 2:14–16)

From the beginning of creation You made us male and female. For this reason a man shall leave his father and mother and shall cleave to his wife, and the two shall become one flesh. So they are no longer two, but one flesh. Therefore what You have joined together, let no one separate. (Matthew 19:4–6; Mark 10:6–9)

The husband should fulfill his marital duty to his wife, and likewise the wife to her husband. The wife's body does not belong to her alone, but also to her husband. In the same way, the husband's body does not belong to him alone, but also to his wife. (1 Corinthians 7:3–4)

Wives should submit to their own husbands as to You, O Lord. For the husband is the head of the wife, as You, O Christ, are the head of the church; and You are the Savior of the body. But as the church is subject to You, so wives should be to their husbands in everything. (Ephesians 5:22–24)

Each husband must love his own wife as he loves himself, and each wife must respect her husband. (Ephesians 5:33)

Wives should submit to their husbands, as is fitting in You, O Lord. (Colossians 3:18)

Husbands should love their wives and not be bitter toward them. (Colossians 3:19)

Marriage should be honored by all, and the marriage bed should be undefiled; for You, O God, will judge fornicators and adulterers. (Hebrews 13:4)

Husbands should be considerate as they live with their wives and treat them with respect as the weaker vessel and as co-heirs of the grace of life. (1 Peter 3:7)

Children

Like Abraham, I should direct my children and my household after me to keep Your way, O Lord, by doing what is right and just. (Genesis 18:19)

I will learn to fear You all the days I live on the earth and teach Your words to my children. (Deuteronomy 4:10)

Your commandments will be upon my heart, and I will teach them diligently to my children and talk about them when I sit in my house and when I walk along the way and when I lie down and when I rise up. (Deuteronomy 6:6–7)

I will lay up Your words in my heart and in my soul and teach them to my children, talking about them when I sit in my house and when I walk along the way and when I lie down and when I rise up. (Deuteronomy 11:18–19)

I will discipline my children while there is hope and not be a willing party to their death. (Proverbs 19:18)

I will train up my children in the way they should go; even when they are old they will not depart from it. (Proverbs 22:6)

If I correct my children, they will give me rest; they will bring delight to my soul. (Proverbs 29:17)

I will not provoke my children to wrath but bring them up in Your discipline and instruction, O Lord. (Ephesians 6:4)

I will not provoke my children, or they will become discouraged. (Colossians 3:21)

Believers

How good and pleasant it is when brothers and sisters live together in unity! (Psalm 133:1)

Lord Jesus, You prayed these words for the unity of all who would believe in You: "I ask that all of them may be one, Father, just as You are in Me and I am in You, that they also may be in Us, that the world may believe that You sent Me. And the glory which You gave Me I have given to them, that they may be one, just as We are one: I in them, and You in Me, that they may be perfected in one, that the world may know that You have sent Me and have loved them, even as You have loved Me." (John 17:21–23)

Lord, may we imitate the faithfulness of the believers in Jerusalem, who continually devoted themselves to the apostles' teaching and to fellowship, to the breaking of bread and to prayer. (Acts 2:42)

I want to speak words of encouragement to other believers. (Acts 20:2)

We must take heed to ourselves and to all the flock of which the Holy Spirit has made us overseers to shepherd Your church, O God, which You purchased with Your own blood. (Acts 20:28)

We have many members in one body, but all the members do not have the same function; in the same way we who are many are one body in You, O Jesus Christ, and individually members of one another. And we have different gifts, according to the grace You have given to us. (Romans 12:4–6)

I will pursue the things that lead to peace and to mutual edification. (Romans 14:19)

O God, You are the One who gives endurance and encouragement; grant that we be of the same mind toward one another, according to Christ Jesus, so that with one accord and one mouth we may glorify You, the God and Father of our Lord Jesus Christ. (Romans 15:5–6)

Since we were called into fellowship with You, Lord Jesus Christ, all of us should agree with one another, so that there may be no divisions among us, and that we may be perfectly joined together in the same mind and in the same judgment. (1 Corinthians 1:9–10)

I will be careful not to let my liberty in You, O Christ, become a stumbling block to the weak. (1 Corinthians 8:9)

If someone is caught in a trespass, we who are spiritual should restore him in a spirit of gentleness, watching ourselves, lest we also be tempted. (Galatians 6:1)

We should bear one another's burdens and so fulfill Your law, O Christ. (Galatians 6:2)

As we have opportunity, we should do good to all people, especially to those who belong to the family of faith. (Galatians 6:10)

In You, Christ Jesus, God's whole building is joined together and growing into a holy temple in You, Lord, in whom we also are being built together into a dwelling of God in the Spirit. (Ephesians 2:21–22)

We should bear with one another in love and make every effort to keep the unity of Your Spirit in the bond of peace. (Ephesians 4:2–3)

Grace has been given to each one of us according to the measure of Your gift, Christ Jesus. And You gave some to be apostles, some to be prophets, some to be evangelists, and some to be pastors and teachers, to equip the saints for the work of ministry so that Your body will be built up. (Ephesians 4:7, 11–12)

Lord Jesus Christ, grant that as Your body, we might reach unity of the faith and in the knowledge of You, the Son of God, so that we will become mature and attain to the whole measure of Your fullness. Then we will no longer be infants, being blown and carried by every wind of doctrine and by the cunning and craftiness of people who scheme deceitfully. Instead, we will speak the truth in love; we will grow up in every way in You, our Head. (Ephesians 4:13–15)

We are to put off falsehood and speak truthfully to our neighbors, for we are members of one another. (Ephesians 4:25)

We should submit to one another out of reverence for You, O Christ. (Ephesians 5:21)

If we have any encouragement from being united with You, O Christ, if any comfort from Your love, if any fellowship of the Spirit, if any affection and compassion, we should also be like-minded, having the same love, being one in spirit and one in purpose. (Philippians 2:1–2)

May we let Your word, O Christ, dwell in us richly as we teach and admonish one another with all wisdom, and as we sing psalms, hymns and spiritual songs with gratitude in our hearts to You, our God. (Colossians 3:16)

We should always thank You, God, for other believers, mentioning them in our prayers. (1 Thessalonians 1:2)

We ought always to thank You, God, for other believers and pray that their faith would grow more and more, and that the love each of them has toward one another would increase. (2 Thessalonians 1:3)

We should always pray for other believers, that You, our God, may count them worthy of Your calling and fulfill every desire for goodness and every work of faith with power. (2 Thessalonians 1:11)

We should ask that Your name, our Lord Jesus, may be glorified in others, and they in You, according to the grace of our God and of You, Lord Jesus Christ. (2 Thessalonians 1:12)

You, O God, are not unjust; You will not forget our work and the love we have shown toward Your name in having ministered, and continuing to minister, to the saints. (Hebrews 6:10)

We should consider how to stir up one another toward love and good works. (Hebrews 10:24)

We must not forsake our meeting together, as some are in the habit of doing, but encourage one another, and all the more as we see the day approaching. (Hebrews 10:25)

I will remember those who led me, who spoke Your word, O God, to me. I will consider the outcome of their way of life and imitate their faith. (Hebrews 13:7)

I will obey those who lead me and submit to them, for they keep watch over my soul as those who must give an account. I will obey them, so that they may do this with joy and not with grief, for this would be unprofitable for me. (Hebrews 13:17)

We should all be of one mind, and be sympathetic, loving as brothers and sisters, compassionate and humble. (1 Peter 3:8)

Unbelievers

How beautiful on the mountains are the feet of those who bring good news, who proclaim Your peace, who bring good tidings, who proclaim Your salvation. (Isaiah 52:7; Nahum 1:15)

You have called us to go and make disciples of all nations, baptizing them in the name of the Father and of You, the

Son, and of the Holy Spirit, teaching them to observe everything You have commanded us. And surely You are with us always, even to the end of the age. (Matthew 28:19–20)

We are Your fragrance, O Christ, to God among those who are being saved and among those who are perishing; to the one an aroma from death to death; to the other, an aroma from life to life. And who is sufficient for these things? (2 Corinthians 2:15–16)

All things are for our sakes, so that the grace that is reaching more and more people may cause thanksgiving to abound to Your glory, O God. (2 Corinthians 4:15)

Knowing what it is to fear You, O Lord, I seek to persuade others. (2 Corinthians 5:11)

All things are from You, O God, who reconciled us to Yourself through Christ and gave us the ministry of reconciliation: namely, that You, O God, were reconciling the world to Yourself in Christ, not counting our trespasses against us. And You have committed to us the message of reconciliation. Therefore, we are ambassadors for Christ, as though You, O God, were appealing through us, as we implore others on Christ's behalf to be reconciled to You, O God. (2 Corinthians 5:18–20)

I pray that words may be given to me, that I may open my mouth boldly to make known the mystery of the gospel. (Ephesians 6:19)

I pray that You, O God, may open to me a door for the word, so that I may speak the mystery of Christ and proclaim it clearly, as I ought. (Colossians 4:3–4)

I should walk in wisdom toward outsiders, making the most of every opportunity. My speech should always be with grace, seasoned with salt, so that I may know how to answer each person. (Colossians 4:5–6)

I am to offer petitions, prayers, intercession and thanksgiving on behalf of all people—for kings and all those who are in authority, that we may live peaceful and quiet lives in all godliness and reverence. This is good and acceptable in Your sight, O God our Savior, who desire all people to be saved and to come to the knowledge of the truth. (1 Timothy 2:1–4)

I pray that the sharing of my faith may lead to a full knowledge of every good thing I have in Christ. (Philemon 6)

I will sanctify You, O Christ, as Lord in my heart, always being ready to give an answer to everyone who asks me to give the reason for the hope that is in me, but with gentleness and respect. (1 Peter 3:15)

I will have mercy on those who are doubting. (Jude 22)

PART THREE

Personal Prayer Pages

Prayer Concerns

Date: _____

_____

_____

Prayer Answered: _____

_____

Date: _____

_____

_____

Prayer Answered: _____

_____

Date: _____

_____

_____

Prayer Answered: _____

_____

Date: _____

_____

_____

Prayer Answered: _____

_____

Date: _____

_____

_____

Prayer Answered: _____

_____

Prayer Concerns

Date: _____

_____

_____

Prayer Answered: _____

_____

Date: _____

_____

_____

Prayer Answered: _____

_____

Date: _____

_____

_____

Prayer Answered: _____

_____

Date: _____

_____

_____

Prayer Answered: _____

_____

Date: _____

_____

_____

Prayer Answered: _____

_____

Prayer Concerns

Date: _____

_____

_____

Prayer Answered: _____

_____

Date: _____

_____

_____

Prayer Answered: _____

_____

Date: _____

_____

_____

Prayer Answered: _____

_____

Date: _____

_____

_____

Prayer Answered: _____

_____

Date: _____

_____

_____

Prayer Answered: _____

_____

Prayer Concerns

Date: _____

_____

_____

Prayer Answered: _____

_____

Date: _____

_____

_____

Prayer Answered: _____

_____

Date: _____

_____

_____

Prayer Answered: _____

_____

Date: _____

_____

_____

Prayer Answered: _____

_____

Date: _____

_____

_____

Prayer Answered: _____

_____

Prayer Concerns

Date: _____

_____

_____

Prayer Answered: _____

_____

Date: _____

_____

_____

Prayer Answered: _____

_____

Date: _____

_____

_____

Prayer Answered: _____

_____

Date: _____

_____

_____

Prayer Answered: _____

_____

Date: _____

_____

_____

Prayer Answered: _____

_____

Prayer Concerns

Date: _____

_____

_____

Prayer Answered: _____

_____

Date: _____

_____

_____

Prayer Answered: _____

_____

Date: _____

_____

_____

Prayer Answered: _____

_____

Date: _____

_____

_____

Prayer Answered: _____

_____

Date: _____

_____

_____

Prayer Answered: _____

_____

Prayer Concerns

Date: _____

_____

_____

Prayer Answered: _____

_____

Date: _____

_____

_____

Prayer Answered: _____

_____

Date: _____

_____

_____

Prayer Answered: _____

_____

Date: _____

_____

_____

Prayer Answered: _____

_____

Date: _____

_____

_____

Prayer Answered: _____

_____

Prayer Concerns

Date: _____

_____

_____

Prayer Answered: _____

_____

Date: _____

_____

_____

Prayer Answered: _____

_____

Date: _____

_____

_____

Prayer Answered: _____

_____

Date: _____

_____

_____

Prayer Answered: _____

_____

Date: _____

_____

_____

Prayer Answered: _____

_____

Prayer Concerns

Date: _____

_____

_____

Prayer Answered: _____

_____

Date: _____

_____

_____

Prayer Answered: _____

_____

Date: _____

_____

_____

Prayer Answered: _____

_____

Date: _____

_____

_____

Prayer Answered: _____

_____

Date: _____

_____

_____

Prayer Answered: _____

_____

Prayer Concerns

Date: _____

_____

_____

Prayer Answered: _____

_____

Date: _____

_____

_____

Prayer Answered: _____

_____

Date: _____

_____

_____

Prayer Answered: _____

_____

Date: _____

_____

_____

Prayer Answered: _____

_____

Date: _____

_____

_____

Prayer Answered: _____

_____

Prayer Concerns

Date: _____

_____

_____

Prayer Answered: _____

_____

Date: _____

_____

_____

Prayer Answered: _____

_____

Date: _____

_____

_____

Prayer Answered: _____

_____

Date: _____

_____

_____

Prayer Answered: _____

_____

Date: _____

_____

_____

Prayer Answered: _____

_____

---❧---

FACE TO FACE:
Praying the Scriptures
for Spiritual Growth

Scripture translation and adaptation by
Kenneth Boa

Kenneth Boa is engaged in a ministry of relational evangelism and discipleship, teaching, writing and speaking. He holds a B.S. from Case Institute of Technology, a Th.M. from Dallas Theological Seminary, a Ph.D. from New York University and a D.Phil. from the University of Oxford in England.

Dr. Boa's previous publications include *Face to Face: Praying the Scriptures for Intimate Worship, Cults, World Religions, and the Occult; I'm Glad You Asked; Talk Thru the Bible; Visual Survey of the Bible; Drawing Near; Unraveling the Big Questions about God; Night Light;* Dr. Boa is also a contributing editor to *The Open Bible* and *The Promise Keeper's Men's Study Bible;* he is sole contributor to the *Two-Year Daily Reading & Prayer Bible.*

Dr. Boa is the President of Reflections Ministries, an organization that seeks to provide safe places for people to consider the claims of Christ and to help them mature and bear fruit in their relationship with Him. Dr. Boa writes a free monthly teaching letter called *Reflections.* If you would like to receive this letter, please call (800) DRAW NEAR (372-9632).

Project management and editorial
by Ruth A. DeJager

Editorial Assistance by Donna Huijsen
and Marjorie Terpstra

Interior design and typesetting
by Sherri L. Hoffman

Cover design by Paula Gibson

Published in association with the literary agency
of Wolgemuth & Hyatt, Inc., Brentwood, TN

Printing and binding by
R. R. Donnelley & Sons, Crawfordsville, IN